A HISTORY OF EDUCATION

THE MACMILLAN COMPANY
NEW YORK · BOSTON · CHICAGO
SAN FRANCISCO

MACMILLAN & CO., Limited
LONDON · BOMBAY · CALCUTTA
MELBOURNE

THE MACMILLAN CO. OF CANADA, Ltd.
TORONTO

A

HISTORY OF EDUCATION

BEFORE THE MIDDLE AGES

BY

FRANK PIERREPONT GRAVES, Ph.D.

PROFESSOR OF THE HISTORY AND PHILOSOPHY OF
EDUCATION IN THE OHIO STATE UNIVERSITY

New York

THE MACMILLAN COMPANY

1915

Norwood Press
J. S. Cushing Co. — Berwick & Smith Co.
Norwood, Mass., U.S.A.

TO

ALBERT ROSS HILL, LL.D.

PRESIDENT OF THE UNIVERSITY OF MISSOURI

PREFACE

THE present publication is intended to meet the demand for a text-book or reference work that will give a comprehensive account of the history of education before the day of the monastic schools. The aim has been to present sufficient material to mark the most significant movements, and disclose the underlying principles, without entering into unnecessary detail, or dwelling upon matters but remotely related to the educational problems of to-day. While there has been no attempt to adduce exhaustive proof of the various theses maintained, it is hoped that enough has been presented to make them acceptable for the occasion, and to serve as an interpretative basis of further study.

An effort has, moreover, been made to see that all interpretations are based upon historical data collected from the sources; and direct quotation of this material has been liberally made throughout. Also, to supply deficiencies in either facts or interpretation and stimulate the student to research or further reading, references to the sources and to collateral works have been given at the end of each chapter. I believe that teachers should encourage their pupils to use this part of the book especially, if for no other purpose than to find a different emphasis and set of generalizations from those of the text, and so realize that no one form of treatment can be considered infallible or final.

The point of view and method of presentation in this book have been worked out in the class-room and in extension lectures. While the treatment is not limited to a history of schools and educational methods, a definite attempt has been made to center the discussion about the schools and render the subject pertinent and profitable for the teacher of the present and future. It is especially desired that it may prove a stimulus and help to the further study of education.

My general attitude is, with Davidson, to regard education as a species of 'conscious evolution,' and to trace throughout the period covered the development of individualism. Accordingly, I have endeavored to point out the traditional forms of expression that have grown up among the various peoples and become fixed by social habit, and the lack of progress that has ensued, until, through some conflict of traditions, the individual is enabled to select a new pathway of expression. By thus adopting a general point of view, I have hoped to bind together all nations and periods in a connected account of world progress.

The method of approaching educational history that is recommended in Chapter I was first suggested to me

by a former pupil of Professor Paul Monroe.   It closely
resembles the plan adopted in the *Text-book in the
History of Education* that has since been issued by that
well-known authority.   Others, notably Laurie and
Williams, seem to have used a similar method more or
less consistently, and the idea was outlined and followed
to some extent by Schmidt in his *Geschichte der Pädagogik*.   Experience has shown that, in a more or less
modified form, this is a natural and effective procedure.

In order to present the education of each period in
its proper setting, and show how its ideals arose, a brief
account of its political and social history has first been
given.   Such knowledge, I have found, cannot be taken
for granted.

I have to acknowledge indebtedness to many persons,
including those who have previously written on this range
of educational history.   Nearly every chapter of the
book has been submitted to some authority in the particular field, and some of the grosser errors eliminated
in this way.   Those that remain are probably due to
my own carelessness or immunity to advice.   Suggestions on portions of the manuscript have been made by
Professors C. A. Ellwood of the University of Missouri,
J. H. Breasted of the University of Chicago, A. V. W.
Jackson of Columbia University, C. M. Sharpe of the
Missouri Bible College, and J. R. Smith and S. C. Derby
of the Ohio State University.   A wider reading of the

manuscript has been made by Professor Jesse H. Coursault of the University of Missouri, Professor Arthur E. Davies of the Ohio State University, and Professor William G. Tousey of Tufts College; and their keen, but sympathetic, criticism has been of especial value. I am also indebted to my wife for careful reading of the proof and for timely suggestions.

F. P. G.

JANUARY 1, 1909.

CONTENTS

CHAPTER I

PAGE

THE STUDY OF THE HISTORY OF EDUCATION . . . I
The Value of the History of Education. How to Study It.

PART I

NON-PROGRESSIVE EDUCATION

CHAPTER II

SAVAGES OR NATURE PEOPLES 8
Nature of Primitive Society. Purpose of Primitive
Education. Its Organization and Content. Its Method.
Summary of Results.

CHAPTER III

BARBARISM OR EARLY CIVILIZATION 20
The Movement from Nature to Culture.

CHAPTER IV

EGYPT 22
Historical Development. Effect of the Nile upon Eco-
nomic Development. Religion and Ethics. Classes of
Society and Position of Women. Cultural Development.
Education.

CHAPTER V

BABYLONIA AND ASSYRIA 43

　　Historical Relations. Social Conditions. Religion and Ethics. Culture. Education.

CHAPTER VI

PHŒNICIA 52

　　Achievements. Character. Education.

CHAPTER VII

CHINA 55

　　National Conditions. Religion and Ethics. Culture. Education.

CHAPTER VIII

INDIA 77

　　Effect of Environment. Religion. Social Conditions. Education.

CHAPTER IX

PERSIA 91

　　Natural Influences. Government. Religion and Ethics. Education.

CHAPTER X

CHARACTER OF THE EARLIEST CIVILIZATION . . . 104

　　Transitional Stage. Restricted Ideals. Occupational Content. Memory Method. Sacerdotal Organization of Schools. Static Results.

PART II

THE BEGINNINGS OF INDIVIDUALISM
IN EDUCATION

CHAPTER XI

ISRAEL AND JUDÆA (THE JEWS) 110

Survey of Jewish History and Religion. Development of Israelite Religion. Educational Ideals. Pre-exilic Education. Post-exilic Education. Educational Method. Effect of Jewish Education on Progress.

CHAPTER XII

SPARTA AND ATHENS (THE GREEKS) 138

Physical and Social Factors in the Progress of the Greeks. Outline of Greek History. Education in Pre-historic Greece. Older Education of the Historic Period. Spartan Education and Its Aim. Infancy. Boyhood and Adolescence. Youth and Young Manhood. Citizenship. Education of Women. Merits and Defects of Spartan Education. Athenian Education in the Old Period. Childhood. Boyhood. Adolescence. Youth. Citizenship. Education of Women. Character of the Old Athenian Education. Athenian Education in the New Period. The Sophists. Reactionary Forces. The Mediators. Socrates. Plato. *The Republic*. Criticism of The Republic. *The Laws*. Influence of Plato. Aristotle. *The Ethics* and *The Politics*. Criticism of The Ethics and The Politics. Influence of Aristotle. Triumph of Individualism. Later Greek Education. Philosophical Schools. Rhetorical Schools. Universities. Extension of Hellenic Culture. Survey of Greek Education.

CHAPTER XIII

ROME AND THE ROMAN WORLD 230

Survey of Roman History. Practical Aim of Education in Early Rome. Informal Acquisition of Abilities and

PAGE

Virtues. Imitative Method of Training. Effect of the Education of Early Rome. Absorption of Greek Culture. Schools of the Hellenized Roman Education. Elementary Schools. Grammar Schools. Rhetorical Schools. Education beyond the Rhetorical Schools. Education of Women. Education Subsidized and Systematized. Decay of Education. Effect of Roman Education upon Civilization.

CHAPTER XIV

EARLY CHRISTIANITY 272

Beginnings of Individualism among the Jews, Greeks, and Romans. Larger Ideals of Christianity. Vicious Conditions that Christianity Needed to Reform. The Earliest Christian Education. The Catechumenal Schools. Amalgamation of Christianity with Græco-Roman Culture. The Catechetical, Episcopal, and Cathedral Schools. Opposition of Christianity to the Græco-Roman Culture. Influence of Greece and Rome upon Christianity. Effect of Organized Christianity upon Society. The Monastic Schools. Summary of Pre-mediæval Progress.

INDEX 299

A HISTORY OF EDUCATION

A HISTORY OF EDUCATION

EDUCATION BEFORE THE MIDDLE AGES

CHAPTER I

THE STUDY OF THE HISTORY OF EDUCATION

A WELL-KNOWN philosopher [1] has treated the history of education as an account of the latest stage in the process of evolution. All the development of the universe that had taken place in the stages prior to the advent of man might, he thought, be considered as the result of a sort of unconscious education. Or better, education might be regarded as 'conscious evolution,' — the stage where the process came to completer consciousness of itself and sought to guide itself more definitely. In other words, at this point man might be said to take himself in hand and endeavor to direct his living toward a higher development or 'ideal end.' From such a

---

[1] Thomas Davidson in *A History of Education*. Cf. Schmidt, *Geschichte der Pädagogik*, Vol. I, p. 1: "Das Wort Entwicklung verrät das Geheimnis alles Lebens," etc. Cf. also Hegel's view of history as 'theophany,' *Philosophy of History*, Introduction, III.

point of view, the purpose of education is to help along this latest and highest movement in the working out of the world. The teacher's function thus becomes the most important of all in society, and the history of education surveys a wider field than any other study in the curriculum.

The Value of the History of Education. — This is an inspiring interpretation, but it is hardly necessary to plunge very deeply into speculation or to study the history of education before man's advent, in order to perceive the dignity and importance of the teaching profession, or to realize the wide range of perspective afforded by a study of educational history. In fact, if the history of education is limited to a record of only typical instances of the moral, æsthetic, and intellectual development of man in all lands and at all periods of civilization, and his efforts to evolve ever higher and more expanding ideals, the student of this subject will find his vision considerably enlarged without reverting to the day of the clod, the plant, the amœba, or our simian ancestry. No teacher can make a survey of even a limited portion of the development of the educational process, which is all that this book attempts, and not find his professional view greatly widened, or fail to appreciate more fully the part which his calling has played in the progress of civilization.

It affords a broad survey, and shows the importance of the teacher.

How to Study It. — But before beginning to study

the educational procedure of even the earliest man, it may be worth while to seek the best avenue of approach to so important a subject. The facts connected with the educational history of any nation or period are found to be so diverse and numerous that one is liable to be lost in the maze unless he holds some silken clew to guide him. If we are to regard education as the gradual realization of a world purpose, and to consider the history of education as a history of progress in which each nation, period, or theorist described represents some stage in the process or embodies some suggestion of advance or retrogression, the most natural method of procedure is to study each topic from the standpoint of progress.

To understand the history of education,

How, then, is progress effected? To understand this, it will be well to see in outline how those social and educational ideals that determine progress are developed. Among every people a number of traditional forms of self-expression grow up and gradually come to be accepted without question. Such, for example, are their religion and philosophy, their government and political institutions, their literature, art, and science, and all the other features of their social and economic life. Many influences may be instrumental in shaping these traditions, and, so far as they have affected them, are worthy of some study in determining the traditions themselves. For example, the race, his-

one must see how progress is effected.

tory, geography, climate, and the surrounding peoples usually play the greatest part in the evolution of the traditions of a nation or period, and must be given due consideration. From these racial traditions those which seem to be most valuable are more or less consciously selected as social and educational ideals for the rising generation, who are guided in such a way as to re-live the experience. Thus they may be rapidly brought to the level of the race without being obliged to pass through all the laborious stages of experimentation by which the race has achieved its standing.

The more the traditions and ideals that have thus evolved are conformed with, the more firmly they become fixed as social habits and the more does progress in these directions cease. Now, in general, these traditional ideals last until, through war, commerce, or social contact within the group, there arises a conflict with other traditions formed under different conditions, when mutual destruction is likely to occur. Then the individual, who is always the progressive factor in social evolution as opposed to the conservative force of the group as a whole, is enabled to select a new form of expression from the best elements of the conflicting traditions. Social habit again fixes the new form of expression, and the individual is emancipated only through another mutually destructive conflict. Thus, broadly speaking, each period in the development of civilization is marked by higher forms of expression than the preceding, and society becomes better organized and its members more individualized as time goes on. Also, as individuals do become more differentiated in society, there is a greater conflict of habits within the group, and more rapid progress is possible.

These social traditions, which also become educational ideals for a nation or period, would, therefore, indicate the stage of development in world progress at which a people have arrived, and the task, in estimating an epoch, is to discover what are its habitual forms of expression. Hence the thread for which we have been looking, that will lead one through the labyrinth of facts in the educational history of a period or people and enable us to classify them best, seems to lie along the way of inquiring the purpose of the education under consideration, for purpose unifies the manifold acts of a people by giving meaning to them.

And to estimate the development of a period, one must first know its educational aim;

The first step, then, in studying the history of the education of any people should be to trace their educational aims, and when these can be established, even if only tentatively, the next move will naturally be in the direction of finding out what attempt was made to realize them. This study of the means of accomplishing an educational purpose may include an investigation of at least three main topics, which are closely connected. In the first place, one should find out

then its content, through what accomplishments or knowledge the education under consideration attempts to reproduce in the younger generation the best of the racial experiences. This educational content may consist of a few simple forms of expression, or, if an educational system has been fully developed, of the actual course of study. *method,* Then some attention should be given to the method by which the instruction was imparted, although in some instances this may be so informal that one would not at first perceive that any definite procedure was followed. This may involve some study of the spirit, ideals, and preparation of the teachers, and their modes *and organi- zation;* of punishment or reward. Finally, it is of some importance to understand the organization and material equipment by which the particular type of education was carried out, although it may be that the experience to be reproduced is so simple that the youth could learn it through imitative play or active participation in the community. When, however, the ideal becomes more complicated and the subjects to be acquired become more numerous and difficult, regular schools are instituted, and the study of organization may include a description not only of the school system with the management and the hours of attendance, but also of the buildings or places for holding the schools and an account of the other equipment.

When the educational system is fairly understood, both

in its purpose and its procedure, the final inquiry will *and finally* naturally be as to its results. Only as its effect upon *the results.* civilization and the people who employed it is known, can its importance as a guide or a warning at the present day be rightly estimated.

But beyond learning and interpreting the facts connected with *the educational purpose* of a country, period, or individual, and the way in which the attempt was made to approach this goal, — *i.e. the matter, method, and organization* of the system, and making some estimate of its *results*, the student of the history of education has no direct concern. This classification is quite obvious in the earliest types of education, but the more advanced the culture, the more complicated does it become. But all historical material, however interesting and valuable in other connections, which does not in some way contribute to these ends, may safely be neglected in this study, as it can throw little or no light upon educational problems of the present, past, or future.

PART I

NON–PROGRESSIVE EDUCATION

CHAPTER II

SAVAGES OR NATURE PEOPLES

"ONE set of savages is like another," said Samuel Johnson, and this dictum of the eighteenth-century sage has stood the test of modern investigation. The government, customs, and mentality of all savages have proved to be strikingly similar in their simplicity and crudity. When the human race is yet in its intellectual infancy, which it seems to be in the case of all primitive peoples both of the present day and the past,[1] society is found to be on a comparatively simple basis, and there is little differentiation of thought or occupation.

[1] It should be remembered that while there is evidence to show that most civilized countries were once occupied by primitive tribes, savagery is by no means limited to antiquity. There are many instances of arrested social development at the present day, such as the savages of North and West Australia, South and West Africa, Malaysia, Tasmania, Sumatra, and the Brazilian forests, and it is from these living examples rather than from the stone implements and ceremonial objects of the past that we gain our best knowledge of savagery.

8

Nature of Primitive Society. — In all primitive society there is recognition of no social tie save that of blood, and the family, clan, and tribe are the highest form of organization of which such peoples are capable. Their affections are, therefore, limited to the members of their clan, although they usually include in this body friendly spirits, especially the ghosts of their ancestors, the 'totem' animals or wild beasts from which they believe they have sprung, and certain other animals which they have tamed or domesticated. *The blood tie.*

This belief of the savage in the existence of spirits and his inclusion of lower animals in his clan, grow out of that view of the world which is known as *animism*, and which is peculiar to all savages at their earliest stage. The savage at first attributes a personality to every object, and explains all phenomena of nature as if they were demonstrations of some personal will. Such an idea cannot, with peoples so crude, be the result of metaphysical speculation, as has been the case with some similar conceptions [1] of antiquity and modern times. It is due to a simple confusion between animate and inanimate objects. Through such phenomena as dreams, unconsciousness from a blow or other cause, reflections in the water, shadows, swoons, trances, or fancied ghost-seeing, savages come to conceive of the *Animistic religion*

and the concept of the 'double.

[1] Compare 'hylozoism' among the Greeks, and the present-day 'pan-psychism' of Royce.

possibility of a separation of the individual from his body, and gradually get to believe that every person has another existence outside his visible corporeal one. This existence can hardly be thought of as a soul, in our sense of the word, for it is not really conceived as immaterial. It is only a kind of more attenuated 'double,' or copy of the body, which exists inside it. The conception is then carried over to the lower animals and inanimate objects. Cattle, horses, trees, stones, and weapons are all regarded as possessing a double of this sort. Hence the savage's possessions, such as his weapons, utensils, dog, horse, or even wife, are often burned or buried with him when he has left this life, that, through their doubles, they may continue to serve or comfort him in the life to come.

Totemism.   A further development of animism appears in that worship of animals which characterizes the higher stages of savagery, and is known as *totemism*. This probably arises, on the one hand, from the close association of savages with wild animals, and, on the other, from the savage's conception of animals as personal beings superior, in some respects, to himself. This leads to a superstitious reverence for these animals, to the savage's naming himself after them, and finally, through a confusion of the name with the animal itself, to the idea that the persons bearing the name of the totem animal are descended from it. Hence the totem animal, as well as all who bear his name, is included in the membership of the clan.

A still further outgrowth in savage society, although it may be considered more characteristic of the stage of human development known as 'barbarism,' is the form of religion called *ancestor worship*.[1] It has already been seen how the totem animal worshiped by the members of a clan is considered their ancestor. Hence, later on in their development when descent comes to be reckoned through fathers,[2] nothing is more natural than that human ancestors should come to be worshiped instead of the mythical animal ancestor. Thus the ghosts of ancestors are also included in the clan.

Ancestor worship.

This animism, totemism, ancestor worship, and other naïve explanations illustrate how little ability the primitive mind has to analyze experience, make abstractions and generalizations, or formulate laws. So it is that while the savage does, to a certain extent, know how to use things, he can understand forces but little or not at all. Not being able to comprehend such a force as fire, his weapons, utensils, and tools are made of stone, wood, clay, bone, horn, ivory, or shell, since

Inability to understand forces

[1] For a detailed account of the various types of primitive religion, see Spencer, *Sociology*, Vol. I, Pt. I, Chaps. VIII–XXII.

[2] In the earliest society, it is held by anthropologists, descent is recorded only through the female parent, largely because the father is often unknown. See Deniker, *The Races of Man*, p. 233.

these can be shaped without its use, as metals cannot be.[1]

Since the implements that the true savage is able to manufacture are so crude, and because he cannot, through a want of abstract thought in other directions, understand or anticipate the future, he does not practice agriculture to any extent, and is largely confined for his subsistence to hunting and fishing and gathering the natural products that are at hand. In fact, the chief characteristic of savages is their inability to control nature, and they are, therefore, because of this bondage, often spoken of as 'nature peoples.'

They are on this account inclined to be nomadic, for after they have exhausted the fruits of the earth and the game in one place, they are obliged to seek them in another. In consequence, they dwell in caves, tents of skin, or rude huts, and their arts are limited to making clothes of wool and skins, roughly shaped utensils for domestic use, and implements for hunting and fishing and sometimes for war.

Purpose of Primitive Education. — Because the life and thought of savages are so crude and undeveloped, histories generally give little or no account of the

---

[1] Food must at first have been eaten raw, and while there is evidence for believing that man early learned to use fire for cooking, it seems that he was much later in smelting metals for tools and weapons. See Starr, *First Steps in Human Progress*, Chaps. I–III.

educational process among the most primitive peoples. Nevertheless, the very simplicity and uniformity of the organization, method, and content of savage education, by constituting an instructive contrast to later complexities, and affording a means of interpreting them, form a natural starting-point for studying the history of education, and would seem to be worthy of some consideration.[1]

Although primitive education is almost unconscious of its own aim, and cannot be said to possess any genuine ideals, political, social, or moral, it must tend to afford a training in two different directions. The aim of a primitive people is the satisfaction of immediate wants, and the young savage must be taught the occupations of his race, in order that he may provide himself with the necessaries of life, — food, clothing, and shelter. This constitutes his practical education. On the other hand, his religion is likewise viewed as a means to a satisfaction of these physical needs. If the mystic powers are appeased, they will serve rather than thwart his purpose. He must, therefore, also receive a theoretical training in learning how to deal with the unseen. He is shown by the medicine-man, exorcist, priest, or whatever the

Aims to satisfy immediate wants (practical education),

[1] Dewey, in his *Interpretation of Savage Mind* (*Psychological Review*, Vol. IX, p. 217 ff.), makes it clear that the present tendency to interpret primitive mentality with civilized mind as a standard, and so in negative terms, has prevented us from grasping the genetic significance in the process of mental development.

and deal
with the un-
seen (theo-
retical ed-
ucation).

interpreter of the invisible may be called, how to explain
or interpret nature, how to propitiate the 'spirits' or
powers, which, it has been seen, are believed to reside
in every person, animal, and object, and how to conduct
the worship of the totem animals or the human ancestors.   It may be noted in passing that these explanations and ceremonials of the medicine-man, crude as
they are, were the first expressions of that tendency
from which all forms of human philosophy, religion,
and science have developed.[1]   Furthermore, the growth
of such training has made possible all our progress in
practical education.

The family is
the means of
practical
education,

Its Organization and Content. — Since the racial experience at which primitive education aims is so simple,
the youth can acquire it largely in imitative play or
by participation in the activities of the community.
Hence no schools are needed, and the means of carrying
out their education, at least as far as the practical side
is concerned, is through the family, or the clan, which
is only a larger group supposed to be bound by the
ties of kinship, and which constitutes the social unit
in savagery.   Through these institutions the young
savage is taught to obtain the necessaries of life.
Individuality is as yet at a minimum, since the same
forms of expression are carried on by all.   The only

[1] For the evolution of the theologian, philosopher, and scientist from
the medicine-man, see Spencer, *Sociology*, Vol. III, Pt. VII, Chap. VI.

division of labor known to the savage is not a distinction between individuals, but that between male and
female, the stronger sex being the protector and pro-
vider, and the other caring for the shelter and preparing the food and clothing.[1] But even at this crude
economic stage, there has been developed some skill
in fighting, hunting, and fishing, and in shaping
weapons and utensils on the one hand, and in tanning
skins, weaving, and possibly cooking on the other,
and these arts must be learned by the future men and
women of the clan.

Outside this practical training, a more conscious and
formal means of education, largely theoretical, is usually
undertaken by the clan.   This is conducted through
what is known by anthropologists as 'initiatory ceremonies' or 'puberty rites.'   The boys of the clan,
at the age of puberty, are definitely instructed by their
elders, especially the medicine-men, concerning their
relation to the spirits and their totem animals, and
acquainted with the religious forms and ceremonies of
their people.   They are also informed concerning their
associations with the other members of their group,
such as subordination to elders, relations between the
sexes, and the sacredness of the clansman's obligations,
especially loyalty in time of war.   Strict silence is

*and the pu-
berty rites of
theoretical.*

[1] An account of the rise of the sex division of labor is undertaken by
Thomas in *Sex and Society*, pp. 123–149.

enjoined upon the candidates concerning the information that is communicated, and to impress it upon their minds, and possibly to test their endurance and bravery, they are required to fast for several days before and after the ceremonies, and are usually mutilated in some way. A corresponding initiation is given to the girls of the clan under the direction of the older women.

'Trial and error.'

Its Method. — The method of the savage in acquiring his practical education is, to a great extent, that of 'trial and error.' The learner blindly imitates, with little or no consciousness, the act of an older member of the family or clan, in hunting or weaving, for example, until he meets with some degree of success, and the right acts are rendered habitual, and the wrong ones eliminated, through the pleasure resulting from successful action. But even in this practical education the young savage must be taught to perform these acts in the exact manner which the experience of the tribe, as interpreted by the exorcist or medicine-man, has prescribed as being the only way that will not offend the spirits connected with the object.

Summary of Results. — Thus the practical education is somewhat regulated by the theoretical. Theoretical training, however, is not confined to explaining the procedure of practical education, as we have seen in the case of the initiatory rites, but gives an interpretation to every experience and problem of life. It prescribes the exact method of conducting one's self toward the other members of the tribe, and of worshiping or of appeasing the totem animals and the spirits on all sorts of occasions.

While this theoretical education is largely in the hands of the medicine-men, under some circumstances the head of the family or clan seems to become the teacher. Neither the priest nor the patriarch, however, assigns to those under his guidance any reason for the procedure he prescribes. As in practical education, the whole matter is mostly one of unconscious imitation.

Thus in all things the savage lives merely from hand to mouth. His social organization is undeveloped, he is absolutely incapable of abstract thought, his religion is superstitious and crude, his occupations are largely limited to securing the products of nature that are at hand, and the education he receives is imitative and fixed. Because he has not developed sufficiently to analyze the conditions about him and pass general judgments upon them, or to treasure his results in a written language, literature, and historic records, he has little idea of the past or future, and is practically *tied to the present*. Therefore, looking upon his physical and social surroundings as unchanging through all time, he seeks no control over nature, and secures his education, both practical and theoretical, by follow-

The savage is tied to the present,

c

ing the example of the tribal exorcists and elders.

and no development of individuality exists. Since he is completely bound down by nature and the customs of the society in which he lives, the habitual forms of expression are the same for all savages of the same sex, and *no real development of individuality exists*. The welfare of the individual is never even considered, except as a member of the clan. Such a training must be conspicuously *non-progressive*. Not until people have come to see beyond the present and control their environment to some extent, do they reach to even a slight degree of culture or civilization. They remain savages, or children of nature.

SUPPLEMENTARY READING

BRINTON, D. G. *Basis of Social Relations.*

BRINTON, D. G. *Races and Peoples.*

CHAMBERLAIN, A. F. *The Child. A Study of the Evolution of Man.* Chap. VIII.

DAVIDSON, T. *A History of Education.* Bk. I, Chap. III.

DENIKER, J. *The Races of Man.* Chaps. V–VII.

LETOURNEAU, C. *L'evolution de l'education dans les diverses races humaines.* Chaps. II–VIII.

LUBBOCK, J. *Prehistoric Times.* Chaps. I and XII–XV.

MONROE, P. *Text-Book in the History of Education.* Chap. I.

MORGAN, L. H. *Ancient Society.* Pt. I, Chaps. I–II, and Pt. II, Chaps. I–II.

SPENCER, H. *Principles of Sociology.* Vol. I, Pt. I, Chaps. V–XXVI, and Vol. III, Pt. VII.

STARR, F. *Some First Steps in Human Progress*. Chaps. I, II, XII, XIII, XXI, XXII, XXIV–XXVI.

THOMAS, W. I. *Sex and Society*. Especially pp. 55–172.

TYLOR, E. B. *Anthropology*. Chaps. I, IV–XII, and XIV.

TYLOR, E. B. *Primitive Culture*. Chaps. II and XI–XVIII.

TYLOR, E. B. *Researches into the Early History of Mankind*. Chaps. VII–X.

CHAPTER III

BARBARISM OR EARLY CIVILIZATION

Barbarism as
a transitional
stage.

The Movement from Nature to Culture. — The progress of the human race from nature to culture — savagery to civilization — is very gradual, and the dividing line is difficult to draw. To make the process clearer, and also for the convenience of classifying a number of peoples who have evidently passed beyond most of the characteristics of savagery and yet can hardly be called civilized, many ethnologists[1] and historians recognize the stage known as 'barbarism.'

Similarity
among
Oriental
nations.

Whether we use the term 'barbarism' or not, it is easily seen that there are many and varied nations which fall under the head of this transitional stage. While, however, they represent several races and a large number of influences, the most typical have all been located in the Orient, and their social characteristics are sufficiently alike to justify treating them in a single group. Their similarity in educational procedure has appeared so great to some writers, that they suggest the omission, in studying, of all these

[1] Compare Tylor, *Anthropology*, p. 24; Morgan, *Ancient Society*, Chap. I; etc.

nations save one, or actually limit their treatment to a single nation as typical of all.[1] It has, however, seemed well to describe here briefly, in their historical order, the more important peoples of barbarism, or early civilization, and afterward endeavor to sum up their common characteristics. The diversities, after all, are worthy of some consideration, as each seems to emphasize more strongly than the others some peculiarity of barbarism, and it would be difficult to state what nation should be made the type. If, however, it is felt that these systems are of little value in a general history of education, the attention can easily be confined to Egypt as historically the most obvious type of transition, and the final statement of features in common[2] may be used as a sufficient summary of the other nations.

[1] See Monroe, *Text-book in the History of Education;* Seeley, *History of Education,* p. 5; and the remarks of A. O. Norton in *School Review,* Vol. XII, p. 823.

[2] See Chap. X.

CHAPTER IV

EGYPT

Historical Development. — Egypt furnishes us with abundant evidence of the early day at which she passed beyond the stage of savagery. Thousands of Egyptian manuscripts, monuments, and mummies, preserved by the dry air and sand, by solidity of structure, or care in embalming, witness the extent to which her civilization was developed tens of centuries before the earliest epochs in Greece. The history of this ancient country extends from the days before the 'dynasties,' 5000 B.C., down to its decline and final conquest by the Persians in 525 B.C., after which the identity of its civilization was lost. It passed through a number of periods in its development, each of which is fairly distinct in its characteristics, but there is an underlying unity throughout the entire history of ancient Egypt. The social, political, and intellectual conditions of each epoch are clearly implicit in the one just before it, and up to the beginning of the period of decadence there is a constant growth in all the marks of its peculiar civilization.

Effect of the Nile upon Economic Development. — The interest which the Egyptians showed in various lines of development, and the extent to which they carried them, were determined in large measure by the peculiar topography of the country.   The statement of the old Greek traveler, Herodotus, that " Egypt was the gift of the river," is true in a wider sense than he intended it.   It is obvious that geologically Egypt is the product of the Nile.   Every year, after the snow has melted and the spring rains have set in, the river reaches its height and appears like a vast lake.   Then it gradually recedes and leaves behind a rich deposit of black mud, which it has gathered from the mountains in the south.   The natural fertility of such a soil, increased by the evenness and warmth of the climate, has caused Egypt, from the days of the youthful Joseph, and even before, to be known as a land of steady and plentiful crops.

Fertility of the soil.

The Nile was largely instrumental also in determining the industrial and intellectual characteristics of the people.   The Egyptians found it necessary to regulate its waters in order to secure the best results.   They had to construct irrigation canals, to conduct the river at its flood into reservoirs and then out into the fields wherever it was most needed.   Their most striking feat of this sort occurred early in their history, when they reclaimed an arid tract called Fayûm,[1] some seven hun-

Skill in engineering.

---

[1] It is not certainly known whether the original flooding of the Fayûm was effected by natural or artificial processes.   The lake of historic times

dred square miles, by constructing a canal through the limestone hills. They also invented devices to raise the water from the canals to the level of the more distant fields as the Nile gradually receded. Other difficulties, such as the arrangement of dikes and the location of landmarks, must have been overcome, and Egypt was thus forced by her river to become the mother of engineering.

Homogeneity and isolation of the people. By affording a means of transportation the Nile was of great assistance to trade and industry, and likewise enabled the Egyptians to become more homogeneous. It furnished a roadway seven hundred and fifty miles long, which connected all parts of the country. They were able to float huge blocks of stone down from the quarries of the south, thus facilitating greatly the progress of architecture, and other intercourse between the various communities was active. This must have done much to moderate the local differences and jealousies that would naturally exist in a country so long and straggling.

As a whole, however, Egypt was quite isolated from the rest of the world. Although she had easy access to the Mediterranean, there were no harbors on the Delta, while the Red Sea, which led to the Indian Ocean and the East, was distant three or four days' journey through

called Moeris was pushed back by retrenchment walls, and its eventual destruction was due to the decay of the embankment through neglect.

the desert, and the 'cataracts' of the Nile made it
difficult to approach the countries south of Egypt.
Similarly, outside influences were slow in affecting the
Egyptians, as whatever foreigners found their way in
from Asia, Libya, or Nubia, were so few at any time
that they were easily assimilated.[1] Their long seclusion
had its effect in developing a unique type of civilization,
with cultural products peculiar to themselves.

Religion and Ethics. — The religious conceptions of
the Egyptians, also, were affected by their natural surroundings. Their earliest deities were the Sun ($R\hat{e}$[2]),
who was universally popular, and the Nile (*Hapi*),
toward which they usually faced their temples. A
myth that became fully as widespread as that of Rê
dealt with *Osiris* (Sun), his sister-wife, *Isis* (Dawn),
and his hostile brother, *Set* (Darkness). Other cults
connected with the sun, such as those of *Horus, Amon,*
and *Aten,* sprang up, but nearly every locality differed
in the names, attributes, and powers that it assigned to
the sun god. When the gods of the various districts
were gradually identified and their names made inter-
changeable, the Egyptian theogony became hopelessly

Worship of the Nile and the sun.

---

[1] The Egyptians, however, learned to use to the utmost their meager
facilities. As early as 2900 B.C. they had commerce with Syria and other
countries on the Mediterranean. By the time of the Empire (1600–
1100 B.C.) they had communication with most of the known world, and
were in turn largely modified in their customs and progress, especially
through Semitic influence.   [2] Pronounced *Ray.*

involved. From this condition it was apparently extri-
cated by the development of a henotheism, with Rê, or
some other god, as the head of the hierarchy. Although
the Egyptians never became acute in their meditation
and reasoning, the more enlightened may thus have
come to conceive of God as one, though worshiped
under many aspects, and to interpret the various myths
in a metaphorical sense. The religion of the common
people, however, was much lower. They regarded certain animals not merely as symbols of the gods, but as
actual deities, and eventually worshiped them.

Yet belief in a future existence was universal. A
small statue of the deceased was set up in the tomb as
an habitation for his *ka*, or double, and the body was
mummified, that the ka might one day return and
revivify it. While this life after death was, in the oldest period, viewed as uneventful and sad, before long
its nature was supposed to depend upon the judgment passed upon one at his trial before Osiris in the
Lower World. If it were favorable, he might be allowed to dwell in the pleasant fields of *Aaru*, or share
in the life of the sun god.

On the whole, however, the religion of the Egyptians
was viewed as a means of propitiation, that their practical needs might not be interfered with, and it had
little effect upon conduct. If we may judge from the
Confessions before Osiris, the *Book of the Dead*, the

Aphorisms of Ptah-hotep, and other moral works that have been found, their ethical doctrines were prudential and sordid. Personal conduct was prescribed largely as a key to success; friendship was considered useful, but not a matter for devotion; the grosser crimes and vices were forbidden, but self-sacrifice and purity were not enjoined; and dealings with the gods were described as compacts. "Sacrifice," says a maxim of Ani, "for God looks on the offerer, but he neglects those who neglect him." Moreover, as in the case of all moral systems that are imposed by some outside sanction rather than developed from within, the ethics of the Egyptians became a veneer under which lay much vainglory, hypocrisy, and immorality.

Classes of Society and Position of Women. — As would be expected in so religious a country, the priesthood finally became the controlling element in Egypt. It possessed most of the wealth and learning, and held many of the political offices. Before the differentiation of the professional priest, the sacerdotal class performed the functions of not only priests and prophets, but of many professional people, such as lawyers, doctors, embalmers,[1] architects, and scribes. By the time of the Empire (1600–1100 B.C.), however, the military class, which was made up of all types of soldiery, including the complement for the navy, became nearly

Privileges of the sacerdotal and military classes.

[1] An important profession in Egypt, ranking as a sort of medical specialty.

equal to the sacerdotal in privilege. Both classes were exempt from taxation, and from their number came the king. The rest of the people, who composed the industrial class, were obliged to support these higher classes, construct the public works, and carry all the other burdens of state. Yet they had definite rights guaranteed them by law.

While the classes were well separated early in the history of Egypt, their number and relative importance varied from time to time. Distinctions grew up especially within the industrial class. At no time, however, was the division between classes absolutely fixed, and no real caste system prevailed. While a son generally followed the occupation of his father, he might through education rise into a higher class.

Kindly treatment, but subordination of women.

Also in the social position allowed to women, Egypt was more advanced than most Oriental countries. As a rule, a man had but one wife, who was recognized as ' mistress of the household,' and, if we may judge from statuary, was treated with great affection. Ptah-hotep gravely advises : " If thou art successful and lovest the wife of thy bosom, fill her stomach and clothe her back. Make glad her heart during the time thou hast." The kings and some wealthy men had concubines, but even then the women were not veiled or immured. Women were allowed some education, although it never extended beyond the rudiments.

Cultural Development. — The advance for which Egypt has been most famed was in architecture. This also was closely connected with religion, and seems to have consisted mostly of temples and tombs, as there are few evidences of domestic or palatial buildings to be found. The temples were at first rude structures of wood or wicker, but before long were built of stone, and continued to increase in number and magnificence. The climax was reached in the later Empire through the completion by Ramses II of the temple of Amon, or 'Hall of Columns,' at Karnak, "the greatest of man's architectural works," the elaborate temple at Luxor,[1] the temple cut from the living rock at Abû Simbel, and the Ramesseum, or mortuary temple of the monarch on the plain of Thebes.

The Egyptian temples were grand in conception and massive in proportions.[2] The great structure at Karnak is judged to have been a quarter of a mile long, with a main entrance of 379 feet, which would make it more than twice the size of St. Peter's at Rome. But the development of architecture in these enormous buildings was limited, for they were all of practically the same conventional type. They were intended not merely as

[1] Karnak was begun in the Middle Kingdom, and Luxor probably so.

[2] Karnak depends upon mass for its effect, but Amen-hotep III's colonnades at Luxor depend upon form. Contrary to the general impression, Luxor exhibits much greater architecture than Karnak. The 'climax' was reached in the Eighteenth Dynasty.

sanctuaries, but as monuments to the sovereigns who built them. In front of the entrance gateway stood twin colossal statues of the monarch, together with a pair of obelisks bearing in hieroglyphics a glorification of his victories and achievements. The gateways were always flanked with towers, and, as luxury grew, the entrances were increased to two or three, which were often separated by avenues of sphinxes.

tombs,

Owing to the solemn prominence connected by the Egyptians with the thought of death, the tomb dominated even the temple. Diodorus said, " The Egyptians call their houses hostelries, on account of the short time during which they inhabit them, but the tombs they call eternal dwelling-places." In the earliest days the tomb was only an oblong pile of stones to protect the body which had been placed below in a chamber hollowed out of the rock. But the tomb was also used as a place where the friends of the deceased could make offerings to his ka and recite a ritual. So, while remaining of the same type architecturally, it soon became a vast structure of stone, sometimes having as many as thirty chambers. It contained a species of conventional chapel, which was adorned with scenes from the life of the deceased.

and
pyramids.

The pyramids, of which remains of seventy or more still exist, are the most impressive of all Egyptian structures. They should, however, be considered achievements of engineering rather than of architecture. One [1] of them is 755 feet square at the base, and rises to a height of 481 feet. It is faced on all four sides with limestone blocks so beautifully joined as to appear like a single surface. The pyramids were erected as tombs for the royal mummies, and, except for differences in size and material, are all alike.

The temples and tombs of the Egyptians were adorned with paintings, reliefs, and statuary. As their painting was done in outline only, it was the same in principle as the relief in their sculpture, except that it was more rapid, cheaper, and less durable. A king's tomb, which was always supposed to be carved in relief, if left unfinished, often had the design completed in painting by his successor.

Formalism of painting and sculpture.

Besides this lack of development, the outline, whether painted or in relief, was thoroughly formulaic. All figures had as far as possible to make every part of the body appear in profile, and they were all supposed to face toward the right, with the further foot and arm in advance. This always gives a stiffness and unnaturalness to Egyptian figures; and where the artist was obliged to face his figure toward the left and simply reversed the design, the effect is sometimes ludicrous.

---

[1] The three 'great pyramids' are those of *Khûfu* (Cheops) and his immediate successors in the Fourth Dynasty, and are located at Gîzeh, almost north of Memphis.

Practically every picture, too, had its typical method of representation, which the artist was required to follow. During the Empire a realistic school of artists flourished to some extent, but was eventually crushed out.

Egyptian statuary also was bound by social custom. The two classes of works that have been found, — portrait statues for the inner chambers of the tombs, and decorative statues of gods, kings, and sacred animals for the temples, have but two types of representation. Although their portraiture reveals the first emergence of individuality, until the time of the Empire the treatment of details, with the exception of the face, is generally as stereotyped as that of the position.

Development of crafts.

In other technical lines the Egyptians showed much practical skill, if we may judge from pictures and descriptions that have come down to us and objects that have been found. At an early day they learned to make bricks and mortar from the mud of the Nile. They worked granite and other stone of the greatest resistance, made the sharpest details, and gave a finishing polish. The smelting of metals was understood by them. They manufactured glass as early as the First Dynasty; and their skill in glazing beads, amulets, bowls, and vases, so as to resemble the most costly gems, and in preparing enamels for the work of the goldsmith, has commanded the admiration of modern experts. They invented a potter's wheel and baked the clay in a stove, but their product, though durable, was not of a high order. The papyrus was manufactured by them into paper, mats, ropes, sandals, and boats, and they were dexterous in weaving and coloring baskets, mats, and clothing. Their fine white linen was famous.

In the sciences, too, the Egyptians made considerable progress. Skill in engineering was forced upon them by irrigation problems, and the erection of the pyramids, the obelisks, and the supporting columns of the temples. This knowledge was purely practical and was discovered empirically. The mathematics underlying it was not a genuine science. Their methods in arithmetic were cumbrous, and small account was taken of fractions. In geometry, so necessary for surface measurement, there was little theory, although their procedure was accurate enough for practical results. Astronomy must have been developed early as a means of calculating the Nile's annual overflow and marking religious festivals. However, while they devised the calendar of 365 days more than four thousand years before Christ, they continued to believe in 'lucky' and 'unlucky' days, according as they were connected with various mythological events. Their knowledge of medicine, which on the empirical side was not inconsiderable, was likewise confused with incantation, superstition, and disgusting compounds.[1] The Egyptians also held music, both sacred

Empiricism of the sciences.

---

[1] Putrid meat, lizard's blood, swine's teeth, and dung were often ingredients.

D

and secular, in high esteem, but the rules for its composition were prescribed and rigid.

Literature was stereotyped and stilted.

The literature of the Egyptians was extensive. Besides the works on religion, morals, and practical pursuits, they wrote fairy tales, travelers' stories, novels, school books, letters, lyrics, and hymns to the gods and kings. While these works were the first in the history of literature to disclose the development of the individual, from a modern point of view they seem stereotyped, lacking in wit and description, and forced and stilted in style. The fiction is uninteresting and licentious. The hymns, except, perhaps, that of Amen-hotep IV, are lacking in devotional spirit, and consist largely of hyperboles and conventional phrases without much meaning. The school books are in the form of an 'instruction' from some wise ruler or teacher to his son or pupil. One of the most interesting is that found in the Sallier papyrus, in which the wise Dauuf thus describes to his son the advantages of the literary life: "Give thy heart to learning and love her like a mother, for there is nothing that is so precious as learning," and so on. As a rule, these instructions struggle after a fixed style and harp tediously on the same ideas.

Education was priestly, practical, and professional.

Education. Its Purpose. — The education of the Egyptians has been variously spoken of as 'priestly,' 'practical,' or 'professional.' From the foregoing account of their history, life, and customs can be seen the significance of each of these terms as descriptive of the forms of expression at which their education aimed. Inasmuch as the sacerdotal class possessed the learning, did the imparting, and dominated the state, the education of the times may well be called *priestly*. Again, education, which was always highly esteemed, was considered important entirely because of its *practical* value. It was intended simply to equip one with some *professional* skill that was in demand, such as that of the engineer, architect, physician, scribe, soldier, musician, or artisan, and thus help him to lead as happy a life as possible in this world, and secure the good-will of the gods in the life to come. It was also indispensable to office, and might enable one to attain a higher position in life than that of his father. " The ignorant man, whose name is unknown," according to one papyrus, " is like a heavily laden donkey; he is driven by the scribe." And another advises, " Set to work and become a scribe, for then thou shalt be a leader of men." The idea of a liberal education, however, never impressed itself upon the Egyptians. Such a notion as the search after truth for its own sake, without utilitarian motive, or the idea of educating for good citizenship or manhood, still awaited a time when people allowed freer play to individuality.

Its Organization and Content. — School life began as soon as the child passed out of infancy, at five years of age. School hours lasted half the day. The state did

Elementary education was possible for all,

not provide an educational system for the masses, but teachers were always to be had, and at a reasonable price, so that any clever boy might obtain a training in the rudiments of reading, writing, and arithmetic.

while higher education at the temples furnished training for the scribes, In the chief cities of the various districts, more advanced instruction leading to the different professions could be obtained at the temples. The chief colleges were at the temples of *Ptah* at Memphis, *Rê* at Heliopolis, and *Amon* at Thebes. During the early days boys of good family were often educated at the court with the sons of the king, and later the various departments of administration came more and more to educate the candidates for their respective official positions. Education was always for a specific profession, and very seldom did a young man change to some other line than that for which he had been trained.

The most general profession was that of the scribe. It was the first step on the ladder of learning, and the beginning of official advancement. While scribes were not needed because of the illiteracy of the people, there was a wide field for the profession. There were sacred manuscripts and official documents to be copied, estates and storehouses to be managed by those who understood accounts, and military, civil, royal, and priestly offices that needed skilled administration. The notarial, or lower-class scribe, after receiving an elementary education, usually secured his special training through apprenticeship in an office, where he learned to write the proper forms and legal documents, and to acquire the hieratic, or cursive, handwriting. One who was ambitious to become a scribe of the higher class went to a temple college, and here, besides learning the hieroglyphic, the hieratic, and, during the later Empire, the still more abbreviated demotic, writing, he was trained in ethics, philosophy, and good manners, and studied law and administration.

In addition to the attainments of the scribe as a basis, each of the other professions had a specific training of its own at the temple colleges. The architects learned, besides mathematics and mechanics, much that was of a sacred or historic nature. The physicians were taught crude anatomy and physiology, the use of remedies and incantations, and in some cases received special training on various organs, such as the eyes, brain, teeth, and intestines. The priests were given a thorough grounding in the old religious documents, ritual and ceremonies, law, mathematics, astronomy, and astrology, and all the other learning of the times.

architects, physicians, and priests.

Its Method. — Not much is known concerning the methods of teaching in Egypt, but considerable time must have been spent in learning the hieroglyphs. The Egyptians had reason to be proud of these characters, which were of their own invention, and were, in spite of their complexity, very easy to read; but the

Memoriter and imitative methods of teaching.

acquisition of some five hundred or one thousand characters was no small task for the memory. During the early Empire, too, the hieratic also came into use and had to be learned. The schoolboy at first imitated with a stylus upon a wooden tablet the copy that had been set for him. As soon as he could write, he was promoted to transcribe or write from dictation upon papyrus passages from some poem, story, religious work, school book of the type called an ' instruction,'[1] or some other good literature. By this means the pupils improved their calligraphy and style. Their literary training must have been carried on largely by imitation, as no vestige of a grammar or lexicon has yet been discovered in Egypt. Large numbers of their copy books, however, have been found in rubbish heaps. These books are easily distinguished by the master's corrections, indicated upon the upper edge of the pages. On the reverse side of the papyrus are often found bills for invoices of corn, business letters, and other practical work, written by the pupils. Any further instruction consisted, as has been seen, in learning a profession, also through memory and imitation from the priests at one of the temple colleges or from one of the higher officials of a governmental department.

Corporal punishment.

Learning by such methods must have been tedious, and discipline had to be severe. A pedagogical maxim

[1] See p. 34.

of the time was, "A boy's ears are on his back; he
hears when he is beaten." Reprimands were also used
as a corrective, and a youth could be punished by con-
finement to the temple for three months.

**Influence of Egyptian Education and Culture upon
Civilization.** — A great deal has been said, especially
in ancient times, about the 'learning of the Egyptians.'[1]
In comparison with other nations of their time, this
fame was undoubtedly deserved. The needs of the
country and their isolation from other nations forced
a higher development, and they contributed greatly to
the advancement of civilization and education, but their
achievements should not be exaggerated.

Great advance for the times,

The limitations of their activities can easily be seen.
Engineering and the other sciences, while appearing
for the first time in history, were at the empirical stage,
and were, in most cases, somewhat mixed with superstition. The industrial arts, as well as painting, relief, and
sculpture, had not received much development, with the
exception of their glazed work and enameling, and there
was an inclination to follow stereotyped rules. Even
their grand architecture, with all its elaborations, was in
the main conventional and fixed. Similarly, while their
thoughts and history were recorded, and they were the
first people to have a large and varied literature, it is repetitious and tiresome, and the style is prescribed and stilted.

but limited in development.

[1] Compare *Acts*, VII, 22.

Again, while the Egyptians held to a rude belief in immortality, and in the case of the priesthood at least had begun to regard God as one, their religion never rose beyond a personification of natural forces at the best and a species of animal worship at the worst. Their profound religious awe, while an advance on the superstitions of animism, totemism, and ancestor worship, must not be mistaken for an outcome of philosophy or analytic thought.   Likewise, their religion seldom bore any intimate relation to conduct,[1] and their teachings were largely prudential and imposed in the form of precept without any appeal to one's inner light.

As a result of the dominance of their superstitious religion, although the classes of society were not organized as an iron-clad system, such as sometimes occurs at this stage of development, they were so arranged as to suppress the individual and give practical control to the politico-religious priesthood.   Similarly, women were held in subjection.   They were not regarded as the slaves or toys of men, as in some countries of antiquity, but they were not allowed much freedom or intellectual training.

The type of education which prevailed among the Egyptians was the result of the social stage they were in, and was, in turn, somewhat calculated to perpetuate it.   By means of education the professions were to be

[1] At one period, however, religion must have had a close connection with conduct to have given rise to the elaborate confession in the Book of the Dead.

handed down, and with them the class distinctions that were connected. The teaching class, however, had not yet been differentiated from the priesthood, although it was recognized that instruction could no longer be carried on in the family. Their method, while somewhat more conscious than mere imitation, did not recognize individuality and was not yet a matter of genuine rationality. Their complex system of writing and their body of traditions required a tremendous effort of memory to learn, which prevented an intellectual development of more value.

With this system of education, great advancement was impossible for Egypt. She produced, to be sure, through the commerce of the Phœnicians, considerable effect upon the art, learning, and religion of the Greeks and other later peoples, and thus contributed her share to the world's progress. But while in many of the fundamentals hers was the earliest civilization, it was, after all, but the first link in the chain. New ideals and forms of expression were needed before civilization could continue its onward march.

Some effect upon progress through the Phœnicians and the Greeks.

SUPPLEMENTARY READING

I. Sources

Diodorus, Bk. I; Eusebius, *Fragments*; Herodotus, Bk. II; Manetho, *Fragments*; Plutarch, *Isis and Osiris*; Strabo, Bk. XVII.

II. AUTHORITIES

BREASTED, J. H. *A History of the Egyptians.*

BRUGSCH-BEY, H. *Egypt under the Pharaohs* (translated).

EDWARDS, AMELIA B. *Pharaohs, Fellahs, and Explorers.*

ERMAN, A. *Life in Ancient Egypt* (translated).

LAURIE, S. S. *Pre-Christian Education.* The Hamitic Races.

MASPERO, G. *L'Archeologie Egyptienne.*

MASPERO, G. *The Dawn of Civilization in the East* (translated).

PETRIE, FLINDERS. *History of Egypt.*

PETRIE, FLINDERS. *Religion and Conscience in Ancient Egypt.*

RAWLINSON, G. *The Story of Ancient Egypt.*

RENOUF, P. LE P. *The Origin and Growth of Religion as Illustrated by the Religion of Ancient Egypt.*

SCHMIDT, K. *Geschichte der Pädagogik,* Vol. I, Chap. I, pp. 194–250.

WILKINSON, J. G. *The Manners and Customs of the Ancient Egyptians.*

CHAPTER V

BABYLONIA AND ASSYRIA

Historical Relations. — The history of Babylonia must have begun a little after 3000 B.C.[1] Her empire, however, came before that of Egypt, for from 2300 to 1600 B.C., beginning with the reign of the famous Hammurabi, Babylonia had extended not only over all the Euphrates-Tigris district, but throughout Syria. During the rule of the Kassite kings, however, the country was greatly weakened, and the city of Assur revolted and eventually developed into the kingdom of Assyria. Then for several centuries Babylonia and Assyria were on terms of equality and diplomacy, broken more or less by short wars for supremacy, but Assyria gradually rose to preëminence, until in the tenth century she had begun to extend her sway over Babylonia and the other surrounding nations, and by 670 B.C. possessed the greatest empire known until that time. However, her splendor faded rapidly. Before the close of the century the mighty empire fell to pieces under

[1] Recent discovery has at last settled the age of Babylonian civilization. Its earliest monuments do not extend back to 3000 B.C. See Breasted, *A History of the Egyptians* (second edition), pp. viii, 419 ff., and 443.

43

the joint attack of the Medes and her southern province, Babylonia, which was at that time dominated by the fierce Chaldeans. Chaldean Babylonia then enjoyed a brief period of restored magnificence, but in 538 B.C. the Medes, now combined with the Persians, completely crushed their former ally.

Babylonia and Assyria are complementary in their history.

Thus Babylonia and Assyria seem to be complementary in their history, which lasts from 3000 to 538 B.C. They may well be considered together, especially as Assyria borrowed the Babylonian learning without making any important contribution in return. The Babylonio-Assyrian civilization was, as a whole, quite similar to that of Egypt, which has been described at length, and therefore, while of great historic importance in itself, will not need an extended account here.

Predominance of the sacerdotal class.

Social Conditions. — The classes of society in Babylonia and Assyria were about as distinct as in Egypt, and the influence of the priests, who also constituted the judges, scribes, librarians, teachers, authors, and other professional men, was almost as pervasive. They ranked, with the nobility, next to the king, and while Babylonia, and even more Assyria, attached greater importance to military affairs than did Egypt, the soldiers never reached the social dignity of the priesthood. The common people seldom owned land and were never allowed any part in public affairs. Since, however, both countries were very accessible, and found it desirable to exchange their agricultural products and manufactures for the stone, wood, and metals they lacked, their commerce expanded early, and the importance of merchants, tradesmen, and artisans increased until they were almost equal in rank with the privileged classes.   Certainly society never stratified into castes. Also women were treated with more consideration than in most Oriental nations, but, as in Egypt, a wealthy man might have concubines, and women were completely under the control of their husbands.

Subordination of women.

Religion and Ethics. — The Babylonio-Assyrian religion was as crude as the Egyptian in its formulation. At the earliest period it consisted in a worship of arbitrary spirits, who could be exorcised by formulæ. While these demons evolved into gods who typified great natural forces, such as the sun, moon, and stars, and the rain, storm-wind, and watery deep, it was still believed necessary to get into harmony with them through astrology and magic.   At first, as in Egypt, each Babylonian city had its own temples and gods, but gradually, as the cities were unified, a pantheon with a supreme god was organized.   This chief deity was *Bel* of Nippur until Babylon rose to prominence and made *Marduk* supreme.   Assyria accepted the pantheon, but placed her own god, *Ashur*, at the head. Probably, as in Egypt, through this henotheism, the priesthood and more intelligent people came to believe in a single

Nature worship,

henotheism,

supreme being, of whom the other gods were merely aspects, and, without giving up their augury and magic, dimly apprehended the ideas of sin, penitence, and dependence on God. This led to some moral aspiration, but unfortunately they were still unable to distinguish between ceremonial and ethical transgressions, and fear remained their moral motive. Superstitious observances continued to cloak cruelty, treachery, and sensuality. Their idea of the future life was generally less hopeful than that of the Egyptians. Except in the *Gilgamesh Epic*, they described the abode of the dead as dark and dreary.

Culture. — In their other intellectual activities the Babylonio-Assyrians were likewise defective. They achieved much in science, but altogether empirically and with a curious admixture of superstition. Both countries were covered each spring with a rich alluvial deposit from the Tigris and Euphrates, and, as in Egypt, the inhabitants were compelled to become skilled in all forms of engineering. Similarly, arithmetic, geometry, and mechanics made some progress, but were entirely practical. They had a complicated numerical system, compounded of the decimal and sexagesimal, and crude measures of length, area, capacity, and weight, derived from handbreadth as a standard. Geometry was used, but largely for mapping out the heavens in augury. They made many astronomical

and ceremonial ethics.

Science was empirical and superstitious;

discoveries, such as the movements of the heavenly bodies, the calendar year, and the calculation of eclipses, invented the signs of the zodiac, and named the points of the compass and several constellations, but astronomy had not yet evolved from astrology, and they used this knowledge mainly for horoscopes and divination. In their theory the earth was an inverted bowl with the edges resting on the waters; mankind dwelt upon the outside and the dead within the crust; while above was the heaven, another bowl, on the under side of which moved the heavenly bodies. Likewise, medicine could not become a genuine science with them, for they attributed all diseases to evil spirits, and while some real remedies were discovered by chance, their treatment often consisted in magic.

The architecture and art of the Babylonians and Assyrians, although comparatively advanced, inclined toward conventionality. While in their palaces and temples technical skill is shown, these structures are now famed for their immense size rather than for variety and beauty. Because of the scarcity of stone, they were always of brick, and were built upon a rectangular platform of the same material some forty feet above the ground. The temples were of the *ziggurat* type; that is, they consisted of a tower of several stories, each smaller than the one beneath. The palaces, especially those of the Assyrian monarchs at Nineveh

architecture and art were conventional;

during the empire, were more elaborate, having halls and galleries lined with sculptured alabaster, but even these were all rectangular, one story in height, and after the same general plan. The Babylonio-Assyrian art, which consisted largely of bas-reliefs and sculpture, was more varied and accurate in detail, and showed greater strength and freedom than in any other Oriental country, yet it savored of stiffness and naturalism. In the arts and crafts, especially baking bricks and pottery, engraving hard stones, weaving woolen cloths and rugs, and, during the Kassite period, coloring glass, these people were also expert, but generally conventional.

and litera-
ture, though
somewhat
advanced,
was repe-
titious and
formulaic.

To judge from the number of libraries of clay books that have been excavated, literature was highly esteemed by both countries. Probably each city of any size had its own library, and that of Assurbanipal (668–626 B.C.) at Nineveh contained books by the tens of thousands. As might be expected, much of this literature was religious and scientific. Numerous prayers, hymns, rituals, and even religious epic poems, including the *Gilgamesh*, which contains in its eleventh book the prototype of the Hebrew account of the Deluge, have been discovered. Cosmogonic narratives also, among them a *Creation Epic* similar to the story in Genesis, have in large part been preserved. Several collections of the science of the day, such as the

Illumination of Bel in seventy-two books, have likewise been recovered. Assyria furnishes especially historical inscriptions and an account of the diplomacy between the two countries from 1450 to 700 B.C., known as the *Synchronistic History of Assyria and Babylonia*. Also royal proclamations, official letters, tribute lists, judicial decisions, and systems of laws, especially the famous *Code of Hammurabi*, give us historical knowledge from the early days of Babylonia down. Reading books, grammars, and lexicons mark the emphasis on education.

While this literature shows some development of imagery and diction, and at times even rhythm and meter, it is made up, in general, of short, simple sentences, filled with imitation, repetition, and formulaic expressions, and consists largely of bare realism. During the Chaldean period it degenerated into great elaboration and artificiality without any new thought.

Aim of Education. — The educational aim of such a people, as in Egypt, was necessarily *practical* in the narrow sense of the word, for it was intended only as a preparation for the various professions. As this professional training was limited to the sacerdotal class, including the scribes, the system may also be described as *priestly*.

Practical and priestly education.

Organization and Content. — Practically nothing is known concerning the schools in which the elements

Elementary and higher education.

E

were taught, but the opportunities to obtain this training must have been numerous and widespread. The
higher education was given in colleges connected with
the temples, although the great libraries must also have
furnished a means of study for all who were ambitious.
A wide range of technical subjects, such as engineering, mathematics, astronomy, divination, natural science, medicine, architecture, art, literature, and history,
must have been taught.

Method. — Teaching seems to have been largely conducted through memorizing and imitation. The Babylonio-Assyrian writing, which consisted of cuneiform,
or wedge-shaped, characters, was, like the Egyptian,
'ideographic'; that is, it had a separate sign for
every idea. When they had learned the characters,
the pupils imitated the copies set them on slabs of
fine clay, which were then sent to the potter to be
baked. Many tablets with school exercises on them
have been found in Babylon. The methods used in
the higher education must have been similar. The
identity of the teachers of the elementary work, who
were probably numerous, and gave their instruction
individually rather than by classes, is unknown. Of
course the priests taught the higher work.

Influence upon Progress. — It will be seen that, although the Babylonio-Assyrian civilization and education were connected with considerable development,

progress in these countries was subject to limitations Greeks, and Israelites. similar to those in Egypt. Conventions controlled their activities, and individuality was largely disregarded. The most evident contributions appear in their influence upon the Phœnician arts and commerce, upon the epic and other literature of the Greeks, and in those legendary conceptions which, purified of their polytheism, the Israelites used as a means of teaching profound religious truth.

SUPPLEMENTARY READING

I. SOURCES

HARPER, R. F.   *Assyrian and Babylonian Literature.*

HARPER, R. F.   *Code of Hammurabi.*

HILPRECHT, H. V.   *Excavations in Assyria and Babylonia.*

JASTROW, M.   *A Fragment of the 'Dibbara' Epic.*

SAYCE, A. H.   *Records of the Past.*   Especially Vol. I, Chaps. I, V–VIII ; and Vol. II, Chaps. VII–IX.

II. AUTHORITIES

GOODSPEED, G. S.   *A History of the Babylonians and Assyrians.*

HASTINGS, J.   *A Dictionary of the Bible.*   Articles on Assyria, Babylonia, Races of the Old Testament, and Semites.

HILPRECHT, H. V.   *Recent Research in Bible Lands.*   Pp. 43–95.

JASTROW, M.   *Religion of the Babylonians and Assyrians.*

LAURIE, S. S.   *Pre-Christian Education.*   The Semitic Races (2).

MASPERO, G.   *The Dawn of Civilization in the East.*

SAYCE, A. H.   *Babylonians and Assyrians : Life and Customs.*

SAYCE, A. H.   *The Origin and Growth of Religion, as Illustrated by the Religion of the Ancient Babylonians.*

SMITH, W. R.   *Lectures on the Religion of the Semites.*

CHAPTER VI

PHŒNICIA

Of the other Semitic nations of the Ancient Orient, the Phœnicians and Israelites are of especial interest to the history of education, because of their influence upon civilization. The history of the Israelites lasted until so much later, and their culture was so superior to that of the other Semites, the nation is treated elsewhere[1] with countries of a higher type. But Phœnicia's development was of a lower order.

Arts and crafts, navigation, and the phonetic alphabet.

Achievements. — Phœnicia itself consisted of a narrow strip between the Lebanon mountains and the Mediterranean less than two thousand square miles in area, but its permanent colonies, which extended over all the islands and coasts of the Mediterranean and Ægean even to Spain, made up an empire of no mean dimensions. This widespread settlement and the influence of the Phœnicians were due to the extent of their commerce and manufactures, in which they surpassed all ancient peoples. They were, like all commercial people, shrewd and ingenious; and, while

[1] See Chap. XI.

somewhat lacking in originality, they borrowed the arts and crafts of the lands they visited. Thus they took from Egypt, Babylonia, and Assyria their architecture, sculpture, and bas-reliefs, textiles, glass-making, mining, ornamental metallurgy, gem-engraving, and ivory-carving, and improved somewhat upon them. They also greatly developed the science of navigation, and spread throughout the known world the systems of weights, measures, and money they had taken from the Babylonio-Assyrians. The greatest debt owed to them, however, is for the phonetic alphabet. While the Egyptians and others had long before invented a method of expressing speech in written form, it remained for the Phœnicians, from the demands of their commercial life, to shorten the process and reduce the ideographs to an alphabet.

Character. — On the other hand, they had all the worst faults of a people absorbed in materialism and money-getting without moral ideal. They were luxurious, sensual, cruel, crafty, hypocritical, and treacherous. The 'Punic faith' attributed to Carthage, Phœnicia's greatest colony, by the Romans, was not merely a hostile slur. Their mythology and religion were connected with the sun, moon, and other nature divinities, as in Egypt and Babylonia, but they rejected even the small spiritual element which they might have obtained from the priesthood of those countries. Their religious

Materialistic and treacherous in nature.

rites were disgusting, and at times included even the sacrifice of their own children.

Industrial and depraved.

Education. — Little is known of their formal education, but from the character of their civilization it would naturally be *industrial and commercial* in aim. In a country where writing was so universal, there must have been schools in which all young people could learn to read and write, and there was probably some means of imparting their arts and sciences to those who could take a higher training. Their ethical teaching must have been most depraved.

Disseminated arts and science, but had a negative effect ethically.

Effect upon Civilization. — Besides extending navigation and inventing the phonetic alphabet, the Phœnicians improved on the other arts and sciences of Egypt and Babylonio-Assyria, and disseminated them throughout the world. They must, however, have failed to make any allowance for the initiative of individuals. As far as their religion, ethics, and character are concerned, their influence was bad; and they have little to teach us now, except the destructive effect of a purely industrial education and absorption in commercial success.

SUPPLEMENTARY READING

HASTINGS, J.   *A Dictionary of the Bible.*   Article on Phœnicia.
LAURIE, S. S.   *Pre-Christian Education.*   The Semitic Races (3).
RAWLINSON, G.   *The Story of Phœnicia.*
SAYCE, A. H.   *The Ancient Empires of the East*, Chap. III.

CHAPTER VII

CHINA

National Conditions. — A type of transitional civilization, differing widely from that of the Semitic nations, is found to the east of them among the Mongoloid peoples that go to make up the Empire of China. This nation extends over a territory almost twice the size of the United States, and contains a population fully five times as large. The country is very unfavorably situated for intercourse with other nations, and such outside relations as it has had, especially on the west, have been of so unpleasant a kind as to crowd it back upon itself. As it possesses a remarkable diversity of climate and a wide range of products, it has been able to keep itself quite independent of foreign nations.

Chinese scholars claim great antiquity for their country, even dating its origin back millions of years to the first man, who is said to have sprung from chaos. While the history of China is known with accuracy only from the seventh century before Christ, there is some reason to accept the implication in the *Book of Historical Documents*, edited by Confucius, that there was a sort of gov-

Its great size and population,

isolation,

and age.

ernment by 2357 B.C.[1] Although the system of education was not instituted in exactly its present form until
617 A.D.,[1] it would seem that, practically speaking,
Chinese civilization and educational procedure have not,
until recently, altered in their type for more than three
thousand years. During the last decade there have been
most sweeping changes in the way of introducing Western education and culture, and a veritable renaissance is
going on at the present day. But while it may not be
long before China is among the leading civilized nations, results are as yet comparatively meager, and the
spirit of the past largely abides.

Effect of
teachings of
Confucius.

About the seventh century before Christ, owing to a
series of weak sovereigns, there was a century or more
of great degeneracy and civil disorder. Through a
widespread feudal system, the nobles became practically independent of the throne, and for a time the
country was in a state bordering on anarchy. This

---

[1] Opinions among European scholars are divided. On the one hand, the
entire oldest history, including that of Confucius himself, has been denied;
on the other, the most insipid tales leading back to the third millennium B.C.
have been taken as fact. Chavannes and Hirth place some confidence
in the accounts of the destruction of the Shang dynasty by Wu-Wang (1122
B.C.), but assign the lives of the earliest emperors to the legendary period.
The Chinese statement that public schools were established under the
Emperor Ti-k'u (2432–2363 B.C.) deserves little confidence, and the foundation of the imperial college and other schools in the twelfth century B.C.
is also open to some question; but it is certain that the Chinese have
taken a great interest in schools throughout their history.

condition was at length relieved through the influence of the teachings of Confucius, who had endeavored throughout his life to restore the ideas and customs of his ancestors. As a prefect he instituted these reforms within his own province, and was at first fairly successful; but he soon met with the frequent fate of reformers, and was obliged to flee and remain in exile until almost the day of his death. Afterward, however, he came to be regarded as a sort of Chinese Messiah, and his writings, which are everywhere used as a guide to life and conduct, are considered sacred.

The works in which his doctrines can be found are the *Five Classics* and the *Four Books*.[1] The former were collected [2] by him from writings of the past, except in the case of the last book, which was of his own authorship. Of the latter, which are in the nature

---

[1] The five *King* ('Classics') are (1) the *Shu*, or *Book of Historical Documents*, covering the period from 2357 to 619 B.C.; (2) the *Shih*, or *Book of Poetry*, which contains 305 odes, ranging in date from the eighteenth to the sixth centuries B.C.; (3) the *Yi*, or *Book of Changes*, an enigmatic and symbolic work on moral, social, and political themes; (4) the *Li*, or *Ritual Books*, composed of three sets of imperial laws; and (5) the *Hsiao*, or *Classic of Filial Piety*, which seems to be an effort of Confucius to construct religion on the basis of the virtue of filial piety. The four *Shu* ('Books') are (1) the *Lun Yu*, or *Discourses and Conversations* of Confucius with his disciples; (2) the *Works of Mencius;* (3) the *Ta Hsio*, or *Great Learning;* and (4) the *Kung Yung*, or *Doctrine of the Mean*, which was peculiarly a Confucian addition to the philosophy of the past.

[2] Probably they were colored somewhat by his own ideas, although he declares that he is a mere transmitter of the doctrine of Yao and Shun.

of exposition, one book was written by him, the second was contributed two centuries later by his disciple Mencius, and the other two are statements of his teachings by still later disciples. Many other commentaries have constantly been produced, to declare and illustrate his teachings.

Religion and Ethics. — Confucius was too absorbed in the practical reformation of morals to speculate on the nature of the Deity. However, while he formed no conception of a living, personal God as the source of authority, he could hardly be considered an atheist. He and his disciples recognized an Ultimate Principle, Supreme Order, or Heaven, which lay outside daily life and apart from men, and existed from everlasting to everlasting. "What Heaven has conferred," he declares,[1] "is called nature : an accordance with this nature is called the path of duty." Thus Chinese religion defines 'nature' as a manifestation of the working of the great Ultimate Principle, but in reality it means whatever is sanctioned by the usage of many generations and especially authorized by Confucius. So, to the Chinese, truth is what has been agreed upon in the past ; and virtue is a knowledge and observance of fixed ideas and customs. Thus, with them, morality becomes purely a matter of knowledge ; and their ethical system, which appears in the form of dogmatic

Custom is the Ultimate Principle,

---

[1] The first sentence of the *Kung Yung*.

precepts, with no appeal to reason, is the result of tradition, and is altogether formal. Many of these moral aphorisms are lofty, but the underlying basis is necessarily prudential and sordid. Under such a system, individuality is crushed, and originality is largely lost.

and the ethical system is traditional and formal.

Socially, this Supreme Order of Confucius is believed to be expressed in the family relationship. In consequence, this institution is treated with the greatest reverence, and the head of the family is endowed with absolute powers. His wife and children must render him implicit obedience in all things, so that women are practically slaves of their husbands. Moreover, the state is supposed to be a development of the family, and the emperor at its head is treated as 'the father of the nation.' He is to be obeyed without question, and has absolute control of the life and death of his subjects. Hence the fourth of the Confucian Classics [1] declares : "When nothing is left incomplete or improperly discharged ; this is what is called perfection. There is a fundamental agreement between a loyal subject in the service of his sovereign and a filial son in the service of his parents. In the supernal sphere there is a compliance with the repose and expansion of the energies of nature ; in the external sphere, a compliance with the rulers and elders ; in the internal sphere, the filial

Absolute control of the father in the family, and of the emperor in the nation, is part of Confucianism.

[1] See the *Li*, Bk. XXII, 2.

service of parents : — all this constitutes what is called perfection."

Numerous rites and ceremonies are pre-scribed.

With so stereotyped a society and moral code, it is not surprising that religious observances in China are also thoroughly formal.   The Classic quoted from above prescribes the exact moral and social acts that are to be performed each day by both family and state, declaring that " of all the methods for the good ordering of men, there is none more urgent than the use of ceremonies." Connected with the abstract pantheism and intellectual ethics of Confucius, there is a yearly ceremonial performed by the state as a whole in the person of the emperor-father,[1] and his various provincial representatives.   It is intended to honor Nature and acknowledge the dependence of man upon the Supreme Order. The family idea of Confucianism is also carried out in a formal worship of ancestors, which, however, is partly the outcome of a fear that these spirits of the departed might, if neglected, visit wrath upon their descendants. But besides these and other features of Confucianism, which is the state religion, though professed only by the better educated people, an idolatrous form of Buddhism,[2] and a still more degenerate Taoism,[2] made up of incantations, exorcism, and spiritism, are adhered to by

[1] See footnote on p. 65.

[2] See *Sacred Books of the East,* edited by Max Müller, Vols. XIX, XXXIX, and XL.

the masses generally. These cults, however, do not conflict, but have tended to amalgamate with the older religion, which had shaped the Chinese character long before the others entered the field.

Culture. — The language and literature of the Chinese have remained quite as undeveloped as their religion and social order. The language consists of monosyllables,[1] and is completely analytic and juxtapositive. There are no distinct parts of speech and no inflections; and the grammatical relations and meaning are indicated by position in the sentence, and by combinations with qualifying words, assisted by tone and accent. There is no alphabet, and the written characters have been modified but little from the original ideographs. The literature of China consists largely of the nine sacred books and numbers of commentaries upon them by later writers. The subject-matter[2] of these works consists for the most part of preceptive systems of morals and ceremonials, barren annals and history, and various types of lyric poems, together with interpretative explanations. Their literature has been greatly hindered by their early activity in this direction, of which they are extremely proud. The language in which this classic literature is written differs so much from the colloquial as to be practically a foreign tongue.

Language is analytic and juxtapositive,

literature is barren and formulaic,

---

[1] This, however, is possibly due to the decay of the original dissyllabic and trisyllabic forms.   [2] See footnote 1 on p. 57.

and the development of science, art, and the crafts has been handicapped.

Because of the Chinese opposition to anything new, there has never been any real philosophic speculation, or any development of physical or biological science among them. The few theories they have invented are almost as devoid of fancy as they are of accuracy. Chinese artists have shown much delicacy of touch in carving fans and card-cases, but while most of their work is pretty, it is cramped and out of proportion. Painting and sculpture have not advanced much beyond rude imitations of nature, and they pay little attention to perspective or shading. From the seventh century A.D. they have made beautiful porcelain, and, from their earliest history, mirrors of bronze, and have at all times woven mats, chairs, and baskets from rattan; but all their patterns are imitative and little subject to change.

The Purpose of Education. — Thus every influence connected with the history of the Chinese has conspired to make them a most conservative people. The isolation of their geographical position, the sufficiency of their natural products, and the national habit that has resulted from such vast numbers of people following a definite bent for thousands of years have done much toward creating an inherent opposition to progress. The preservation of the past has become the great essential, and all originality is regarded as impious and unpatriotic.

Naturally, the educational aim is a reflection of their social ideals. As far as it is conscious, the purpose of education is to maintain conditions as they have always been, and, by means of literary training of a most stereo-typed order, to reduce to uniformity a numerous and heterogeneous people. It is not intended to advance the individual or social welfare of the people, but to enable the pupils to pass examinations upon certain definite requirements fixed for centuries past. Hence the Chinese system has often been referred to as the most perfect type of *static*, *ancestor*, *family*, or *formal education*.

Intended to maintain conditions as they have been.

Means of Education. — The means for providing this training is ingenious. The administration of a school system for some four hundred million people might easily be felt to be too cumbersome for any state to undertake. At any rate, the Chinese Empire has not attempted this, but it does encourage all private endeavors by limiting eligibility for every national position of trust and dignity to the educated, and it allows to practically all classes the privilege of securing an education and competing for these honors. Yet, while schools exist everywhere, and no boy is excluded from rising to the highest office under the empire, the attendance is smaller than it should be. This is because the only real value of Chinese training is to enable one to pass examinations leading to offices of profit and honor, and

No national system, but private schools encouraged.

the educated man is actually unfitted thereby for any other employment, except teaching, without loss of prestige. So only one pupil in twenty passes beyond the elementary work, and but a small fraction of these remains long enough to secure even the lowest degree. Except in the case of a few wealthy families, where the training is entirely private, girls are not allowed any education beyond the household arts and fitting deportment, and women cannot compete at the examinations. Such a school system is necessarily ineffective, in spite of its apparently being so general.

Twofold organization: (1) Elementary schools;

The organization of education is twofold, and consists of a system of schools and a set of examinations. The schools, which are usually concerned with elementary training only, are seldom held in buildings designed for the purpose. The master's own dwelling or that of some wealthy patron, an old pagoda or temple, or even a shed, is ordinarily used as a schoolhouse. The schoolrooms are, as a rule, far from attractive. In them are generally a study-table and armchair for the teacher, and a picture or altar of Confucius in one corner of the room. The boys bring their own tables and chairs or stools, and provide themselves with books, paper, pencils, and India ink. Much ceremony is practiced, and is, doubtless, necessary to keep alive any respect under such bare surroundings. When a pupil first goes to school, about the age of seven, he is dressed in festal garb with a tasseled cap. As soon as he has entered the room, he prostrates himself before the picture of Confucius,[1] and then with almost equal reverence he bows to the teacher. Thereafter, he begins every morning of his school life with these two ceremonies. Dr. Martin tells us: "In no country is the office of teacher more revered. Not only is the living instructor saluted with forms of profoundest respect, but the very name of teacher, taken in the abstract, is an object of almost idolatrous homage."

As the tasks are most severe, school hours last from sunrise to five in the afternoon, with an intermission from ten to eleven for luncheon; and school is in session practically throughout the year. Thus the schoolboy, being excluded from all companionship with those of his years, becomes the veriest drudge.

While students are generally obliged to continue their work beyond the elementary grades by themselves, a few academies for higher training have been founded under private auspices, or through the endowment of wealthy men and public officials. These academies prepare for the government examinations, which comprise the higher part of the scholastic organization, and

(2) Examination system for higher work.

[1] On the last day of 1906 Confucius was, by imperial edict, raised to the same rank as Heaven and Earth, who are worshiped by the emperor alone. This action is supposed to have been taken in deference to the increasing number of Christian students, who object to bowing to Confucius.

F

are more distinctively Chinese.   From the ranks of the successful are filled the various offices of the empire, and in this way the order of the government and of society is preserved without change.   After two preliminary, or, as as we might say, 'entrance' examinations, there are tests of three grades, each of which, **with degrees.** if passed, leads to a degree.   An idea of the precise and formal character of these examinations, and the way in which those who succeed are rewarded, can be gained with a fair degree of accuracy[1] from the tabulated outline on pages 68 and 69.

Those who have attained the doctor's, or 'fit for office' degree, may take a fourth and final examination, and, upon passing it, become life members of the *Han-lin Yuan* ('forest of pencils'), or Imperial Academy.   The members of the Han-lin are the official poets and historians of China.   They virtually serve as the emperor's cabinet, and, although as such their educational prerogatives are only advisory, other offices of great importance are also granted them.   Sometimes the emperor designates the one who most distinguishes himself in the final examination as the literary leader of the nation, and this man is held in great reverence by all as the very flower of their genius.

There is no age limit for any of the examinations,

---

[1] Authorities differ in their descriptions, and the details are too numerous to be given in full.

and not infrequently a youth has undergone the ordeals
at the same time with his father, and even his grand-
father. During the entire time of an examination the
candidates are locked up in cells, and are not allowed
to leave under any circumstances. Even their meals
are eaten there. The strain under which they labor
must be tremendous; and often serious illness, or even
death, results. The examinations, however, are not
always conducted honestly, for, despite a vigorous
searching of the candidates beforehand, small editions of
the sacred books, or essays prepared in advance, are sometimes smuggled into the examinations in their sleeves,
and officials have been known to be open to bribery.

Subject-matter of the Course. — The entire course of
study in the Chinese schools may be divided into three
grades. In the first, or elementary period, the pupils
learn the most important characters in the language
and commit the nine sacred books to memory. The
characters, as has already been indicated, do not represent sounds, but ideas, and a different symbol is used for
every word. There are, therefore, fully thirty thousand
ideographs, although only about five thousand appear
in the Five Classics and the Four Books. In acquiring
these characters, some six or seven schoolbooks [1] are com-

In the elementary period, the most important characters are learned and the sacred books committed.

---

[1] The first schoolbook, or primer, is the *San-tsz King*, or *Trimetrical
Classic*, from which the pupil acquires some five hundred symbols. It receives its name from the fact that it is rhythmically constructed, having three

EXAMINATIONS FOR DEGREES IN CHINA

	First	Second	Third
Place held . . .	County seat [1]	Provincial Capital [1]	Capital of the Empire
Number of centers	252	18	I
How often . . .	Twice every three years	Every three years	Every three years
Length of session	One day and one night	Three sessions of three days each	Thirteen days
Presiding officer	Provincial examiner	Two examiners from the Han-lin	The Han-lin (Imperial Academy)
Nature of the examination	Two prose essays, and one poetical, on themes from the sacred books	Five or six essays on each of the first two days; and five questions on the history and economics of China, for the third day	
Number of candidates . . .	500 to 2000	4800 to 10,000	
Number that pass	About 1 in 35 [2]	One in 120 [2]	A larger proportion than in the two other examinations

EXAMINATIONS FOR DEGREES IN CHINA — *Continued*

	First	Second	Third
Degree received	'Flourishing Talent.' Cf. our 'Bachelor'	'Promoted Scholar.' Cf. our 'Master'	'Fit for Office.' Cf. our 'Doctor'
Other distinctions	Gilt button on cap	Gilt button of higher order on cap, a couple of flagstaffs before the gate, and a tablet on the door	
Privileges . . .	Chief place at banquet and funerals; spared all toil through support of relatives; may obtain subordinate official position, though no right to expect it [3]	Privileges of the first degree; but also sure of an office after a year or two, and sooner, if influence enough	May claim a county magistracy at once; from their numbers are filled all the higher civil and educational offices

[1] China is divided into 18 provinces, and these are subdivided into 252 counties and 705 districts. The preliminary examinations are held in the districts, and the tests for the degrees are conducted at the centers of the larger divisions.

[2] The examination is repeated, if too large a proportion pass on the first occasion.

[3] See especially Smith, *Village Life in China*, pp. 132–133.

mitted before the sacred books are taken up. All of these texts, including the nine sacred works, are intended at this stage simply to give a command of the characters, and no attention is paid to meaning. Even if the ancient literary language were understood, the subject-matter is treated in far too condensed and abstract a fashion for a boy to comprehend.

During this period also the pupils learn to write, although without any relation to what they are reading. Arithmetic, which is very necessary to them in calculating their exceedingly small currency, is never taken up in the school, but must be acquired afterward in the course of practical business. This elementary period of education, which lasts some five or six years, usually represents the limit for most boys who go to school at all.

In the second period, the books are translated;

In the second stage the nine sacred books are translated into more modern Chinese, although at first no explanation is given by the teacher. Later, commen-

characters to each line, and it treats of a number of duties and the rules for study. Following this comes the *Pih Kio Sing*, or *Century of Surnames*, from which they learn some four hundred family names. The *Tsien Tsz-wan*, or the *Essay of a Thousand Characters*, is studied next. In this the characters are arranged in two hundred and fifty columns of four symbols each, so as to secure rhyme and rhythm, but without much regard to continuity or sense. There are also used the *Yiu Hioh Shi-tieh*, or *Odes for Children*, the tractate on *Filial Duty*, called the *Hiao King*, and finally, the *Siao Hioh*, or *Juvenile Instructor*, all of which contain moral ideas in the form of story or precept.

taries are taken up, and the meaning made clear. The and in the third, essays are modeled after them. third period is occupied with the writing of essays and poems after the style and thought of the Five Classics and other fixed models. These latter stages of education last indefinitely, as they may continue until the student passes the governmental examinations, — or finally dies in the attempt.

Method of Teaching. — The Chinese methods of The boys memorize books by shouting, teaching are formal in the extreme. They are based upon mere memorizing and exact imitation. While each teacher has charge of from twenty to forty pupils, the instruction is not by classes, but by hearing of individuals. The words of the lesson are read out by the teacher and repeated in concert by the pupils, each of whom has a book open before him, until they can pronounce a line without assistance. Every one then shouts out the line until it is fully impressed upon his mind, when he hands his book to the teacher, turns his back, and rapidly repeats this portion in a shrill voice without any idea of the meaning. After all have committed the line, the next one is taken up in the same way. Of this method of teaching, Dr. Smith dryly remarks : "Every Chinese regards this shouting as an indispensable part of the child's education. If he is not shouting, how can the teacher be sure that he is studying ? And as studying and shouting are the same thing, when he is shouting, there is nothing more to be

and learn to write by tracing;

desired." Writing is learned by having the teacher's copy under the paper and tracing it with a brush until some facility is obtained. The pupils then imitate the copy without tracing until they can finally draw the characters from memory. The easiest symbols are learned first, and the writing is gradually made smaller as skill is acquired.

while higher education is obtained by committing lectures and phrases.

The higher education in explaining the sacred books and in essay writing is similarly crude in method. Explanatory lectures on the Five Classics and the Four Books are given at the private and public academies, and are largely committed to memory. Prose and verse composition on the topics discussed are also written at frequent intervals. These essays cannot show any originality, but must employ the thought, style, and meter of the sacred books or of certain distinguished scholars whose productions are memorized for this purpose.[1] Such a method would be about equivalent to requiring our American schoolboys to produce compositions after the style and subject-matter of Wyclif or Chaucer.

Teachers are unskilled,

No examinations or licensing of teachers, or supervision of their work, is attempted by the government. The elementary schools are generally taught by those who have obtained only the first degree and have as yet

[1] The slow and stereotyped fashion in which composition is learned is more fully described by Martin in his *Lore of Cathay*, pp. 293–294.

found no official opening, or often by those who have failed to secure even this distinction. We are, therefore, not surprised to learn from an eminent authority [1] that "To the enormous oversupply of school-teachers it is due that one of the most honorable callings is at the same time one of the most ill-paid." In the higher work, however, where the salaries are much better, even the 'doctors' are, as a matter of preference, sometimes engaged. With methods so poor, it is not surprising that an artificial stimulus is necessary, or that the bamboo is frequent and merciless in its applications.

and discipline is harsh.

Results of Chinese Education. — Thus every feature of the social and intellectual life of the Chinese has in the past stamped them as non-progressive. While they have not been altogether as stationary as sometimes described, and at present are introducing European civilization at a most surprising rate, their advancement in the past has been in spite of themselves. The chief tenets of the prevailing religion are the maintenance of an unchanging order and a static system of ethics. The worship of antiquity and ancestors, and the formal ceremonial, together with the family ideal of government at home and in the state, are natural outgrowths. The rules for conduct are prescribed, and must be committed to memory. In consequence, moral judg-

[1] Smith, *Village Life in China*, pp. 73–74.

ments are not well developed with them, and often no distinction is made between an accidental and an intentional lapse. The Chinese are sober, industrious, and thrifty; but beneath the surface of their fine ethical precepts, they are often vain, cunning,[1] servile, and immoral.

Their education is the product of this society, and is subject to the same limitations. While all boys are allowed to obtain school privileges, and it is possible for any one who can pass the first examination to secure social standing and an official position, because of the time and money needed to secure it and its worthlessness to one who fails at the examination, education is not common among the masses of the people. So, although the nominal opportunities offered prevent the formation of any definite system of castes, and may help to keep the people contented, the social order is in reality largely predetermined by an aristocratic edu-

The Chinese are bound to the past, and individuality is suppressed.

cation. Not only does this training tend to bind society to the past, but it more directly prevents progress by suppressing individuality. The subjects offered are purely literary and must be learned after a stereotyped fashion. Even the ruling of the paper, the formation of the symbols, and their exact position is prescribed. Mental training, therefore, consists mostly in the devel-

---

[1] Commercially, however, the Chinese have a reputation for formal honesty. Most of the cashiers in the Japanese banks are Chinamen.

opment of retention, and the more important powers of analysis and reasoning are neglected. The pupils are forced to load their minds with numerous details, and to make unessential distinctions. Failing to do this, they are severely punished. Little attention is given to anything that might foster initiative and originality, or fit the pupil for concrete living, except in so far as he obtains from his education certain rules for practical conduct, or through it secures the right to an official position. No training in calculation, geography, science, manual arts, or other subjects needed in actual life, is afforded.

No initiative or originality, or training for concrete living is possible.

Thus Chinese society and education have remained of much the same type throughout their history. In them the past is continually preserved, and progress is forbidden. As a result, the Chinese Empire has already endured for several millennia, and if outside influences were not interfering, it would continue in its way indefinitely. Where no change is permitted, stability is an easy matter; but it may be doubted whether permanence without progress can be accounted real existence after all.

SUPPLEMENTARY READING

I. SOURCES

MÜLLER, MAX. *Sacred Books of the East*, Vols. III, XVI, XIX, XXVII, XXVIII, XXXIX, XL.

II. Authorities

Douglas, R. K. *China.*

Douglas, R. K. *Europe and the Far East,* Chaps. I–VIII.

Hirth, F. *The Ancient History of China to the End of the Chóu Dynasty.*

Laurie, S. S. *Pre-Christian Education.* The Uro-Altaic Races, Chap. I.

Martin, W. A. P. *The Chinese; Their Education, Philosophy, and Letters.*

Martin, W. A. P. *The Lore of Cathay.* Especially Bk. IV.

Monroe, P. *A Text-Book in the History of Education,* Chap. II.

Smith, A. H. *Chinese Characteristics.*

Smith, A. H. *Village Life in China.* Especially Chaps. IX, X, and XII.

Williams, S. Wells. *The Middle Kingdom.* Especially Vol. I, Chap. IX.

CHAPTER VIII

INDIA

Effect of Environment. — The Aryan nations, which will now be viewed, were by nature more emancipated from superstition and bondage to the past than the other countries belonging to the transitional stage of culture. The strength of their intellect was largely due to the invigorating surroundings amid which they were originally placed. The cradle of the Aryan race, according to the view now prevailing,[1] is generally regarded as Europe rather than Asia, but those characteristics which more commonly mark the European Aryan did not survive in that branch of the family that went south and dispossessed the aboriginal tribes of India. The enervating climate of this great peninsula, the chronic lassitude of the older inhabitants, and their own inactivity eventually had its effect upon the Aryan conquerors. They must have entered India somewhere about 2000 B.C., and for nearly eight hundred years they preserved their peculiarities to a greater or less extent. In the earliest

The Aryans in India.

[1] However, the recently discovered cuneiform material in Asia Minor tends to show the Asiatic origin of the Iranians, and hence of the Aryans.

portions of their sacred writings, the Vedas, their thought so closely resembles the primitive form of the Persian religion, which never lost its Aryan vigor, as very clearly to suggest a common origin. During this early period they evidently worshiped the various powers of nature, especially *Agni*, the Fire, and *Indra*, the Thunder-storm,[1] and their religion was without an element of weakness or inaction.

Religion. — Gradually, however, the debilitating climate, together with various other causes, led to the formulation of Brahmanism, with its mystic philosophy, which is almost the opposite pole of the Aryan individualism and activity. The old Vedic gods and the sacrificial ceremonies were retained, but it was held that nothing except *Brahma*, the one universal spirit, really exists. Whatever else appears to have separate existence, even the earlier gods, is in reality identical with that spirit; and while men seem to be temporarily allowed an individuality of their own, they should seek an ultimate reunion by absorption into the great eternal spirit. With this is joined the belief in *metempsychosis*, or transmigration of souls. It was held that every creature must be repeatedly reborn in various forms until he is purified of all desires; and thus, by gradually doing away with activity and deeds, he becomes united with Brahma, or pure existence.

Mystic philosophy of Brahmanism.

[1] See Tiele, *History of Ancient Religions*, p. 113.

This pantheistic conception was, however, reserved for the Brahmans, or priestly class, who had grown into a hierarchy, and kept intensifying the lines between the castes. The masses were taught only a polytheistic worship, which, although based upon Vedic beliefs, embodied the fetishism of the older inhabitants, and multiplied sacrifices and ceremonies, and so eventually degenerated into an absurd idolatry. As a reform, Buddhism arose about 500 B.C., although it did not become a real rival to Brahmanism for two centuries and a half. It was founded by *Gautama*, more often called Buddha,[1] who, being himself only the son of a warrior, and not a Brahman, taught disregard of caste distinctions. It also insisted upon the uselessness of sacrifices, ceremonial, and prayers, and held that the goal of life was a complete extinction of desire, which would result in a state known as *Nirvana*. This is equivalent to self-annihilation, rather than absorption into the world-spirit. Feeling the hollowness of this transitory world, the Buddhists advocated monastic life in the forests.

Buddhism arose as a reform from ceremonial and class distinctions;

Such a negative ideal of life, together with the Buddhist substitution of an atheistic belief for the older pantheism, enabled the Brahmans about 500 A.D. to crush the schism completely. By the thirteenth century of our era, Buddhism had been altogether exiled to

but was crushed, and united with Brahmanism.

[1] Gautama has been known as *Buddha* ('the enlightened one') among Europeans.

Ceylon, Burmah, Siam, Thibet, China, Japan, and other places, or had lost itself in the modified form of Brahmanism known as Hinduism. Since then, education in India has consisted almost entirely of a training in Hindu principles and lore.[1]

The four castes,

Social Conditions. — A Hindu boy's whole situation in life, including the education that he receives, depends upon the occupation of his father, for the people are divided into hereditary classes, or 'castes.' As a result of the prominence of the religious element in their civilization, the priestly caste, or the *Brahmanas*, which also embraces all those skilled in law, medicine, architecture, music, legislation, and other learning, is the highest. It outranks that of the *Kshatriyas*, or warriors, which includes all those engaged in the administration of the country. The honor attached to leisure by the religion of the Hindus has caused those who carry on the industries to be looked upon as inferior to the former two classes. The third caste is, therefore, that of the *Vaisyas*, which is composed of merchants, farmers, and other employers of labor. The fourth, or lowest of all, including all outcasts, is looked upon as 'unclean,' and it comprehends, under the name of

---

[1] Great Britain, the present ruler of India, has transplanted there a complete school system of her own type, and the various Christian churches, the Mohammedans, and the Parsis have interested themselves more or less with education; but the most influential factor is still decidedly Hinduism, and with its peculiarities alone are we concerned here.

Sudras, the serving class and all menials. Numerous subdivisions [1] are also made within the castes, especially the third and fourth, and many former distinctions have now disappeared. Outside the social order altogether are the *Pariahs*, who, with the Sudras, are probably de- *and the Pariahs.* scendants of the original inhabitants. The Brahmanas seem to be of pure Aryan extraction, and the second and third castes of various degrees of mixed blood. But the first three castes are sometimes grouped together as *Aryas*, or nobles born, as distinguished from the serving class, the Sudras.

A man may marry a woman of a lower caste than his own, but not of a higher. So one may fall into a caste below, but he cannot rise. Neither wealth nor other success in life, nor any amount of philanthropy or exhibition of any virtues, can lift him a single notch beyond the point at which his family has been for centuries. Loss of caste by one person in a family will degrade all the rest. But the Brahmans have never been able, since the influence of Buddhism was felt, to place so strict an interpretation upon the caste system; and it is now generally admitted that even the lowest orders may sometime attain to absorption in Brahma. All the castes are also allowed to know a little of the pantheistic teachings. Eventually, with the growth of humanity, the caste system must altogether disappear, but, for a

[1] See *Code of Manu*, X.

G

long time to come, it is likely to be the curse of India, and to mark its system of education.

In such an organization of society, it is not surprising that woman is not held in proper esteem. It is true there have been some notable exceptions at all times, like the wife of *Rama*, the legendary prince of ancient India, whose memory is worshiped as the ideal type of womanhood; and there are instances cited in which poëtesses composed Vedic hymns, and a woman discussed philosophic questions. But woman's position in India has generally been to minister to the comfort and pleasure of man, and to bear children. The ancient laws tell us: "In childhood, a female must be subject to her father, in youth to her husband, and in widowhood to her sons; a woman must never be independent. Though destitute of virtue, or seeking pleasure elsewhere, or devoid of good qualities, a husband must be constantly worshiped as a god by a faithful wife." While a campaign is being vigorously waged by Christian missions against various revolting practices, yet even now, in keeping with the Hindu code, girls are in their infancy[1] still sold for wives, a gross polygamy is allowed,[2] and perpetual widowhood[3] of a degrading sort is still prevalent. The position of women in much of Hindu society is little above that of slavery.

Woman is supposed only to minister to man, and bear children.

[1] *Manu*, IX, 88.   [2] *Ibid.*, III, 12–13, and IX, 85–86.
[3] *Ibid.*, V, 160–164, and IX, 65.

Aim of Education. — Thus, ever since Brahmanism and brooding reflection first controlled the Hindus, the aim of education has been to prepare for the life to come and absorption into the Infinite, rather than for achievements in this life. The chief object is to fill the pupils with the tenets of their religion, and to teach them how to carry out its injunctions. Incidentally, education is intended to preserve the caste system commanded by Hinduism, and to keep all within the sphere of their occupation. The three upper castes are nominally supposed to gain a knowledge of the sacred works, but, outside the Brahmans, custom dictates that not many take advantage of the opportunity. The warriors are expected to pay more attention to martial exercises, and the industrial caste to acquire through apprenticeship the arts necessary for its hereditary occupations. The Sudras have been allowed to receive no education at all, and it has at times been even deemed a crime punishable with death to let them learn anything. It is intended that women shall remain uneducated, and it is considered a reproach to them even to know how to read or write, as they might thereby be tempted to neglect their domestic duties. So, throughout Hindu education, mental development for its own sake is entirely unknown.

Preparation for the life to come.

Means and Content. — All of the castes, however, except the Sudras, may now learn reading, writing, and

Elementary subjects and traditions are

learned at home, and later in local schools.

the elements of arithmetic, together with the special requirements and religious observances suited to each caste. They receive this training to some extent from the laws, traditions, and customs of the country through the medium of the family; but also in a more formal way from the elementary schools, which are a modern institution. These schools are held in each village under the trees in the open air, or, during bad weather, in covered sheds; and besides the subjects mentioned, since the early centuries of the Christian era, the pupils have been taught fables, parables, and allegories. The best known collection of these stories is the *Panchatantra*.

Higher education is carried on at Brahmanic colleges,

The higher education, from about 1000 B.C., has largely been carried on in Brahmanic colleges called *Parishads*. These were originally conducted by three Brahmans, but the number has gradually been increased until twenty-one are considered the ordinary corps of instruction. Even before these institutions were founded, however, during the Vedic period, higher schools for the study of the religious works and practices were held at the houses of the teachers or at the different royal courts. There are now also private schools that are not necessarily for Brahmans, in which the tuition may be paid for by services.

When a Brahman has attained a complete education, he has committed to memory various sacred books.

The chief of these is the work known by the collect-
ive name of *Veda* ('knowledge'). It includes four
manuals, each of which is also called Veda.[1] These
Vedas are arranged as rituals for the four orders of
Brahman priests, when engaged in sacrificing. To
each of these metrical portions are appended various
prose writings[2] which are intended as commentaries on
the hymns and prayers and on their application to the
sacrifices. "Every Brahmanic family," writes Professor
Bhandarkar, in the *Indian Antiquary*, "is devoted to the
study of a particular Veda; and the domestic rites of
the family are performed according to the ritual described in the Sutra connected with that Veda."

*by commit-
ting the
Vedas and
works drawn
from the
commen-
taries.*

From the different commentaries on the Veda has
been drawn the nucleus for metrical books of laws, like
the *Code of Manu*, which is a collection of traditional
customs; and for philosophical and scientific works,
such as the six *Angas* on Phonetics, Etymology, Meter,
Astronomy, Grammar, and Ceremonial respectively.

In all this hereditary knowledge of the Hindus, which
has been a natural fruit of their contemplative life, the
Brahman may also be instructed. The learning that

---

[1] These are (1) *Rigveda*, a collection of the earliest hymns; (2) *Sama-
veda*, and (3) *Yajurveda*, which are largely made up of verses from the
Rigveda, the one consisting of chants and the other of prayers and ritual;
and (4) *Atharaveda*, a composite collection, popular rather than hieratic
in its character.

[2] *I.e.* the *Brahmanas*, *Sutras*, *Aranyakas*, and *Upanishads*.

has been handed down in this way is not inconsiderable. To the Hindus we are indebted for our numerical notation, often wrongly attributed to the Arabs. During the fifth century after Christ they invented an algebra superior to that of the Greeks, although they were probably assisted by the work of the latter. They early learned how to calculate eclipses and find the location of planets by means of tables. They seem also to have had some knowledge of medicine. By 300 A.D. they possessed a treatise on rhetoric, and had worked out a logic two centuries before the time of Aristotle; while in the science of grammar, as early as the fourth century B.C., they were so far advanced that the Western world first learned what philology was when the study of Sanskrit was opened to Europe a hundred or more years ago. To complete his course of study has always taken the young Brahman from eight to twelve years; and he may, if he undertakes the entire range of Hindu knowledge, spend a lifetime in the work.[1]

Method of Teaching. — Since all learning has been preserved by oral tradition, it is not remarkable that

Pupil commits by singing aloud.

---

[1] We learn from *Apastamba-sutras*, I, 2, 12: "He who has been initiated shall dwell as a religious student in the house of his teacher, for forty-eight years (if he learns all four Vedas), for thirty-six years, for twenty-four years, for eighteen years. Twelve years (should be) the shortest time." Max Müller (*Origin of Religion*, p. 156) shows that at present a student requires fully eight years to learn the various sacred books.

practically the only method of instruction, even since writing has been used, is a *memoriter* one. Even the later texts are so written as to be easily committed. The alphabet and some ten or twenty pages of the text are taught before any explanation is given. The teacher pronounces two or three words at a time, which the pupil repeats after him; and, when two or three verses have been read, they are sung aloud by the boy until he has committed them. Each lesson consists of 125 to 175 verses. The higher education is imparted in a similar way. Writing is learned by practicing the teacher's copy on the sand with a stick, then on palm leaves with a stylus, and finally on plane leaves with ink.

The teachers are always Brahmans, and, to teach even the elementary work, are required to pass through the complete course of higher study.[1] Naturally they are treated with the greatest respect.[2] They are not directly paid for their services,[3] but collect 'presents' from the parents, especially the wealthier men. It is considered a grave offense to study the sacred works without an authorized instructor.[4] Older students, however, are often used by the master to teach the younger pupils, and it was from India that the idea of the 'monitorial' system was first obtained by Andrew

Teachers are treated with the greatest respect.

[1] Max Müller, *Origin of Religion*, p. 154. [2] *Manu*, II, 191–208.
[3] *Ibid.*, III, 15. [4] *Ibid.*, II, 242.

Discipline.

Bell, and others before him.   Although individuality is entirely neglected in this system of sheer memory, discipline, owing to the unassertiveness of the pupils, is mild, except in very serious cases, when a pupil may be beaten upon the back with a rope or a split bamboo.[1]

Effect upon Hindu Character. — Thus education in India is based upon a gloomy religious belief and the rigid caste system accompanying it.   The Hindu boy is impressed with the unreality and wretchedness of this life, and is enjoined to escape from it as soon as possible through reflection and inactivity.   He also learns to regard members of the other castes not merely without sympathy, but with positive hatred.

Most of the people are uneducated, and even the Brahmans have only traditional learning; hence there has been little progress or ambition.

In consequence, education has been forbidden to ninety-eight per cent of the population,[2] and, as far as it does exist, it is a mere stuffing of memory.   It is as little concerned with real mental culture as it is with training for manhood or citizenship.   Also, as has been seen, while the Brahmans have handed down much traditional learning, it is blended with superstition, and new knowledge of any sort is barred.   All science and inventions are naturally beside the mark when emphasis is laid chiefly on the life to come, and it is known that

[1] *Manu*, VIII, 299–300.

[2] There is, however, a remarkable stir in education to-day.   The *Gaikwar of Baroda* first introduced free and compulsory education throughout his state, and other *rajahs* are following his lead.

no amount of advance in methods, implements, and mental development can make the slightest change in one's position during the present life. The Hindus still plow with sticks of wood, as their remotest ancestors did, and their wonderful soil fails to produce a tithe of what it might. Their crops are harvested and threshed by devices equally antique. They bake their bricks, work their metals, and weave their cloth with appliances that might have seemed crude to the early Egyptians. In fact, they still live in the first, rather than the twentieth, century.

Similarly, the Hindus have, until recently, been greatly lacking in ambition, self-reliance, and personal responsibility, and have never come to any feeling of solidarity or national unity. They have cultivated the passive virtues, — patience, resignation, gentleness, peaceableness, and docility, and they are polite, respectful toward their parents and elders, and obedient to authority; but they have accomplished little for themselves or civilization, and have been conquered by one nation after another. The Macedonian Greeks, the Mohammedans, the Turkomans and Mongols, the Portuguese, the Dutch, and the British have successively been masters of their land. To them progress, prosperity, and patriotism are foreign ideas. Despite all the Hindu's fineness of intellect and his idealistic religion, India seems typically 'barbarian.'

SUPPLEMENTARY READING

I. Sources

Müller, Max. *Sacred Books of the East.* Vols. I, II, VII, VIII, X, XIV, XVII, XX, XXII, XXV, XXVI, XXIX, XXX, XXXII, XXXVI, and XXXVIII.

II. Authorities

Dutt, R. C. *Ancient India.*

Dutt, R. C. *The Civilization of India.*

Laurie, S. S. *Pre-Christian Education.* The Aryan Races (A).

Letourneau, C. *L'evolution de l'education.* Chap. XIV, A and B.

Müller, Max. *The Origin and Growth of Religion as Illustrated by the Religions of India.*

Ragozin, Z. A. *Vedic India.*

Sayazi, Rao. *Articles on Education by his Highness the Maharaja Gaikwar of Baroda.*

Taylor, H. O. *Ancient Ideals.*

Tiele, C. P. *Outlines of the History of Religions* (translated). Chap. IV, I and II.

Williams, M. M. *Brahmanism and Hinduism.*

CHAPTER IX

PERSIA

Natural Influences. — The Persians seem to have had much the same origin as the Hindus. The environment into which they moved, however, was far different, and they never lost the energy and aggressiveness of the Aryan. Instead of the enfeebling climate of India, with its prolific soil and dreamy inhabitants, they met with the stern conditions of a barren country and warlike peoples, and were spurred to greater activity by the bracing air of their surroundings. They came to dwell on the high table-lands, hedged on all sides by still loftier mountains, south of the Caspian Sea, and east of those Semitic countries at whose development we have already glanced. Although their country was grooved with many productive valleys, and was extremely fertile on the north as it sloped toward the Caspian, as a whole it was an arid land, and required a constant struggle to yield the barest living. Thus the Persians were soon tempted to prey upon the wealthy civilizations to their west, especially since these countries had been overcome by luxury and sloth.

who absorbed all the surrounding nations.

About 550 B.C. the Persians absorbed their relatives, the Medes, who had themselves already (606 B.C.), in conjunction with the Chaldean Babylonians, come into possession of Assyria. Bactria and Elam had also been amalgamated with Persia, and Cyrus, king of the combined countries, set out to extend his empire. After conquering Lydia (545 B.C.), which had previously reduced most of Asia Minor, the Medo-Persians turned against their former allies, the Babylonians, who were attempting to stay their progress, and easily overcame them (538 B.C.). Cyrus died a few years later (530 B.C.) while reducing the Scyths. His son and successor, Cambyses, carried the Persian conquest into Egypt, where he, too, met with death (525 B.C.). The next sovereign, Darius, cousin of Cambyses, pushed his way into northern India (520 B.C.), and carried on aggressions in Thrace (515 B.C.), where the Persians came into close contact with the Greeks, and were led into the struggle (500–479 B.C.) which ended so disastrously for themselves. Out of this, too, grew the conquests of Alexander (336–323 B.C.), and the final downfall of the Persian Empire.

An excellent organization was formed in the provinces,

Government. — But for some time Persia ruled over the largest empire the world had known. Darius displayed much wisdom as a statesman. He followed the Assyrian plan in dividing his dominion into 'provinces,' but greatly improved upon it. Each of the twenty provinces was placed under a *satrap*, or governor, appointed by the Great King to act in his stead. This viceroy had as his assistants a civilian secretary, with a council, and a general, commanding an army. While the Persians insisted on firmly maintaining their rule and crushing any rebellion with great severity, they granted complete local autonomy. Each province was required to pay tribute in proportion to its means, but was allowed absolute freedom in its customs and religion. Under such a centralized government these warlike nations were really better able to preserve and advance their civilization than if they had each been entirely independent.

The administration at home was equally wise and strong. It was organized as a bureaucracy, and had seven tribal princes, seven judges, and various other officials who administered affairs, under the Great King. The laws were just and humane. In consequence, practically all within the Persian Empire came to feel a personal responsibility for its welfare, and, in spite of the way in which their dominions were spread out and separated by impassable mountains and unnavigable rivers, for a long space of time there remained a sense of national unity and a willingness to work together. *and at home.*

Religion and Ethics. — As might be expected from the national characteristics, the religion of the Persians, *Mazdeism*, was a militant one. It recognized two *Militant and dualistic religion.*

antagonistic spirits, *Ahura-Mazdah*,[1] or Ormazd ('Lord Wisdom'), the omnipresent and omniscient creator and nourisher of all mankind, and *Anra-Mainyu*, or Ahriman ('Enemy Spirit'), who arose from the conflict of forces when Ormazd created the universe, and was the source of all things evil in the world. It was believed, however, that Ahriman was inferior to Ormazd, and would eventually be vanquished by him.

Zoroaster introduced spiritual conceptions, This spiritual conception seems to have been formulated first about 600 B.C. by a reformer named *Zarathushtra*, or Zoroaster, as he is now commonly called. Somewhat before his day there existed a primitive worship of natural forces[2] not unlike the Vedic. The earlier belief remained, but the good elements were treated as ministering angels of Ormazd, and the evil as subordinate demons of Ahriman. The chief good angels were thought to be the divinities of fire and light.[2] Holy fires were consequently tended by an hereditary priesthood called the *Magi*, and the sun was worshiped by all.

Light, however, was regarded by the more advanced merely as emblematic of truth, wisdom, virtue, and

[1] Compare the warrior deity, Ashur, whom the Medes may have adopted while in captivity to the Assyrians, 2200–800 B.C., and later identified with Mazdah. The Medo-Persians gained much from their contact with Şemitic peoples.

[2] Compare Agni and Indra, p. 78. See also Sayce, *The Ancient Empires of the East*, pp. 256–257.

purity. Hence men were urged, by overcoming evil impulses and desires, and by extending the power and civilization of their native land, to enter the contest of life on the side of light, and aid Ormazd in his ultimate victory over Ahriman. Professor Tiele says of Mazdeism: "The whole life of the believer is a constant conflict with evil, in which, as is universal in antiquity, little difference is made between physical and moral evil. Agriculture, likewise, and the care of clean animals and plants are powerful means of weakening the kingdom of impurity. But the love of truth, also vigilance and activity, are weapons which win the victory in this contest."

But, as in most of the other barbarian countries, the higher ideals were held only by the most intelligent people; and while they determined the general condition of religion and society, were not at all understood by the masses, who largely retained the original worship of natural forces. Yet even in this case there was no suggestion of idolatry, if Herodotus[1] is to be credited, when, before describing the more overt ceremonies of the Persians, he says: "It is not their practice to erect statues, temples, or altars, but they charge with folly those who do so; because, as I conjecture, they do not think the gods have human form, as the Greeks do."

but the masses retained the worship of natural forces.

[1] I, 131.

Moreover, a belief in bodily resurrection was generally held by the Zoroastrians.   At death a man's good
deeds were supposed to be weighed against the evil,
and if the good prevailed, he was sent to the 'Abode
of Song,' where dwelt Ormazd and the saints; but if
the evil surpassed the good, he was cast into the ' Lower
World,' to be tortured by demons.   Should the balance stand even, a period of second probation was
allowed him.   It was believed, however, that even the
wicked would in the end be purified and counted among
the blessed.

Virtues
that were
inculcated.

Clearly Mazdeism was an ethical religion and gave
some value to personality and the desire to work out
one's own salvation.   The chief virtues, as would be
expected in a religion of light and individual responsibility, were truth, justice, gratitude, courage, and self-
control.   There were naturally no castes, except possibly in the case of the hereditary tribe of priests, the
Magi.   While, according to Herodotus,[1] polygamy and
concubinage were common, women were held in higher
esteem than with most Orientals, and the Persians were
naturally domestic.   Children rendered a willing obedience, and the family tie was held to be sacred.   It was
believed that he who slew a parent must be a change-
ling or a bastard, for it was hardly to be supposed that
one's own legitimate offspring could act in this way.[2]

[1] I, 135.   [2] See Herodotus, I, 137.

The Zoroastrian ideas of religion are found in the sacred books known as the *Zend-Avesta* ('The Law and Its Interpretation'). Although Mazdeism began to creep into the old nature worship possibly about 900 B.C., it was not made a definite system before the time of its great prophet, Zoroaster, whose *Gathas* ('Psalms') contain the most exalted and spiritual thoughts of the religion. The Zend-Avesta as a priestly code was hardly formulated into a canon until a hundred years or so after his time.[1] In its present form it does not date earlier than the third or fourth century of our era, and it has probably been affected somewhat by Greek philosophy, and possibly also by Judaism and Christianity. There remains but a small portion[2] of the original work, containing, perhaps, one tenth the material in our Bible. These Zoroastrian scriptures

The Zend-Avesta, or sacred books.

---

[1] The Greeks, however, speak of Zoroaster's having composed a million verses, and the Zoroastrian tradition itself asserts that there were two archetype copies of the Avesta, written on twelve thousand parchments, and that these two copies were destroyed by Alexander.

[2] The Avesta was neglected during the Greek (336–250 B.C.) and the Parthian (250 B.C.–226 A.D.) dynasties, but under the Sassanian monarchs (226–652 A.D.), who restored Mazdeism, about one third of the original text was recovered. It was, however, even more scattered by the conquest of the Mohammedans (652 A.D.), who have ever since been in control of Persia. The remaining portions of the work have been preserved by the few thousand adherents of Zoroaster that still live in Persia, chiefly in Yazd and Kirman, and by the nearly one hundred thousand *Parsis*, who are scattered through India, and more fully represent Zoroastrianism.

H

may be divided into six parts.[1] The first four contain litanies and hymns of praise of greater or less importance, the fifth [2] is a collection of religious rules and legends, and the sixth consists of a set of fragments and glosses. Most of the Avesta, except the *Gathas*, or its oldest psalms, is simple in thought and style. The metrical parts have considerable merit, but the prose is generally tiresome and lacking in spirit.

The Aim of Education. — The Persian ambition, however, was not literary or scholastic. Under the circumstances it was but natural that they should strive principally to produce a nation of soldiers, with all that implies in the way of physical education and training in valor and other virtues.

Military purpose.

Its Organization and Content. — Until he was five, the young Persian was trained at home by the women. According to Herodotus,[3] his father never saw him, in order that he might not be grieved if the child should die in infancy. During this period the boy was supposed to be completely unmoral, and was not expected to distinguish between right and wrong, but simply to obey the directions given him. Girls were at no time allowed anything further than domestic training.

Religious training was given at home;

At five the boy's formal education began. Through the family he was inducted into the national religion

---

[1] I.e. *Yasna, Visperad, Yashts*, and a group of *Minor Texts*.
[2] *Vendidad*.   [3] I, 136.

6255

and its observances.   Unless he belonged to the
wealthier classes, this haphazard knowledge, except
possibly apprenticeship training in some occupation,
constituted his entire education.

The more aristocratic boys, however, after this had *and possibly physical*
some military training.   Possibly something not unlike *and ethical,*
the rigorous plan of the Spartans was in vogue in
Persia.[1]   Boys may have been exposed to hardships of
all sorts in their daily living as a preparation for warfare.   They were probably also given a careful physical and ethical training.[2]   In the open courts before the
palace of the Great King or one of his satraps, it is said
that they learned horseback riding, and shooting the
bow, casting the sling, and throwing the javelin.   It
has been given as an instance of their skill that they
could jump on or off the horse, or hit their mark, when
the animal was going at full speed.   On the other hand,
they were taught to speak the truth,[3] and cultivate
justice, gratitude, courage, purity, and self-control.   By
means of their national traditions, they were inspired to

[1] The *Cyropædia* ('Education of Cyrus') of Xenophon professes to
describe this education, but we cannot put full confidence in its account.
It is generally considered a story intended to laud the Spartan system of
education, and pictures it in Persia as the ideal training.   Modi describes
it as a mixture of facts and fiction rather than merely a 'political romance.'
In either case, its statements should be verified before they are accepted.

[2] Herodotus, I, 136.

[3] The importance of truth is emphasized again and again in the great
cuneiform inscription of Darius on the Behistan Rock in western Persia.

noble deeds, while by instruction in the prayers, myths of the gods, and other religious doctrines of Mazdeism their moral life was fostered.   Other than in this indirect way, they probably received no literary or intellectual education.   Reading and writing were scarcely taught at all.

and military training by the state.

At fifteen, it has been supposed, the boys were considered youths, and began their secondary education, which was even more specifically military.   This brought them for the first time into the service of the state, and the event was attended with important religious ceremonies.   The boy was bound with the sacred girdle as a protection against the demons of Ahriman; he recited a ritual from parts of the Avesta, and swore to maintain the law of Zoroaster.

The Magi alone required a higher education.   This must have consisted in the study and explanation of the sacred writings, and may have included a limited training in philosophy, astrology, medicine, law, and finance, so that they were able to become advisers to the Great King and his satraps.

They were taught by example and imitation.

Method. — Since there was no intellectual education save this given the Magi, there was no opportunity for any real method in teaching.   What there was must have been very informal.   In the case of military training, it consisted largely in consciously imitating the example of men of dignity and good repute at the various courts.   The moral education came from pre-

Gra 678 v. 1

cept, example, and the traditions of the nation, and was impressed by constant practice.

Results. — Of all the nations in the transitional stage, the Persians, as a consequence of their educational system, probably furnish the closest approach to a regard for individuality. Their religious conceptions, which have so close a connection with the educational, show almost as large an ethical element as those of Israel, which is to be classed among the nations that first tended to recognize personality in their education. Although the same intensity of moral sentiment and the compulsion of the sacerdotal law were not felt by the Persians, for that very reason, perhaps, they were freer in their moral judgment and less in bondage to hidebound legalism than the Jews. On the other hand, while the Persians had no real caste system, their priesthood was hereditary, women were not educated, and, as education existed mostly for the sake of occupation, the great mass of the people, who were not allowed to enter the army, received but little training of any sort. The government, too, was thoroughly despotic.

In Persia was the highest development of individualism among transitional nations.

These latter characteristics, together with the natural lack of geographical unity in the nation, contributed not a little to the downfall of Persia. As long as military achievements were going on, the people at home and in the various provinces felt that they were part and parcel of a great empire, and no oppression was

Downfall of Persia occurred when military achievements ceased.

noticed.　But when the Persians came into possession of the entire Eastern world, with its great wealth and high culture but low morals, they were overpowered by vanity, luxury, and idleness, and dissensions and discord arose.　The size and heterogeneity of the country and the remoteness of the various parts afforded an excellent opening for corruption and intrigue.　The majority of the people had never been taught to understand the lofty religion fully, and even with those who did, it became debased through contact with grosser beliefs and through the loose living of its adherents. The Persian education, too, which fitted them for warfare and physical endeavor, despite its ethical elements, had neglected to prepare them for the arts of peace and the enjoyment of leisure, and left them unequal to the moral strain.　Degeneration was rapid, and at the first onset of the vigorous Macedonians, the great empire burst into fragments, and left practically no impress on civilization.　Persia, which might have proven the first type of Aryan progress, was forced to hand over the torch to the Athenian Greeks.

SUPPLEMENTARY READING

I. Sources

MÜLLER, MAX (editor).　*Sacred Books of the East.*　Translated by various scholars.　Vols. IV, V, XVIII, XXIII, XXIV, XXXI, and XXXVII.

II. Greek Authorities

HERODOTUS, Bks. I and II; STRABO, Bks. XI and XV; XENO-
PHON, *Anabasis*, Bk. I, and *Cyropædia*, especially Bk. I,
Chap. II.

III. Other Authorities

JACKSON, A. V. W. *Persia, Past and Present.*
LAURIE, S. S. *Pre-Christian Education.* The Aryan Races **(B).**
LETOURNEAU, C. *L'evolution de l'education.* Chap. XIV, C.
RAWLINSON, G. *The Origin of Nations.* Pt. I, Chap. VI.
RAWLINSON, G. *Religions of the Ancient World.* Chap. III.
RAWLINSON, G. *The Seven Monarchies of the Ancient World.*
Vol. II, Media and Persia.
SAYCE, A. H. *The Ancient Empires of the East.* IV and V.
TIELE, C. P. *Outlines of the History of Religions* (translated**).**
Chap. IV, II.
VAUX, W. S. W. *Persia.*

CHAPTER X

CHARACTER OF THE EARLIEST CIVILIZATION

Transitional Stage. — It can be seen from the fore-going account of certain typical peoples in the barbarian stage, that, while they differ much in details among themselves, certain common tendencies appear through-out their education and their civilization in general. A study of their ideals, together with the way in which they were carried out, and of the results, makes it evident that, although superior to primitive conditions, their civilization had not yet attained to the level of later times.

The Oriental peoples had begun to control nature; Their advance over savagery is revealed in their growing ability to analyze experience and to make generalizations that were impossible for the primitive mind. They must have obtained some insight into nature and learned to formulate her laws. The use of fire became generally understood, and the metals were molded into weapons, utensils, and tools. They no longer wandered over the face of the earth in search of sustenance, but settled down and depended more or less upon agriculture. The sciences sprang up, and art, architecture, and handicrafts began to appear. A division of labor naturally followed, and the blood tie of clan and tribe was gradually displaced by the relationship of kindred occupations.

Restricted Ideals. — However, with the exception of the Semitic nations, whose more advanced civilization imposed itself upon all with whom they came in contact, without being much affected in return, these peoples were largely isolated, and by an imperceptible selection of satisfactory activities, traditional forms of expression gradually grew up. After these had been conformed with sufficiently to fix them as social habits, they became ideals for education as well as for society in general.

Thus, although social organization had become much more complex, the educational ideal, as in savagery, may be described as the satisfaction of immediate needs. While among primitive tribes education was the same for all individuals of the male sex, it had now, because of the division of labor that had grown up, become more differentiated and fitted for specific professions. In this way arose class distinctions, which in India at least were hardened into hereditary castes. All of these nations intended that young people should be educated according to the position in society they desired, expected, or, among the Hindus, were required to fill. _but had class distinctions, and opposed the development of the individual._

They seem never to have realized the importance of

the individual as the progressive factor in civilization. They supposed that all innovations were opposed to the welfare of the social group, and made a special effort to suppress the individual by every agency possible. Education was never regarded as a universal right or of universal value. It did not aim, apparently, to make the perfect man or citizen, but to maintain conditions as they had existed in the past.

Occupational Content. — Thus it came about that the industrial classes, who were engaged in the commonplace task of furnishing means of subsistence for all the people, and to some extent the warriors, who guarded the nation, received little education beyond reading, writing, and apprenticeship in the occupations they were to follow. Similarly, women were allowed no education at all except that which would aid them in their chief function, — keeping the home. While those who entered the sacerdotal class did secure some knowledge of the arts, sciences, and various learned professions, this was to be used merely for practical purposes, or for convincing the masses of the influence of the unseen in the providing of these immediate needs.

Education consisted in training for the occupation one was to follow.

Memory Method. — This professional knowledge would seem to have been largely traditional and was insured against any change by being embalmed in the sacred books of the various countries. The method of teaching it naturally required a memorizing of the symbols in the text rather than a realizing of the meaning of these symbols as part of the pupil's life. Instruction did not consist in mere imitation, with practically no consciousness, as among primitive peoples, although it must have come very close to that line in China and India, and it nowhere became genuinely rational. No effort was made to give a reason for the customs and traditional knowledge that were taught. Individuality was ignored, and all were taught alike, irrespective of interests and capabilities. When individual instincts revolted at this procedure, corporal punishment forced them to submit.

While the method was not merely imitative, it was memoriter and never genuinely rational.

Sacerdotal Organization of Schools. — Obviously, with this development of education, the training could no longer be accomplished through imitative play or by participation in the activities of the group. The family and the clan had, therefore, to yield to the school as a medium. Both elementary and higher schools were gradually instituted. Education, however, seems to have retained some connection with the priesthood, as, from the nature of the subject-matter, higher education, except in China, was largely conducted at priestly colleges, and the teachers did not become separated from the sacerdotal class.

Elementary and higher schools were instituted, but the latter were largely for the priesthood.

Static Results. — The effect of such an organization of society and education was that it rendered progress practically impossible, as all innovations were discour-

Thus they allowed no freedom to the individ-

ual, and were in bondage to the past; and progress was rendered practically impossible.

aged. This was seen not only in the immobility of the political, social, and other external conditions of the countries, but in the products of their inner life. Although their religion was of a much higher order than the crude animism and totemism of the savage, and its more advanced speculations approached monotheism, it was bound down by superstition and ceremonial. It had little effect upon their ethics, which were, for the most part, preceptive and prudential. Their art, architecture, and handicrafts, while sometimes developed to a marked degree, especially among the Semitic peoples, were stiff and conventional. Although they produced considerable literature, it was stilted, repetitious, and formulaic. What science there was appears to have been traditional and mixed with charms and superstition.

So, while these nations in the transitional stage had largely overcome the primitive enslavement to nature and the necessities of the present, they allowed *no freedom to the individual*, and were subservient to the conventions of their society. They were completely in *bondage to the past*. Education with them, as with the primitive tribes, may well be described as *non-progressive*. They appear, however, to represent a definite step in the evolution from nature to culture. Although they had obtained some control over nature, with them the process of evolution had not yet become quite conscious of itself, and man had not come to strive for a realization of what he believed to be ideal in this process. Later on, society will be found to look to the future rather than the past, and to make a self-conscious attempt to promote human development in accordance with its remote ideal progressively revealed to thinking men.

PART II

THE BEGINNINGS OF INDIVIDUALISM IN EDUCATION

CHAPTER XI

ISRAEL AND JUDÆA (THE JEWS)

THE Hebrews, or at least that portion of them known as the Israelites, while classed among the nations of the Ancient Orient, deserve a separate treatment, because their history continued so much longer, and the stage of culture at which they arrived was so much higher in type.

Survey of Jewish History and Religion. — According to the record, these people first appeared in a migration of tribes that started from the east side of the Euphrates,[1] under the chieftainship of one Abraham, about twenty-three hundred years before Christ. They eventually arrived in the land of Canaan, now called Palestine. After some centuries of nomadic life in this country, a portion of the Hebrews,[2] known as Israelites, or de-

---

[1] *I.e.* 'Ur of the Chaldees.' See *Genesis*, XI, 28 and 31.

[2] Hebrew probably meant ' dweller on the other side.'

scendants of Jacob, the reputed grandson of Abraham, wandered with their flocks and herds by successive migrations into the pasture lands of Goshen, or northeastern Egypt. This was probably during the reign of one of the later Hyksos, or Shepherd Kings, who were possibly themselves of Semitic origin.[1] Within the land of the Pharaohs they continued their own pastoral pursuits, clan institutions, and language, until there arose a new dynasty and "a king over Egypt which knew not Joseph," who sought to deprive them of everything distinctive of their nationality, and force them into a degrading serfdom.

From this desperate situation they were delivered by the leader Moses. This hero introduced among them the conception of *Jahweh*, or Jehovah, as a national deity who would protect his people if they were righteous. Having inspired them with this idea, he seized the opportunity during a series of scourges in Egypt to lead out some two million of them across the Red Sea into the desert of the Sinaitic Peninsula. This brought them just south of Canaan and near to the other people of Hebraic origin, — the Edomites, Moabites, and Ammonites.

Introduction of religion of Jehovah.

At first the Israelites were held back by the vigorous

[1] The whole question of Israel's abode in Egypt is one of peculiar difficulty, and there is a wide variety of opinion among scholars regarding it. The racial relationship of the Hyksos is also very uncertain.

Canaanites from proceeding further, and were obliged to remain in the desert for some forty years. During this time the national feeling was further developed; and Moses, possibly aided by the priesthood, exercised legislative and judicial functions on the authority of Jehovah. From the decisions and advice obtained in this way, traditions were rapidly built up and transmitted as the *Thorah* ('Law'), although probably not committed to writing for many centuries. In the course of time the older generation was replaced by a hardier one born in the desert, and during a quarrel between their kindred tribes and the Amorites they were able to cross the Jordan. After many small wars Canaan was conquered by the Israelites and partitioned among the Twelve Tribes some thirteen or fourteen hundred years before Christ.

The judges. While dwelling in this land, for two or three centuries there was little community of feeling, and dissensions were common. "Every man did that which was right in his own eyes," although at times there arose local chiefs, or 'judges,' some of whom attained to a greater or less degree of intertribal recognition. Their internal quarrels, however, were finally pacified by their common resistance to the Philistines, who had overwhelmed the Israelites, and carried off from the shrine at Shiloh the 'ark,' or sacred symbol of Jehovah. For this reason, too, a war-chief became necessary, and, through the offices of the judge Samuel about 1095 B.C., a gigantic The kings. and impetuous Benjamite named Saul was chosen king and general. This warrior soon unified the undisciplined tribes and decisively defeated their various enemies.

The selection of a king did not constitute the only service of Samuel in drawing the nation together. He perceived that the religious and patriotic enthusiasm engendered by the pressure of the Philistines might be used for the restoration and development of the religion of Jehovah. He organized into regular 'schools' the The prophets. 'prophets,' or bands of fanatical devotees of the national God, which in Israel, as among other Eastern peoples, were in the habit of traveling through the land in a state of emotional excitement. At various centers these religious revivalists were gathered together and dwelt in crude huts of their own erection. Their spiritual insight was systematically trained by a course of religious and lyric instruction, and they in turn diffused among the common people a knowledge of the essential truths of the religion of Jehovah. Thus during the following five centuries much was done through these schools of the prophets to develop the national religion and further unite the nation.

Saul, however, deprived by death of Samuel's guidance, gradually degenerated, and was succeeded by Degeneracy of the kings. David, a Judahite. This king recovered the ark, and,

I

placing it in Jerusalem, did much toward securing permanency of religious and political conditions. In the reign of David's son, Solomon, the long-planned temple was built, science and literature were advanced, commerce and wealth were largely increased, and much was **and the division of the kingdom.** accomplished for the internal administration. The king himself, however, succumbed to luxury and indulgence; and under his weak son, Rehoboam, in 930 B.C. the ten northern tribes revolted, and formed the kingdom of 'Israel,' with Samaria as the capital. The two tribes that remained loyal to the house of David became known thereafter as the kingdom of 'Judah.'

The exile. This disruption eventually led to the downfall of both kingdoms. Israel, from its position, was constantly under the burden of warfare, and was finally overrun by Assyria in 720 B.C. Its inhabitants were deported and thus became 'the ten lost tribes.' Judah was rendered more stable through its isolated position and the influence of its prophets, who continually sought to keep the kingdom out of the swirl of international politics. But in 586 B.C. Jerusalem was stormed by the Chaldean Babylonians, the temple was destroyed, and the people deported to Babylon.

Foundation of Judæa. After the Persian conquest of Babylonia, the transplanted inhabitants of Judah and their descendants were allowed in 536 B.C. to return to Jerusalem and rebuild the temple. However, not much was accomplished toward the culture of the religion of Jehovah until the new immigration under Ezra and the arrival of Nehemiah as governor nearly a century later. Then there was founded a religious state known as Judæa,[1] which, while under the nominal protectorate of Persia, left the real power in the hands of the high priest and his council of priests, scribes, and elders.[2]

Through this polity was produced a new movement in the religion of Jehovah. Probably during the reign of Josiah, just before the Babylonian exile, the traditional rulings known as the *Thorah* were written down. While the people of Judah were in captivity, this code was the means of holding them distinct. Many additions, especially from the teachings of the prophets, were made during the exile; and when Ezra, supported by Nehemiah, promulgated the Law upon their return, it must have contained the main stock of the present Pentateuch. Many amendments were afterward made, but from this time it became the *magna charta* of Judaism. With its publication revelation was supposed to be complete. The prophets had now disappeared, leaving behind a rich inheritance of exalted utterances, and the scribes became the recognized authority in matters of religion under the name of

The scribes and their works.

---

[1] Since then these people have been known as Jews rather than Israelites.

[2] The *Sanhedrim*, which arose under the Maccabees, may have been an outgrowth of this Council.

Sopherim ('Scripture scholars'). Before the captivity their duties had been mostly clerical, but they now interpreted and administered 'the Law and the Prophets,' and added to them by their commentaries. Their works were finally collected and are known as the *Talmud*.[1] They include the *Mishna* ('repetition'), which is the oral law that had been handed down as distinguished from the Thorah, and affords an account of various ceremonies and ordinances, and the *Gemara* ('supplement'), which is composed of interpretations of the Mishna. These works have for the Jews an importance second only to that of the Scriptures.

Later history. Meanwhile, Judæa as a state continued its existence for a few centuries longer. In 323 B.C., upon the death of Alexander, who had conquered Persia, Judæa for nearly a century came under the sovereignty of the Ptolemies. Then for another hundred years it writhed under the rule of the Syrians; but, after a struggle of a quarter of a century, it was able to set up an independent religious state under the Maccabees (142–64 B.C.). However, through sectarian quarrels, Rome was enabled to reduce Judæa to a dependency, and, after various insurrections, in 70 A.D. Jerusalem was taken and the temple again destroyed. Since then, the Jews,

---

[1] There are two Talmuds, called the 'Palestinian' and the 'Babylonian' respectively, after the place of their compilation. They differ in minor respects only.

deprived of political existence, have spent their energy
on the culture of their religious patrimony. Although
scattered throughout all lands and nations, and universally oppressed, they have through all these centuries
preserved their identity and strength by the force of
their long history, remarkable traditions, regard for
education, and lofty religious conceptions.

Development of Israelite Religion. — While the Israelites made a great advance over previous religions, in that
Jehovah was from the beginning conceived to some
extent as a god of ethical attributes, who preferred
righteousness to sacrifice, yet the real development of
their religious ideas was of very gradual growth. As
already indicated, their religion was probably given its
distinctive form by Moses, and was most effective during
the great emergency of escaping from the Egyptian
bondage and settling in Canaan. The conception of
Jehovah probably existed before this time, but possibly as
of a deity belonging to one or more Israelitish tribes, —
at least, it was much less developed than with Moses.
There is some evidence also of the existence of polydemonism, if not polytheism, in the pre-Mosaic religion,
and traces even of animism and totemism seem to survive from an earlier time in the Mosaic rites and worship themselves.[1]   Certainly neither religious reflection

Mosaic and pre-Mosaic conceptions.

---

[1] Sacrifice must be regarded as a gift of food to the god, and a communion with the deity by partaking of the same flesh or being sprinkled

nor moral principles could have been present, except in embryo, before the time of the exodus; and for a long time after the introduction of the religion of Jehovah, custom was the all-prevailing influence.

Henotheism. Even the religion of Moses should be described as a henotheism rather than a monotheism, for probably Jehovah was still regarded as one god among many, although the most powerful. He was simply the 'God of Israel,' the protector and de-liverer of his people, and the only one who could claim their gratitude, obedience, and worship. Nor did the religion of the Israelites become an absolute monotheism for a long time after their settlement in Canaan. As Israel came to participate in the agri-culture and viticulture of the Canaanites, they saw no inconsistency in adopting also the various Ba'als,[1] that presided over the several districts. In course of time, as the people of Canaan were subdued more and more, Ba'al was gradually repudiated by the Israelites, and his property and functions absorbed by Jehovah. However, they appear to have seen no reason why the Canaanites should not worship him. For a similar reason, the erection by Solomon of shrines in honor of

with the same blood; and a similar idea underlies the ' covenant,' where the contracting parties walked between pieces of the animal laid opposite each other. Circumcision, too, is customary even at the initiatory ceremonies of savages as a sign that the youth has entered among the warriors of the tribe.

[1] These Ba'als were identified with Dionysus by the Greeks.

Ashtoreth, Milcom, Chemosh, and other deities, to please his foreign wives, was probably regarded rather as unpatriotic than sacrilegious. And even the prophet Micah, as late as the eighth century, recognized the existence of other gods, though subordinate, when he said: "For all people will walk every one in the name of his god, and we will walk in the name of the Lord our God for ever and ever." [1]

Moreover, for many centuries the Israelites had an anthropomorphic, if not lower, conception of God. Jehovah was described as of human form, and his presence was made concrete by images and even symbolized by the bulls of Jeroboam at Bethel and Dan. Also mention was made of the existence of demigods, — 'sons of gods,' [2] — who consorted with mortal women; while 'angels' were viewed as a sort of intermediate being between God and man.

Anthropo-morphism.

The transformation of these narrow conceptions and the real development of Israelite religion came about largely through the instrumentality of the prophets. Although they were laymen, in their fidelity to Jehovah and their zeal, they far outstripped the professional priesthood. At first they supported the throne, although, as in the case of Samuel, Nathan, and Elijah,

Loftier con-ceptions of the prophets.

[1] *Micah*, IV, 5.
[2] *Genesis*, VI, 4, and *Job*, I, 6. These conceptions were probably importations from foreign sources, as Egypt or Persia.

they never hesitated to rebuke the king when they felt that he had sinned. But as the religious degeneracy, especially of the northern kingdom, grew, they came to oppose the rulers openly, as well as the beliefs, tendencies, and customs of the times. They did their best to awaken the consciences of the people to nobler conceptions and loftier morality; and prophesied the downfall of the kingdoms, if the Israelites did not obey the laws of Jehovah in deed and spirit, and reject Ba'alism. Elijah especially fought most strenuously the coördination or identification [1] of Jehovah with Ba'al. In the ridicule he heaped upon the prophets of Ba'al,[2] he went far beyond the henotheistic position and completely denied the existence of other gods than Jehovah. Other prophets also declared that " Jehovah is the only true God, and beside him there is none ; " and while they described him nearly always as working for his own people, they taught that all nations would eventually be brought within his plan of salvation for the world.

Again, while the prophets resorted occasionally to anthropomorphic descriptions, there is in them no trace of the original naïve belief in a human form, and they

[1] The reaction from this inconsistent syncretism produced such extreme individuals as the Nazarites, who insisted upon abstinence from the use of wine, as savoring of the Ba'al cult, and the Rechabites, who went so far as to protest against all civilization with agriculture in it, and even tried to revive the nomadic life of the desert.   [2] 1 *Kings*, XVIII, 17–40.

waged a ceaseless warfare against the use of images. These they felt to be unworthy of his universality and his superiority to restriction in space or time. Through them he was invested with all the qualities of morality and holiness.

However, with the return from the Babylonian captivity and the growing prominence of the scribes, there was a descent from the lofty teachings of the prophets. As the Mishna and the Gemara expanded, the religious life of the Judæans more and more became one of formal observance. Ceremonial, legal dicta, and other prescriptions rapidly multiplied and flourished. Formal obedience to the Law remained, but it took on more of the character of a business contract with the Deity, in which each party was obligated to fill his own part, although even in this a moralizing tendency was apparent.

Formalism of the scribes.

Thus, beginning with Moses, the religion of Jehovah grew and expanded. Through all its stages, — the formulation of priestly tradition, the spiritual development of the prophets, and the formal interpretations of the scribes, it emphasized the moral law, and generally regarded God as an Infinite Being in personal touch with man.[1] The people of Israel were probably not

Summary of religious development.

[1] The later Judaism hardly regarded God as in contact with man. In fact, God was highly transcendent, so that intermediaries were considered necessary between God and the world. Hence arose their

the first to grasp the henotheistic conception, as can be seen from the history of other Oriental peoples, and possibly the Hindus and Zoroastrians at least may be said to have anticipated them in attributing the characteristic of universality to their deity; but they certainly were the earliest people to develop monotheism, and to grasp the conception of God as a self-existent, moral personality in vital relations with his people.

Educational Ideals. — Thus it can be seen that throughout all periods of their history the Jews had ingrained in them the conception of God as the preserver and lawgiver of his people. This was accompanied by the belief that to act in harmony with the Divine will was the highest duty of man. All law, civil and ecclesiastical, was, in consequence, regarded simply as the expression of the will of Jehovah, and no distinction was ordinarily made between patriotism and religion.

Religious and moral aim.

The chief aim of education, therefore, was *religious and moral.* As early as Deuteronomy the command appears: "Thou shalt love the Lord thy God with all thine heart, and with all thy soul, and with all thy might. And these words which I command thee this day shall be in thine heart, and thou shalt teach them

'angelology,' borrowed from Persian and other sources, and the apotheosis of the *Thorah* and of the *Memra* ('word') of Jehovah. See Schürer, *History of the Jewish People in the Time of Jesus Christ.*

diligently unto thy children." [1]   The building of character was looked upon as the one goal to be achieved, and
but little stress was placed upon knowledge of any sort
except as it achieved this end.   So from the first the
pupils were trained preëminently in that 'fear of the
Lord,' which 'is the beginning of wisdom'; [2] and, as
traditions developed, this came to include an acquaintance with ritual and ceremonial duties.   In keeping with
their moral aim, the Jews strove also to make their
training *practical*.   "Not learning, but doing, is the
chief thing," declares the Mishna, [3] and their education
always contemplated a preparation for the concrete
duties of life in matters of trade and occupation, as
well as of religion and ceremonies.

Pre-exilic Education. — Until after their exile there
was no public means of education among the Jews.
Children were taught in the family by their parents.
During their earliest childhood both sexes were under
the mother's care; but later, boys accompanied their
fathers to the field or workshop, while the girls remained
at home with their mothers.   Thus, through the family, Family as
was given that religious and ethical instruction which the means.
is especially characteristic of the Jews.   The boys and
girls alike learned the history of their own people and
of God's dealings with them, the different codes of the

[1] *Deuteronomy*, VI, 5-7.   [2] *Proverbs*, IX, 10.   See also I, 7.
[3] *Aboth*, I, 17.

Pentateuch, the beautiful lyrics of the Psalms, and the wisdom of the Proverbs. Also at the appropriate time their parents explained the significance of their religious observances, such as the festival of the Passover, commemorative of their escape from Egypt, and that of the Pentecost, which celebrated the reception of the decalogue on Mount Sinai. At the same time with this ethical and social training, and as part of it, every boy was fitted for the practice of a trade through his father; and the girls were taught such arts as cooking, weaving, and clothes-making, in the home by their mothers.

Facilities for formal schooling practically did not exist before the Babylonian captivity. Reading and writing were at first not taught at all, but some knowledge of these rudiments may have been given in the larger cities after the founding of the kingdom. Also, when the Israelites were well settled in Canaan, possibly tutors were sometimes employed by the wealthy, just as Solomon was instructed by the prophet Nathan; but, as a rule, such elementary education as they had was carried on by the parents.

Schools of the prophets.   Higher education was scarcely known until after the exile. Even the priesthood and scribes were limited to a certain knowledge of law, and of historical and judicial literature. In the schools of the prophets, besides theological interpretation and the law, they apparently learned only the arts of sacred music and poetry, whereby they were to be stimulated to greater ecstasy, and were instructed in the compilation of maxims, narratives, and annals. It has been claimed that they were taught some mathematics and astronomy, to mark off the religious festivals, but this is very doubtful.

Post-exilic Education. — During their captivity the Jews had an opportunity to see schools for higher training, which were well developed in Babylon. These were, however, intended only for the priesthood and aristocracy ; but the extension of such opportunities to all classes, which was effected upon their return, originated distinctly with the Jews. But even with them, while there was theoretically no distinction in classes, the degree of culture customarily obtained by the priest, prophet, scribe, and lay aristocracy was greater than that of the ordinary man.

This provision for a higher education was probably Higher schools. made shortly after the return of Ezra by the rebuilding of the Temple and the foundation of synagogues. These latter institutions were originally not places of worship, but of religious instruction. In order that the Thorah, which had now been promulgated and accepted by the people, should be generally studied and read, systematic exposition and instruction by such qualified teachers as the scribes were necessary. After the third century B.C., the scribes gave this instruction within the porticoes of the Temple also, and sometimes in their own homes or those of wealthy patrons. A little later, when elementary schools had also been established at the synagogues, this college of the scribes came to be known as *Beth ham-Midrash* ('House of Instruction'); and in Jerusalem every scribe of note had a following of his own.

Content of the higher course.

The teaching at these colleges was intended for those who wished to make a deeper study of the Law, and was advanced in character. It was given the youth after the reading, writing, and other elementary education had been furnished at home. It consisted, if we may judge from the Proverbs, of instruction in such virtues as prudence, temperance, chastity, truthfulness, charity, and diligence, and in disputations concerning the interpretation of the Law, the ritual, and other prescriptions. Possibly it was influenced also by the educational ideals of the times, especially of the Greek schools; and afforded a training in mathematics, astronomy, geography, and such other sciences as were known, and in foreign languages, especially Greek, which, after Hebrew, stood highest of all literature in the estimation of the Jews.

Elementary schools.

In the second century before Christ the public elementary school began to grow up, and in the end became the most prominent feature of the Jewish education. After the spread of Greek ideas, such an institution was naturally started in Jerusalem as pre-

paratory to the higher education of the scribes. This
school, however, was probably also taught by scribes,
and was in close connection with the synagogue, which
had now been established even in every village. It was
generally held in a room of the synagogue, or in the
house of the scribe who was teaching it. The famous
scribe, *Simon ben Shetach* (' Simon, son of Shetach '),
had attendance at these schools made compulsory
upon all children in Jerusalem as early as 75 B.C.;
and, in 64 A.D., the requirement was extended by
Josue ben Gemala (' Joshua, son of Gamaliel ') to every
province and town. That the training might be effective, Joshua also required that, after the number of
pupils in a school had passed beyond twenty-five, the
teacher must be given an assistant; and when it ex-
ceeded forty, two teachers must be employed. Rich
and poor alike might attend these schools without a
fee, but the wealthy probably paid a special school
tax. After the fall of Jerusalem, these elementary
schools, now known as ' rabbinical ' [1] schools, became of
the utmost importance, as they were the great means of
preserving the faith of the Jews, wherever they wandered in their dispersion. A well-known maxim of
these people was : "A town without schools and school
children should be destroyed."

*Held in
connection
with the
synagogue.*

*Made com-
pulsory in
all towns.*

---

[1] About the time of Christ the scribes came to be called *Rabbi* ('master'), and soon displaced the priests altogether.

Internal
organization.

In the first elementary schools the children stood or sat upon the ground and faced the teacher, who was seated a little above them, also upon the ground. Later on, benches, and even stools and cushions, were introduced. The pupils sat in front of the teacher, in order that, in keeping with the words of Isaiah,[1] they might watch his face as he spoke. The school hours lasted all day with the exception of a short recess at noon, although possibly games were interspersed or the monotony was varied by the recitation of parables and legends from the Mishna. School was held every day, except on the Sabbath and on feast days.

When the children came to school at six years of age, they had already learned from their parents select Proverbs and verses from the Psalms, and had

Content of
the elemen-
tary course.

been taught the significance of the various religious ceremonies. Between six and ten they were taught reading and writing, mostly from the Pentateuch as text, and a little arithmetic. Especial attention was given to correct pronunciation and due reverence in reading. Then, until they were fifteen, the teacher explained the Mishna or oral law to them; and if their studies were continued beyond this in a synagogue, they consisted, as already seen, in a discussion and criticism of the Gemara, and embraced all the subjects necessary to throw light upon the interpretations. Besides these

[1] *Isaiah*, XXX, 20.

religious and literary studies, all pupils, rich or poor, were obliged to learn some handicraft. " As it is your duty to teach your son the Law, teach him a trade," reads the old maxim. This was partly for the sake of breadth, but it was largely intended as a recreation and rest.

Girls must have been trained as well as boys, for it is well known that the mothers of Judæa have always been of great importance in educating the family. Probably the training was more emotional than intellectual, — 'to fear God and keep his commandments.' Although girls were taught to read, the deeper study of the Thorah was not encouraged, and the domestic arts, dancing, and music largely took the place of science.

Education of girls.

Educational Method. — The method of learning in the Jewish elementary schools was not unlike that of other Oriental peoples. Frequent repetition was required for the purpose of committing a text and obtaining a distinct pronunciation, and the loud tone in which this was done suggests the memorizing of the Chinese and Hindus. The Jews, however, had learned to make a practical appeal to various memories through the different senses, — to the visual memory by reading, the motor by pronouncing and writing, the auditory by hearing, and the musical by singing, the portions to be committed. It was realized that much

K

Appeal to
memory
assisted by
mnemonics.

care should be exercised in the beginning, as what is learned then remains in the mind 'like ink on fresh paper.' Also many mnemonic helps were at all times used to impress the memory. Catchwords, symbols, numerical groupings, and other devices were invented. The most ingenious of these was probably that of the 'Athbash,' by which the initial words of lines or verses in a passage were so arranged with consecutive letters of the alphabet as to be easily recalled.[1]

Pedagogical
wisdom.

The Jews also had sufficient practical knowledge of psychology to realize that different types of mind must be approached by different methods. The Talmud recognizes four classes of pupils, — the 'sponge,' who absorbs everything; the 'funnel,' who retains nothing; the 'sieve,' who catches the illustrations, but lets the main argument slip by; and the 'winnow,' who fans away the illustrations, but holds the more solid portion. Much other good pedagogical advice can be found in their sacred literature, although, with the *memoriter* method in vogue, it may be questioned whether some of these recommendations were not rather ideal than realized in practice. For example, Rabbi Akiba's advice that "the teacher should strive to make the lesson agreeable by clear reason" is hardly compatible with the system of literal memorizing. However, the statements of the Talmud that, in pre-

[1] The whole of *Lamentations* was constructed after this plan.

senting a lesson, the teacher should be careful not to digress and so confuse the pupil, that he should not assign too much at one time, and that pauses should be periodically given that the pupil might have time to rest his mind and digest the matter, seem to be sensible suggestions which could very well have been applied. Also the use of various rites as object lessons [1] to arouse inquiry leading up to an explanation is known to have been very successful in religious instruction; and the general advice to the teacher to pique the curiosity of the pupil by asking odd questions may also have produced good educational results.

Writing was taught by following the copy on a wax tablet with a stylus, and when the pupil was more advanced, on papyrus or parchment with a pen. The higher education was nominally conducted in the form of a disputation, but was, nevertheless, rather dogmatic in character, and the final *dictum* of the teacher was literally memorized. Some of the interpretations must have been very artificial. Every line of the sacred literature was given a microscopic examination by the scribes, and frequently a very far-fetched meaning [2] was read into it.

Methods in writing and higher education.

All teachers were held in high esteem, as they were the interpreters of truth and morals, and were largely

Esteem for teachers.

[1] See *Exodus*, XII, 24–28; XIII, 5–10 and 14–16; *Joshua*, IV, 6–8.

[2] See Farrar, *History of Interpretation*, Lecture II.

looked upon as the mouthpieces of Jehovah.   Disrespect toward them was treated as irreverence and severely punished.   The Talmud says: " You should revere the teacher even more than your father.   The latter only brought you into this world ; the former indicates the way into the next."   On the other hand, much was required of them.   For the sake of morality a teacher had to be married, and he was expected to be able, experienced, and not too young.   " Instruction by a young teacher," declares the Talmud, " is like sour grapes and new wine ; while by an old teacher, it is like ripe grapes and sweet wine."   Many bits of advice are also given the teacher concerning his education, piety, self-control, and veracity.

Their quali-
fications.

Although the teachers usually combined their profession with the practice of some trade, probably they were often compensated, except in the higher subjects. No definite fee was paid, but probably presents, especially from the wealthier pupils, were given them.

Rigorous
discipline.

The discipline of the Jewish schools must, from the nature of the subject-matter and the methods of teaching, have been rigorous.   Corporal punishment is constantly advised in the Proverbs,[1] although wise reproof is recognized as better on some occasions.[2] After the pupils were old enough to make an appeal to

[1] *Proverbs*, XIII, 24 ; XIX, 18 ; XXIII, 13–14; etc.
[2] *Ibid.*, XVII, 10.

their honor effective and have their pride hurt by a
whipping, the form of punishment was not so severe.
Where corporal punishment was used at all with older
boys, it was applied not with the rod, but with the thong
of a sandal.   In Talmudic times, especially after the
advent of Christ, discipline became much milder, but
chastisement was still recognized.   A new type of borrowed interest was also added in the shape of various
rewards, such as sweetmeats and dainties, which were
used as a stimulus to good conduct.

Effect of Jewish Education on Progress. — Thus the
education of the Jews was the typical religious and
moral training of antiquity, and through it they became
the religious people *par excellence*.   As soon as he was
old enough to understand, even before his formal training in the schoolroom, every Jew had ingrained in
him the idea of Jehovah as a God of moral attributes,
who is in touch with man and requires of him righteous
conduct as the ground of approval.   Human personality he learned to regard as a reflection of the Divine.
Such conceptions of God, man, righteousness, and duty
are easily seen to be far nobler than any that had
previously been formulated among the other peoples of
the Orient.   Through them a new factor, the development of moral personality, was introduced into education.

Religious
and moral,

Even the extensive ceremonial and overelaboration
of the Law introduced through the scribes could not

despite the
ceremonial.

altogether destroy the spirit underlying the formalism. While the Law has always been obeyed in all respects as an absolute authority, and so has become an external sanction rather than an appeal to reason and the inner light, it has been a moral law, filled with high principles, and could not altogether fail as a stimulus to moral action for any, while to a few moral geniuses in every generation it has been the inspiration of loftiest motives.

It is this ideal and content alone which distin-guishes the education of the Jews from that of all other Oriental nations.   In the organization of education, they do not compare favorably with China or India.   For a thousand years they had no such institution as a school, and it was not until a few centuries before their extinc-tion as a nation that they founded any real public schools.   Elementary education did eventually become universal among them, but that was only six years prior to the fall of Jerusalem.   Their methods, while apply-ing some very clever pedagogical devices, were almost as largely *memoriter* and imitative as those of barbarian peoples, and the discipline accompanying them was in-clined to be severe until late in their educational history.

Literature limited to re-ligion,   The objective products of this type of education are illustrative of its merits and defects.   The literature was naturally limited to an expression of the Jewish idea of God's dealings with the world, and the devotion that should go out to him from the pious soul.   Art

and science were almost entirely unknown, except as
they threw light on some religious festival or custom.
On the other hand, the effect of their religious and
educational ideals has always been seen in the beautiful family life and other social relations of the Jews.
Women were never held in degradation among them,
as often among the other Oriental peoples, but were
generally shown esteem; children were treated with
kindness and thoughtful care; while reverence toward
father and mother was one of the virtues first taught to
the Jewish child.

Thus through their high concepts of God and of
human obligations, the Jews have been held together
through centuries of trials and persecutions, and have
found their religion and education a comfort and a con-
solation in the midst of them all. No other Oriental
nation of their day has remained, but the Jew with
his moral discipline is with us yet. Had their ethical
ideals been kept clear of excessive ceremonial, formalism, and narrowness of view, and developed as in the
days of the prophets, they might indeed have become
'the light of the world.' As it is, they gave birth
to the great religion which was needed to emancipate
them from the bondage of form and restricted vision,[1]

Marginal notes: and art and science almost un-known, — but their family life was beautiful. — Their edu-cation has preserved them for centuries.

---

[1] A most remarkable attempt to give the Jewish religion this universality was made by Philo the Jew in the first years of the Christian era.
This seems also to be the aim of the advanced wing of Judaism to-day.

and which has made its resistless way to all nations. This result, however, was not accomplished until contact with the Graeco-Roman civilization had enlarged the horizon of philosophy and religion.

SUPPLEMENTARY READING

I. Sources

JOSEPHUS, OLD TESTAMENT, TALMUD.

II. Authorities

CORNILL, H. H. *History of the People of Israel.*

GELDER, H. *Die Volksschule des Juifs.*

GRÄTZ, H. H. *History of the Jews.*

HASTINGS, J. *A Dictionary of the Bible.* Articles on Education, History of the Israelites, and Religion of the Israelites.

HOSMER, J. K. *The Jews, Ancient, Medieval, and Modern.*

KENT, C. F. *A History of the Hebrew People.*

KITTEL, R. *A History of the Hebrews.*

KOHLER, DEUTSCH, and JACOBS. *Jewish Encyclopedia.* Article on Education.

LAURIE, S. S. *Pre-Christian Education.* The Semitic Races, B.

McCURDY, J. F. *History, Prophecy, and the Monuments.*

MARCUS, S. *Die Pädagogik des Israelitischen Volkes.*

MARCUS, S. *Zur Schul-Pädagogik des Talmud.*

MARTI, K. *Religion of the Old Testament.*

MONTEFIORE, C. G. *The Origin and Growth of Religion as Illustrated by the Religion of the Ancient Hebrews.*

PETERS, M. C. *Justice to the Jew.*

RENAN, E. *History of the People of Israel.*

ROBERTSON, J.   *The Early Religion of Israel.*

SAYCE, A. H.   *The Early History of the Hebrews.*

SCHÜRER, E.   *History of the Jewish People in the Time of Jesus Christ.*

SIMON, J.   *L'education et instruction des enfants chez anciens Juifs.*

SMITH, H. P.   *Old Testament History.*

SMITH, W. R.   *The Prophets of Ancient Israel.*

SPIERS, B.   *The School System of the Talmud.*

STRASSBURGER, B.   *Geschichte der Erziehung und des Unterrichts bei den Israeliten.*

WELLHAUSEN, J.   *Prolegomena zur Geschichte Israels.*

CHAPTER XII

SPARTA AND ATHENS (THE GREEKS)

OF all people in ancient times, or, as some believe, in all history, the Greeks have had the greatest influence upon civilization. Certain it is that they not only gave a wonderful impetus to educational theory and practice in their own time, but ever since then the world has had constant recourse to Greek thought for inspiration and counsel. In some respects their development of individuality was superior even to that of the Jews, and in any account of educational history they are worthy of extended notice.

Physical and Social Factors in the Progress of the Greeks. — Both the natural and the spiritual environment of Greece favored the development of lofty and original ideals. The mild and even climate tended toward happiness and equanimity, and the bracing air was stimulating to thought. The coast line was broken by many gulfs and bays, and its almost unlimited harborage proved most hospitable to commerce. Happily, this was especially true of the eastern coast, so that Phœnicia and other advanced countries were enabled to bring in with the wares of the Orient its arts and civilization.   Thus every physiographic and social feature combined to make old Greece broad-minded and eager to adopt from foreign countries such ideas as would improve her society and laws.

Outline of Greek History. — But let us see what is meant by 'ancient Greece.'   We find that old Greece, — or Hellas, to use her proper name, was not a single nation, but was made up of an aggregation of states on the southeast peninsula of Europe and on those adjacent islands to which the population had overflowed.   The various states of Hellas, largely as a result of topography, were never really unified into a confederacy, except in small groups and for short periods of time.[1] The mountain ranges with which the entire peninsula is covered, or the Mediterranean itself, isolated the different centers from each other, and, by making connection between them difficult, prevented the rise of any great likeness of thought or sentiment.   The states, in consequence, varied considerably in character, government, social conditions, and even in the dialect spoken. Community of interest appeared only when they banded together to repel a common foe, such as the Persians, or gathered upon stated occasions at the great national games, such as the Olympic, Isthmian, and Nemean.

Effect of the isolation of the Greek states.

---

[1] Some attempt at a complete confederation was made toward the end of Greek history in the formation of the Ætolian and Achæan leagues, but these were unsuccessful and short-lived.

Sparta and Athens.

The most important and typical states were Sparta and Athens, and, as they will amply illustrate the evolution of educational theory and practice in Greece, attention will here be largely confined to them. In fact, the really distinctive contributions that Hellas made to civilization grew up in Athens alone from about the middle of the fifth century onward. Athens before that time, and Sparta throughout her whole history, were controlled by an education that was at best but little beyond that of the Orient. This type of training is of importance here simply as it throws light upon the development of those social products that are typical of the Greeks, and from which modern culture has sprung.

Prehistoric period.

The accounts of earliest Greece are mythical, and extend back, as nearly as can be estimated, to at least the twelfth or thirteenth century before Christ. This prehistoric period includes the Tribal Age, when the Greeks were in the nomadic stage; the Mycenean Age, when, through contact with the Orient, they learned to build cities and practice agriculture; and lastly, the Epic Age, which seems to bring them a little further toward civilization. While not much is known of actual events during the prehistoric period, we can, from the *Iliad* and *Odyssey* of Homer, and from excavations at Mycenæ, Argos, and Cnossus, gain some knowledge of how the Greeks lived at the time.

Really authoritative records, however, can be said to date only from the first Olympiad, 776 B.C. During historic times Sparta seems to have been the first of the Greek states to become prominent. This was due to her military system of education, which in turn arose as the result of social conditions. Somewhere about the eleventh century the Dorian tribe, to which Sparta belonged, had pushed aside the primitive inhabitants from their homes in the Peloponnesus, and had taken their place. Thus the citizens of Sparta, while in their own land, dwelt in the midst of hostile people. In the surrounding towns and country were the *periœci* ('dwellers around'), who were free, but paid large taxes for the use of their lands, and largely supported the Spartans. Then there were the *helotes* ('captives'), who had been taken in war, and were forced to remain in serfdom and do all the menial work for the citizens. So it came about that there were in all about two hundred and fifty thousand of the subject people to not more than nine thousand Spartans; and the latter were constantly menaced by an uprising of the conquered tribes, as well as by attacks from the outside. These dangers were aggravated by the notorious slothfulness in military matters into which they had fallen.

To guard against this, it became necessary for the entire body of free Spartans to organize themselves into a citizen army, and arrange for a system of education

Origin and effect of a military system in Sparta.

that would produce a race of warriors. A statesman named Lycurgus, in whom they had great confidence, was selected to formulate a code of laws that should be binding on all and would transmute the desired ends into national habits. This was probably as early as the middle of the ninth century, but the scheme of education remained in vogue almost without change until the Greek states lost their independence. Although toward the end the system degenerated somewhat, during the early days it gave Sparta a decided advantage, especially as the other states tended to neglect military training; and by the middle of the seventh century she had become the leading state of Greece.

Athenian development.

Meanwhile, in the north, Athens had been greatly developing in intelligence and polity. The monarchy was eventually displaced by an aristocracy in 753 B.C. Then the oppression of this type of rule was gradually removed from the people through the publication of the laws by Draco (621 B.C.), the freeing of the masses by Solon (594 B.C.), and the crushing of the nobles by Pisistratus and his sons (560–510 B.C.), until finally it was possible for Clisthenes (510–508 B.C.) to declare the most thoroughgoing democracy in all history. As a result of his reforms, every matter of importance was settled in the public assembly by vote of all the citizens; public officers were chosen by ballot, or even by lot, so high was the general intelligence; and the people were

annually permitted by a secret vote known as *ostracism* [1]
to exile any man, however aristocratic, whose presence
was felt to be inimical to the general welfare.

Under such circumstances, Athens came rapidly to   Supremacy
self-consciousness, and, feeling her superiority to Sparta,   of Athens.
eagerly sought occasion to prove it. The opportunity
presented itself in the outbreak of the Persian wars in
500 B.C. In the course of the three expeditions (492,
490, and 480–479 B.C.) that Persia made against Greece
and in which the Persians were so thoroughly repulsed,
Athens displayed the greatest wisdom and valor, and
stood preëminent in defense of the entire country.
Toward the close of the contest with Persia (479 B.C.),
she became the head of the alliance known as the *Confederacy of Delos*, which was formed at this time to
prosecute the war.   Gradually the allies of Athens were
reduced to subjects; and, under the influence of Pericles, an imperial policy was formally adopted, and the
treasury removed from Delos to Athens in 454 B.C.

The culmination of Athenian prosperity is seen in the   The Peri-
enlightened period called the *Age of Pericles*, from the   clean Age.
leading statesman of the time. This great leader felt
justified in expending the funds of the Confederacy of
Delos to beautify the city with architecture, sculpture,
and painting ; and soon became known as a patron of
art and literature. As a result, these cultural features

---

[1] From the *ostrakon* (' tile '), upon which each ballot was inscribed.

came to flourish as never before in the world's history. On the Acropolis and other heights arose the most beautiful temples, such as the Parthenon, the Erechtheum, and the Theseum. These and other structures were adorned by the marvelous statues of Phidias and Myron, and the lifelike paintings of Polygnotus. Nearly all types of literature also go back to this period for their origin. The 'father of history,' Herodotus, and the most illustrious of ancient historians, Thucydides, and the graphic Xenophon appeared; the great trio of tragic writers, Æschylus, Sophocles, and Euripides, and the most famous of comic dramatists, Aristophanes, produced their masterpieces; and a period of enlightenment in philosophy dawned with the sophists and Socrates.[1] Industries and commerce were also extended, and a remarkable development in politics and practical affairs took place. This was the day of Cimon, Themistocles, Aristides, Cleon, Nicias, and Alcibiades, as well as of Pericles.

Peloponnesian War and the hegemony of Sparta.

However, the political supremacy of Athens before long came to an end in the conflict with Sparta known as the Peloponnesian War (431–404 B.C.). This struggle was inevitable from the intense rivalry of the two great states, but it was begun and continued through a

[1] The impulse given to culture in Athens did not altogether cease with the Age of Pericles, as such names as Plato (427–347) and Aristotle (386–322), Demosthenes (384–322) and Praxiteles (born about 392), indicate.

number of more immediate causes. At first Athens was decidedly successful, but, owing to her grasping selfishness, she was at length completely humiliated, and Sparta once more obtained the hegemony.

But at the height of Spartan power, the Thebans in 379 B.C. shook off the oligarchy established in their city by Sparta, and eight years later overcame the Spartans themselves and ravaged their country. While the Thebans, after the death of the leader Epaminondas (362 B.C.), could not maintain their leadership, Sparta was never able to regain her prestige. *Rise and fall of Theban power.*

It now became obvious that no single city could hope to rule Greece, and for a time all the states were quiescent. During this brief season Athens was perhaps the most considerable of the Hellenic states; she was commercial and wealthy, and peace suited her. But a foreign foe soon threatened Athens and the rest of Greece in the person of Philip, king of Macedon. By military achievements and intrigue this warrior gradually made his way into Greece, until in 338 B.C. he overwhelmed the combined armies of Athens and Thebes at Chæronea. The next year he had himself elected commander-in-chief of all the Greek forces for an expedition against Persia, but he was shortly assassinated, and the conquest of the Orient (334–323 B.C.) was left for his brilliant son, Alexander, to achieve. *Macedonian conquest.*

Greece remained a dependency of her northern neigh- *Roman rule.*

L

bor until the great world power of Rome arose. In three wars (215-167 B.C.) Macedon herself was then slowly overcome by the Romans. While at first this looked like an emancipation for Hellas, her territory, too, was eventually invaded by Rome, and in 146 B.C. she became a Roman province under the name of *Achaia*. But while the political independence of Greece had passed, her intellectual conquest of the world had, as will be seen, but just begun.

Education in Prehistoric Greece. — But before discussing the world dominance of Greece, we must view the development of her system of education while she was unconsciously preparing to become schoolmistress of the world. To begin with, a general picture of prehistoric society and education may be obtained from Homer. In these days social conditions seem to have been very simple, and but little beyond those of the primitive stage. The people had already settled in rudely fortified towns, but their organization was tribal, and their king was but a sort of chief who held his office not so much through heredity as by virtue of his physical and mental qualifications. He did not scorn to perform pastoral, agricultural, or industrial duties, if necessary, and he mingled freely with his people. In the council every free-born head of a family was allowed full liberty of expression and a vote.

Thus, whatever training was given the youth of this

Simple conditions in prehistoric society.

primitive period must have been intended to fit them for practical life.   This ideal is obvious throughout Homer, and is, perhaps, most succinctly stated in the well-known speech of Phœnix to Achilles:—

> "Peleus, the aged knight, from Phthia sent
> Thee, yet a boy, to Agamemnon's aid,
> Unskilled as then thou wert in cruel war
> And martial councils, where men also gain
> A great renown,—he sent me with thee, charged
> To teach thee both, that so thou mightest become
> In words an orator, in warlike deeds
> An actor." [1]

The ordinary aim of education, then, was twofold,— to make the pupil wise and eloquent in council, strong and courageous in battle.   It could not have included any literary, scientific, or artistic elements.

In fact, there were as yet no real schools, either ele- mentary or higher, and, with the exception of Achilles, no one is mentioned as having a specific teacher.   The training was obtained through actual life in the family or community.   The young people learned how to sat-isfy the wants of nature,— food, clothing, and shelter,— from their parents, and acquired their other activities by following the example of the adults whom they met. Where some living man would not serve the purpose, the example of an ideal person such as Odysseus, the

---

[1] *Iliad*, IX, 438 ff., Bryant's translation.

embodiment of wisdom and craft, or Achilles, the model of bravery and action, was presented.

It should be noted that while the method of teaching was that of imitation, it was imitation of a living or a personal example rather than of some precept embalmed in sacred books as in the Orient. It was more rationalized, and gave some opportunity for the selective element of personality to enter in. It is this imitation of an example not fixed and stereotyped, but with possibilities of growth, that is evidence of the leaven which eventually enabled Greece to rise above all previous peoples in civilization.

Even at this early period there can thus be seen the germ of the ideal to free the individual from complete subserviency to the social whole. Moreover, throughout the times depicted by Homer, while the welfare of the group is obviously the prime object of each member of society, every one has a voice in deciding what action is most to the common interest. Tradition and custom still hold sway, but they already have to be of a reasonable type to be accepted, and are constantly subject to the modification of individuals.

Older Education of the Historic Period. — When Greek history actually becomes authoritative, the tribal organization of the prehistoric period seems to have given way completely to that of the city-state, into which the tribes had been amalgamated. So the social bond is no longer even nominally the tie of blood, but ownership of land in the same community; and the central virtue and aim in life have more explicitly become service to the state. While even at the first the duties of the individual were not definitely laid down, and he was allowed some personal development, every one was expected to expend almost his entire energy, and surrender his life, if necessary, in promoting the welfare of the state. This ideal is apparent in the two leading systems of education, — the Spartan and the Athenian.

Spartan Education and Its Aim. — Sparta, which possessed the earliest education of which we have extended information, is the most complete illustration of this type. Its social and political conditions, as has already been pointed out,[1] made it necessary to produce a race of hardy warriors and patriotic citizens; and strength, courage, and obedience to the laws were held as the aims of education. The Spartan educational system was intended to serve the state, and it was supported and controlled by the state. It is the one recorded instance of a complete system of moral and social education in a socialistic state.

Infancy. — State control began with birth. The infant was immediately inspected by a council of elders, who decided whether he was strong enough to be allowed to live. If he were sickly or deformed, he was

Exposure of sickly or deformed infants, and strict training of the strong.

---

[1] See pp. 141–142.

exposed to die in some wild glen of Mount Taÿgetus,[1] unless adopted by the periœci or the helots. If he appeared promising enough, he was formally adopted by the state and left with his mother for rearing until he was seven years of age. He could not be swaddled, lest his limbs should be checked in growth; and he had to be left alone in the dark and not permitted to scream, that he might from the first become hardy and learn self-control.

Boyhood and Adolescence. — At seven the Spartan boy was put in charge of a state officer called the *pædonomus* ('boy trainer'). With the aid of certain assistants, this official supervised the life and education of all the Spartan youth. The boys ate and slept in common in public buildings not unlike present-day barracks. Here they were divided into squads and companies, which were in charge of the older and stronger boys, and were classified according to their ages into three groups. According to Plutarch, "Of the boys he who showed the best conduct and most courage was made captain of the company. The others kept their eyes always upon him, obeyed his orders, and underwent patiently whatever punishments he inflicted; so that their whole education was an exercise of obedience." [2]

The life of the boys during this training was one of

The boys lived in common,

---

[1] In earlier days he was cast down a precipice of the mountain.
[2] *Lycurgus*, XVI.

continual hardening and discipline.   They slept without
covering, at first upon pallets of straw, and after fifteen
upon rushes, which they plucked from the banks of the
Eurotas, as they were not allowed the use of a knife.
They went without shoes winter and summer; and
after they became twelve years of age their entire dress
consisted of a single garment.   They were given little
food, that they might learn to endure hunger; but to
school them in craft for purposes of war, they were permitted to forage for additional food.   If, however, they
were detected in the act by any one, they were considered in disgrace and at once handed over to the
assistants of the pædonomus for a severe whipping.

and had a
rigorous
regimen

The more direct training consisted of a graded course
in gymnastics.   The exercises began with running,
jumping, and ball playing; but as the boys grew older,
they were trained also in throwing the discus, casting
the javelin, wrestling, and boxing.   They were occasionally allowed to engage in the *pancratium* ('a complete
combat'), a contest in which any means of overcoming
one's antagonist, even by kicking, biting, scratching, or
gouging, was permitted.   These events were carried on
in the open air and in the presence of any who wished
to attend, so that they were subject to the criticism,
favorable or otherwise, of the entire city.   Thus a con-
testant would suffer anything, at times even death,
rather than fail to exert himself to the utmost.   The

and severe
physical
training.

intention, of course, was not to make athletes or promote beauty or dexterity, but simply to toughen the boys and cultivate qualities of value in warfare. Dancing supplemented the gymnastic training. This, too, did not aim at developing grace and skill, but a patriotic and religious spirit, for it consisted mostly of war dances, sometimes in full armor and following out military evolutions, and sacred dances in honor of the gods. The boys often gave exhibitions of dancing and gymnastics at various religious festivals, especially those in honor of Apollo.

Intellectual and moral education at a minimum.

The Spartan boys, however, received little that could be strictly accounted an intellectual or moral education. While teachers of reading and writing may have existed, these accomplishments did not ordinarily form part of the training. The laws of Lycurgus and selections from Homer, which had been set to music, and other songs that they chanted in the simple and dignified Doric measure, were seldom written down, but were committed to memory. This music must, like the dancing, have afforded some religious and patriotic inspiration.

Conversation of older men at the table,

The young Spartans obtained further ethical and intellectual training by listening to the conversation of the older men at the meals or in the street, and by being at all times subject to approval or disapproval for their conduct. In this way they learned respect for their elders, honesty, and self-control. The boys were themselves also often required by the youth in charge of the common table to sing a song or give a concise and sensible answer [1] to such a general inquiry as " Who is the best man in the city ? " or " What do you think of this action ? " or some similar question put to test their powers.   The boy whose answer proved unfitting or too wordy had his thumb bitten by the youth in charge ; and this official in turn was sometimes judged after the meal by the older men present, and punished if his decisions were not considered wise.[2]

A more specific means of moral training was the selection of some particular boy as a comrade by every male adult.   This, Plutarch tells us, was a perfectly honorable attachment, and where two or three chose the same lad, instead of provoking jealousy, it only drew them nearer together through mutual interest and friendly rivalry in strengthening the boy's character.[3]

and comradeship with elders.

Youth and Young Manhood. — When a youth reached eighteen, he began his distinctive study of warfare.   For the first two years he was known as a *melleiren* ('budding youth '), and was trained in the use of arms and skirmishing.   He was given a rigorous examination

Training in use of arms.

---

[1] Several instances of such brief, incisive answers are given in Plutarch's *Lycurgus*. They are characterized even to-day by the term ' laconic.' See especially *Lycurgus*, XIX–XX.

[2] See Plutarch's *Lycurgus*, XVIII.

[3] The adult was usually held responsible for his protégé's conduct, and might even be fined if the boy misbehaved. See *Lycurgus*, XVIII.

every ten days, and had his courage and physique tested by being whipped before the altar of Artemis Orthia. Plutarch tells us that these scourgings were so severe that death not infrequently resulted.[1] At

and real military life. twenty the young Spartan became an *eiren* ('youth'), and his training was practically that of real military life. He regularly entered the army and took the oath of loyalty to Sparta. For ten years he lived upon the coarsest of fare, practiced hunting and swimming, and was set to guard some border fortress.

Citizenship. — When the Spartan reached thirty, he was considered to have entered manhood. He then became a member of the public assembly and was

Control of the state even after maturity. required to marry at once. But even then he had no home, and could visit his wife only clandestinely. Until late in Spartan history, he was still obliged to eat at the common tables with the boys,[2] and to spend much of his time in observing their education. Not only was every citizen expected to correct any boy or youth he found acting improperly, but it was considered disgraceful if he did not establish a specific relationship with some particular youth. He also continued in military service.

Women were trained similarly to **Education of Women.** — The education of Spartan women was very similar to that of the men. While

---

[1] See Plutarch's *Lycurgus*, XVIII.

[2] For further details, see Plutarch's *Lycurgus*, XXIV.

the girls were allowed to live at home, they were the men, and had much influence.
trained in running, jumping, hopping, throwing the
discus, hurling the javelin, and even wrestling, in a
regular course.   Dancing and singing were also taught
the girls, and on certain public occasions they joined
with the youths in choral dances and hymns in honor
of the gods.   The aim was, of course, to enable them
to become the mothers of sturdy sons, and to hand
down a religious and patriotic spirit to them.

Merits and Defects of Spartan Education. — Thus, Subordination to the state,
while the laws of Lycurgus, unlike the sacred books
of the Oriental nations, consisted of broad principles
rather than specific precepts, and so admitted of the
development of some individuality in working out details, they were shaped entirely with reference to the
welfare of the state.   "The Spartans," said the exile
to Xerxes, "are the best of all men when fighting in
a body; for, though free, yet they are not free in all
things, since over them is set law as a master, which
they fear much more than your subjects do you."[1]
Their educational system served well its purpose of
creating strong warriors and devoted citizens, but it
failed to make for the highest manhood.   The Spartans and failure to make for the highest manhood.
for centuries excelled all the rest of Greece in courage,
endurance, and self-control; their women were virtuous,
active, and high-spirited; and the youth showed a

[1] Herodotus, VII, 104.

heroism under pain and privation, and an obedience to their elders, that became a model for many philosophers and moralists. Yet they failed to recognize that harmony and balance which was the underlying ideal of the Athenian education, and they lacked entirely in all the finer traits of human nature. They developed practically no art, literature, or philosophy.

The country remained stable, Their education did result in great military achievements and in keeping the country stable, while it remained in force. But the entire system was based on a state morality rather than on individual responsibility, and as soon as the Spartan was removed from his own country and was no longer subject to this outside sanction of the law, his ethical life was completely disrupted. After the Peloponnesian War, when the hegemony of Greece passed from Athens to Sparta, the latter showed herself quite unequal to the task of leading, since she lacked both in moral strength and adaptability to the **but at the expense of progress.** new situation. Moreover, stability is purchased too dearly when accomplished at the expense of progress. Even during the period of her supremacy, Sparta produced little that tended to promote civilization. She has left to the world nothing but examples of heroism and foolhardiness alike, as illustrated in the case of Leonidas and his three hundred warriors, who, even when betrayed and deserted by their allies, calmly met death rather than break the cast-iron laws of their country by a wise retreat. Sparta may occasionally have proven an inspiration, but never an enlightenment. Had the Greeks paused with her development, they would have made no great contribution to civilization beyond that of the Orient. Our chief interest in Spartan education is, therefore, because of the way in which it leads up to the culture of Athens.

Athenian Education in the Old Period. — For many centuries Athenian education, like that of Sparta, aimed primarily at promoting the welfare of the state without much consideration of individual interests. But the view-point of Athens, even at first, differed considerably in its angle, and its range was much broader. Her citizens were to be trained for peace much more than for war, and education in the spirit of Athenian institutions, as well as a course in physical training, was given her boys. Her constant effort was to make well-balanced men. Every one had his place in the service of the state, but it was felt that he could fill it best by securing the most complete development personally. For that reason, while the Athenian curriculum resembled that of Sparta, there was a marked difference in purpose and in the relative importance attached to the various subjects; and even the earlier education at Athens demands a separate treatment.

Childhood. — The more liberal spirit of Athens is made apparent in the fact that the state did not as

Old Athenian education considered state welfare of prime importance,

but felt that personal development was necessary for this.

Life and education of

the child was controlled by the father rather than the state.

completely control the life and education of the young as in Sparta. The method of their rearing was not as rigorous, or so definitely prescribed. While the newly born were often exposed, this was because the father, rather than the state, felt that the child would not be a credit to him, or that his family was already large enough. The mother, and not the state, had nominal charge of the boy, as well as the girl, until he was seven, although the real care devolved upon the slave nurse. By listening to nursery-rhymes, folk-lore, and stories about gods or héroes from Homer and Hesiod, and memorizing them, there was early cultivated within him the germ of that imagination and poetic feeling for which Athens became famous.

Boys went to school in the care of a slave.

Boyhood. — At seven the boy was sent to school in the care of a slave known as the *pædagogus* ('boy leader'), who carried his lyre and other school appurtenances. This functionary was ordinarily one who was unfitted for other duties by age or other physical disability, but he had complete oversight of the boy's morals. The youngster was expected to obey him, and he could enforce his discipline with whipping, if necessary; but it may well be imagined that his youthful charge had but little respect for him. It would seem from this intrusting of the child to the moral care of slaves, such as the nurse and pedagogue, that Athens, while broader than Sparta in its training, was less strict about habit formation in early life.

The training in these schools to which the Athenian boys first went, was not, as in Sparta, provided by the state or altogether under state control. But any father who failed to provide his boy with an education could not, by the laws of Solon, in his old age claim support from his son. Education was mandatory, but individual responsibility was encouraged. So the schools were generally private ventures, and were held in houses or rooms provided by the teachers, or possibly, in some instances, rented to them by the state. All schools were, however, subject to state supervision, probably through the Council of the Areopagus. The exact course that the boy should take and the length of time he should remain in school were matters also to be determined by his father, although the state required in general that every one should be taught gymnastics and 'music.'

These subjects he learned in two different elementary schools, — the *palæstra* ('wrestling ground'), for physical training, and the *didascaleum* ('teaching place'), or 'music'-school. The palæstra seems to have been simply an open space covered with sand, having a racecourse on it, and may sometimes have been connected with the didascaleum, after the fashion of the modern schoolyard or playing fields. While school hours lasted the entire day, from early in the morning until almost sunset, as so much of the course consisted in physical exercise and 'activity' studies, and holidays in honor of the gods were frequent, the work was probably not as strenuous as in Sparta.

(1) the palæstra, for physical training;

The instruction in the palæstra was given through the *pædotribes* ('boy kneader'), who had assistants to anoint the pupils with oil and scrape them after the exercise was over. As in Sparta, the course was graded, and besides simple calisthenics and ball-playing, the *pentathlum* ('fivefold contest'),[1] which included running, leaping, throwing the discus, casting the javelin, and wrestling, formed the staples of the curriculum. Boxing was not allowed until the boys were older, lest they might be permanently disfigured.

The purpose of this physical training in Athens differed from that in Sparta. As might be expected, it did not aim to serve the state by creating a race of soldiers, but to cultivate ease and grace of bearing, adroitness, and strength, and so to heighten the morals and intelligence of the future citizens. Running and jumping were intended to develop the lower limbs, endurance being especially cultivated by long runs, and concentration of energy by sprints and all varieties of jumping; the discus and the javelin afforded special training for the eye-and-arm adjustment, and the former especially aided that poise and symmetry which com-

---

[1] It is questionable whether these games were organized enough to be known by this term before the time of the 'new' education.

posed the Athenian ideal of beauty;[1] while all these objects were furthered by wrestling, and the moral quality of self-control strengthened in addition.

Naturally, intellectual, æsthetic, and moral education was more specific in Athens than Sparta. The effort to furnish this was first made through the *didascaleum*, where the study was of ' music,' which was said to be for the culture of the soul just as gymnastics was for the body. ' Music,' however, had a broader scope than is now intended. It included all that came under the patronage of the nine muses, — literary subjects, as well as musical in the narrower sense. At length, when various lyric, elegiac, and other poems, as well as the epic, had come to be recited to musical accompaniment, the memory became overtaxed, and it was necessary for the musicians who used them to commit them to writing. Consequently, no distinction was made between musical and literary training, and both were furnished by the same teacher, the *citharistes* ('lyre-player'), or 'music'-master.[2]

As elements of the literary training, reading and writing were studied. After the boy had learned his letters by tracing them in sand, he was taught to copy verses and selections from well-known authors, at first upon

and (2) the didascaleum, for intellectual training.

At the didascaleum were taught reading, writing, and literature,

[1] This canon of the human figure is embodied in the familiar *discobalus* of Myron, which is still preserved in the Vatican museum.

[2] Later, the term *grammatistes* (' teacher of letters ') was used to designate the instructor in literature and rhetoric.

M

wax-tablets with a stylus, and later upon parchment with pen and ink. " In the works of the great poets," says Plato, " are contained many admonitions, and many tales, and praises, and encomia of ancient famous men, which he is required to learn by heart, in order that he may imitate or emulate them and desire to become like them." [1] The writing lesson of one day served for the reading of the next; so that if the copy appeared illegible, the boy had his own carelessness to blame. As punctuation and accents had not yet been invented, and a passage was written without spacing between the words, the younger boys seem to have been obliged to have the teacher separate the words and clauses before they began to read. And the older boys must have found it something of an intellectual test to divide the writing mentally, and read with the distinctness and expression that was required of them.

and music. Instruction in music proper, until the fifth century, consisted in learning to chant religious or patriotic poems, and gradually to accompany one's self on the seven-stringed lyre. Only the strong, simple, Doric airs were used, and anything like professional skill was tabooed as being unworthy of a liberal training. These lyrics were taught the boys, " in order that they might learn to be more gentle, harmonious, and rhythmical, and so more fitted for speech and action; for the

[1] Plato, *Protagoras*, 325 D.

life of man in every part has need of harmony and rhythm."[1] It was necessary for the pupils to understand the rhythm and melody, that they might bring out the meaning of the poem, and the older boys were often required to improvise an accompaniment that should express the theme. Thus music constituted an intellectual and ethical, as well as an æsthetic, training.

There was one other subject in the elementary curriculum at Athens, — dancing. This is difficult to classify. It might well be considered under either gymnastics or music; and, as a fact, while the instruction probably took place in the palæstra, it was conducted by the citharist. One object seems to have been, as in music, to express the meaning of some poem and arouse a patriotic and religious spirit. The dancing consisted in a rhythmical swaying of the entire body, expressing by a sort of pantomimic ballet the sentiment which was at the same time sung in words and accompanied on the lyre by a musician. Thus dancing was intended to train the whole being, — body and soul. It seems to have been a point of contact between two seemingly diverse branches of education, and made apparent their essential relation and harmony.

Dancing was a point of contact between physical and intellectual education.

This programme of elementary education in Athens was much richer in possibilities than would appear from the fewness of subjects. Until the fourth century it

Value of the content was greater than it seems.

[1] Plato, *Protagoras*, 326 A.

contained practically no arithmetic or other mathematics, but left these to be acquired in practical life; drawing also was not added until later; and none of the other elements that now seem necessary appeared there as separate subjects. But the material read and memorized, sung and danced to, was filled with valuable experience and moral teaching, and the explanations and interpretations given by the teachers had to bring in all the learning of the times. Expositions of Homer and Hesiod, Tyrtæus, Alcman, and Sappho, Theognis and Solon, in bringing out the inspiration of a noble literature, would require a considerable range of information concerning religion, ethics, politics, and social life, and could easily be correlated with any study in our curriculum to-day. The moral, æsthetic, and general cultural value of these studies must have been far greater than would be suggested to the modern educator from the meagerness of the course.

Methods of teaching were not much developed. On the whole, however, teaching had received as yet but little development in Athens. The pupil learned to write by imitating the copy of his teacher. Reading was taught by the alphabetic, rather than the phonetic, method; and the boys repeated the letters and poems after the teacher, and sang or read them in concert. This memory work was carried on with little idea of the meaning, although it was afterward explained to the pupils.

Nor were there any qualifications for becoming a schoolmaster, and teachers were, in consequence, not much esteemed.[1] In discipline, too, the appeal was made to extraneous motives, either fear of punishment or hope of reward. Rivalry, which played so important a part in all phases of Greek life, must have been largely depended upon in Athenian schools.

Adolescence. — At fifteen the Athenian boy, if he belonged to the wealthier and more cultured class, entered what might be considered his secondary education. Most of this was carried on at one of the exercising grounds in the thick groves just outside Athens. These were called *gymnasia*,[2] and the teachers came to be known as *gymnastæ*. Unlike the palæstra and the didascaleum, these institutions were maintained at state expense. The course consisted largely of physical training of a more advanced character; the features of

Secondary education in the gymnasia.

[1] This may, however, have been due in part to the fact that the elementary teachers, both pædotribes and citharists, charged a fee, as the Athenians could not conceive of a proper relation between teacher and pupil that did not exist purely from mutual regard. Compare the Athenian estimate of the sophists, p. 174.

[2] Two of these had been established early in the sixth century by Solon: the 'Academy' on the northwest in the valley of the Cephissus, intended for Athenians of pure blood, and under the protection of Athene; and the 'Cynosarges,' on the east at the foot of Mount Lycabettus, for those of mixed blood, which had Heracles as a patron. Plato afterward taught at the Academy, while the Lyceum, which was not founded until the time of Pericles, and was near the river Ilissus, became the seat of Aristotle's lectures.

the palæstra were continued, but made more severe, and certain more vigorous exercises were added. The running was now done in armor, and wrestling became rougher and more complicated. It was also supplemented by boxing, and the pancratium was sometimes allowed. Swimming and hunting were engaged in outside the gymnasia, although the latter could not possess the same allurements that it did in the more sparsely settled and hilly country about Sparta.

The youth was now given much liberty, although responsible to his father and the Areopagus.

At this stage the boy passed from the surveillance of the pedagogue, but was still under the care of his father or guardian, who continued to be responsible for his conduct. The adolescent was also subject to the Council of the Areopagus, which could punish him severely for any breach of morals, and each gymnasium was under the strict supervision of a state official known as the *sophronistes* ('regulator'), or censor of morals. Such care was necessary, as this was a critical period in the boy's life. He had been given a sudden access of liberty, which he might at first be tempted to abuse. He was now allowed to go wherever he wished, — into the *agora*, the courts, or the theater, as well as the gymnasium; and became acquainted with public life through first-hand contact. So, too, while he was given no direct instruction of an intellectual character, not even in political science, yet at this most impressionable period he learned, through informal intercourse with his elders, to discuss and converse, and acquired a knowledge of ethics and of civic and social affairs that fitted him well for the duties of citizenship.

Youth. — At eighteen the young man finished his secondary education and was presented by his father as a candidate for citizenship. If it could be shown that he was legitimate and born of Athenians of pure blood, and was up to the physical, intellectual, and moral standards, his name was entered upon the register of citizens, and he was publicly introduced by the king-archon. He was then armed with spear and shield by his father, or, if his parent had perished in battle, by the state, and was permitted at the shrine of Aglaurus to take the oath of loyalty to the gods, state, and traditions of Athens.[1]

The youth now came directly under the laws of the state, but he was considered a novice, and did not share in civic affairs. During this period he was known as an *ephebus* ('youth') or cadet, and for two years continued his education with a course in militia duties. The first

Ephebic, or cadet training.

---

[1] The oath ran as follows: "I will never disgrace these sacred arms, nor desert my companion in the ranks. I will fight for temples and public property, both alone and with many. I will transmit my fatherland, not only not less, but greater and better, than it was transmitted to me. I will obey the magistrates who may at any time be in power. I will observe both the existing laws and those which the people may unanimously hereafter make; and, if any person seek to annul the laws or set them at naught, I will do my best to prevent him, and will defend them both alone and with many. I will honor the religion of my fathers. And I call to witness Aglaurus, Enyalius, Ares, Zeus, Thallo, Auxo, and Hegemone."

year the ephebus spent in the neighborhood of Athens. Here he led the usual life of a soldier; he slept in the open air, drilled, and garrisoned the city, and might at any time be called upon for active service. At the end of a year he took a public examination in the use of arms and was then transferred to some fortress on the frontier, where he acted as a sort of rural police and acquainted himself with the topography of Attica. After another year he took the examination for citizenship called *dokimasia*, and when he passed, became a full-fledged citizen.

Citizenship. — But even with the attainment of citizenship, the education of the Athenian did not cease. Throughout the rest of his life he was constantly surrounded by the means for a liberal training. The drama, architecture, sculpture, and art of ancient Athens everywhere furnished him with noble ideals toward which to struggle; and the civic problems, religious festivals, and literary contests all stimulated him to intellectual and æsthetic efforts of the highest sort. While the Athenians were not, like the Spartans, bound by state regulation to eat in common or assist in the education of the youth, they endeavored always to advance the state by the quality of their manhood and citizenship.

Education of Women. — The education of women was purposely neglected by the Athenians. They felt, as

Even after citizenship, education continued through environment.

Women were trained only

did the Spartans, that education existed only for prac- *in house-*
tical activities ; but unlike their great rivals, they held *hold affairs.*
that men alone should take part in public life, and
so only their sex required specific training. Woman,
whose duties of wife and mother lay entirely within
doors, needed no knowledge beyond ordinary skill in
household affairs; and those who possessed any intellectual attainments were necessarily regarded as
wanting in moral sense and conduct.

Character of the Old Athenian Education. — Hence, in *More oppor-*
the rights of women and in habit formation among chil- *tunity for*
dren, Athens was excelled by Sparta; but upon the *development*
whole, the Athenian education was far superior to the *Sparta,*
Spartan in allowing more opportunity for individual
development. Except in general principles, the laws did
not interfere with the parents in the details of educating their children, and private life was not altogether
crushed out. The course admitted of a more rounded
education than that of Sparta, and was rich in intellectual, æsthetic, and moral content. During youth and
manhood especially, the Athenian was given great latitude in the development of his character, and had every
opportunity to secure a liberal training. Consequently,
while Athens for many years retained a kind of state
morality and was somewhat dependent upon tradition,
elements of individualism and some development of
personality were manifest in her education even at an

early day.   Where Sparta educated preëminently for military service and citizenship, Athens endeavored to train for manhood, that the more efficient citizen might thereby result.

but so great a similarity that both systems were included under 'old' Greek education.

Nevertheless, until about the middle of the fifth century B.C., despite wide divergences in ideals and details of accomplishment, Athenian education resembled the Spartan in its purpose, organization, and content.   For that reason, the early history of Athens is usually grouped with that of Sparta throughout as representative of what Aristophanes called the 'old' education, where personality was given less recognition, and the individual was subordinated to the good of the whole.   This characterization is, of course, in contrast to Greek education in the 'new' period, which is represented by Athens alone.

Factors in the change to the new ideals.

Athenian Education in the New Period. — This new type of education may in some measure be considered a natural evolution from the old.   The gradual rise of broad democratic ideals and the opportunities arising from the supremacy of Athens, culminating in the enlightened Periclean age, which have already been sketched,[1] seem to be a legitimate outcome of the old concept of developing the individual for the sake of the state, and a move toward strengthening the demand for an education that should more adequately recognize the

[1] See pp. 143–144.

interests of the individual.   To this extent, the old theory of education appears to have committed progressive suicide.   But as the result of the Persian wars, a decidedly revolutionary tendency was also at work in Athenian society and was probably more effective in producing the transition in ideals and practice.

The extended conflict with a powerful people from the Orient, possessing a well-organized but widely different body of traditions, the political and commercial intercourse with a variety of other states and nations, which ensued from the formation of the Athenian Empire and the social contact with foreigners from every land that were thronging the streets of Athens, resulted in an interchange of customs and ideas that greatly broadened the views of the Athenians, stimulated their intellectual activity, and led to a reconstruction of their practices and beliefs.   A growing familiarity with new traditions and activities brought about a toleration of them and a comparison with the old, with the inevitable rejection of any portion of either that could not stand the test.

Certain conditions seem especially symptomatic of this break-up of old traditions, and are characteristic of the increased emphasis upon the individual.   In theology, the stories about the old gods and their rather arbitrary control of the world were replaced by more scientific attempts at an explanation of nature.   Philos-

Changes in theology, philosophy, and literature especially resulted.

ophy also shifted the emphasis of its search after ultimate reality from nature to man. The content of
literature showed the change in a similar way. It
came gradually to concern itself with more human interests, such as are contained in the dramas of Euripides,
rather than with such stern old notions of duty and fate
as appear in the *Prometheus* of Æschylus or the *Œdipus
Tyrannus* of Sophocles.

Confusion in
society was
evident.

As a natural concomitant of this rapid transition,
society seems for a time to have been completely disrupted. The old was shattered, and while new ideals
were being constructed, a groping ensued. While the
latitude given the individual was destined, as always,
to produce progress in the long run, and was of great
ultimate service to the world, more immediately a low
ebb in morals at Athens resulted. If we can rely at
all upon Aristophanes, even after his witty exagger-
ations have been properly discounted, it would seem
that children became impudent, cunning, and impure;
wives turned shrewish, extravagant, and unfaithful;
husbands neglected their duties as householders and
citizens in a search for disreputable and dishonest
gain; slaves became disobedient, lazy, and disloyal;
skepticism and license were rampant, and confusion
was general. It was individualism run riot.

Individual-
ism was re-
flected in
education.

Education especially reflected the conditions of the
period. Its ideals became more and more individual-

istic. The times demanded a training that would promote the happiness of the individual with little or
no consideration for the welfare of the state as a
whole. The old education seemed narrow and barren
of content; and there arose a desire for all sorts of
knowledge that might contribute to one's advancement, whether it increased his usefulness or not. Skill
in debate and public speaking was especially sought,
because of the unusual opportunity for personal
achievement in politics.

The Sophists. — To meet these demands, a new set
of teachers, who called themselves *sophistæ* ('wise
men'), came into prominence. They were generally
colonial Greeks[1] who had acquired much knowledge
and experience through wide travel. Hence they
were able to view the traditional Athenian education
from the outside and detect its inability to adapt itself
to the new situation. They especially professed to be
competent to prepare young men for a career of glory
and profit, and some of them even claimed to teach
any subject whatsoever, or how to defend either side
of an argument successfully. This, together with the
want of modesty implied in the name they had assumed,
was quite opposed to the Athenian notion of integrity

The sophists,
who pro-
fessed to pre-
pare young
men for a
career, were
in disrepute.

[1] The new tendencies arose in the colonies, where the first conflict
of traditions naturally took place. From these points of unsettled conditions the sophists emigrated to Athens.

and proper balance of mind; and they further offended the national sense of propriety by charging a fee for their services.[1]

In consequence, the orthodox citizens of Athens were very suspicious of these 'foreign' tutors, but it must not be concluded that the sophists as a class were wanting in character. While there were undoubtedly charlatans among them, as is likely to be the case with any new movement, their number, nevertheless, also included many worthy men, such as Protagoras of Abdera, so much admired by Socrates, and Gorgias of Leontini, who rendered such distinguished service to oratory. Most of these teachers afforded their pupils as thorough a course in natural science and political and economic problems as was possible at the time, and trained them honestly and carefully in rhetorical presentation. Sometimes, to be sure, especially in later days, the sophistic discipline consisted in acquiring superficial information and *bon mots*, and memorizing set speeches upon a variety of topics; and, with even the best of the sophists, mere form, pretentious argumentation, and word quibbles [2] played an important part, and instruction, rather than a training in moral habit, became characteristic of their education.

---

[1] See footnote on page 165.

[2] Prodicus of Ceos was especially famous for his distinctions between synonyms.

The effect of this teaching was naturally felt most strongly by the adolescents in the gymnasium stage of education. These young men were ambitious to distinguish themselves in politics, and the physical training which had hitherto dominated the course in the gymnasium could not be of much service for statesmanship. Consequently, this kind of development was abandoned for the study of grammatical and rhetorical subtleties; and, as Aristophanes phrases it, the youths became narrow of chest and glib of tongue. Whenever a sophist appeared in the street, the *agora*, or the house, the young men crowded about him to borrow from his store of experience and wisdom, and acquire his method of argument.

Its effect felt by those in the gymnasium especially,

But the influence of the sophists also extended somewhat to the ephebic and younger citizens, and the new ideals likewise reacted on the lower schools. The exercises of the palæstra were no longer intended to secure the proper balance and endurance, that better citizens might be made, but for the sake of the glow of health, or for obtaining such form and grace as would impart æsthetic pleasure. The rigor of the training was greatly abated, and warm baths replaced the cold plunge that had formerly braced their sinews. The literary work in the didascaleum, besides epic poetry, which was now considered out of date, came to include the reflective and didactic poems of Simonides, The-

but also by the ephebes, the younger citizens, and those in the lower schools.

ognis, Archilochus, and others, who aimed at teaching morals in aphoristic form; and much fruitless discussion concerning their meaning was carried on. Music was now taught, not so much to stimulate patriotism or to foster intellectual attainments for the sake of the state, as to enable the performer to secure pleasure or exhibit individual skill. Instead of the old patriotic and religious songs sung to the simple Doric airs and accompanied upon the seven-stringed lyre, there were introduced complicated instruments of all sorts, requiring much skill, rhythms like the Lydian and Phrygian, which pleased the ear and were difficult in execution, and other musical novelties.

Extreme individualism of the sophists.

All this inroad upon the time-honored curriculum shows how fully the sophists embodied the individualism of the times. In all matters they represented the unlimited inquiry and discussion that was going on, and the consequent subversion of Athenian tradition and civilization. While the sophists criticised, they made no effort to stay the disintegration, and offered nothing to take the place of the old that was being destroyed. Their attitude was purely negative. Although they held no body of doctrine common to them all, they were generally at one in their position of extreme individualism. They often went so far as to insist that there could not safely be any universal criteria in knowledge or morals; that no satisfactory interpretation of life could be made for all, but that every fact and situation should be subject to the judgment of the individual. No doubt the formula attributed to Protagoras, "Man (*i.e.* the individual) is the measure of all things, both of the seen and the unseen," would have expressed the attitude common to most of them.

Thus the sophists were only carrying to its legitimate conclusion the complete reaction from the old ideal of subordination of the individual to the state; and, while their doctrine of individualism was temporarily connected with much social disorder, it was prophetic of a higher civilization. Destruction must sometimes prepare the way for reconstruction, when social conditions become too hard and fast. As a body, the sophists were earnestly, though perhaps unconsciously, striving to close the period of unreflective acceptance of tradition, and awaken within every one a sense of individual responsibility. While others were required to rebuild the social and ethical structure, theirs was the first step toward moral freedom.

Reactionary Forces. — Meanwhile, the conservative element in society was making its usual attempt to adjust the unsettled conditions by suggesting a return to the old. Various schemes had been advanced, even before the sophists had come into prominence. The plan most completely worked out, both in theory and

System of Pythagoras.

N

practice, was that of Pythagoras (about 580–500 B.C.). He formulated a socialistic system in opposition to the growing individualistic tendency as early as the latter half of the sixth century. Adopting an analogy from the 'harmony' of the celestial bodies and from the relation of the powers in the individual to each other, he arranged a definite hierarchy in society, so that each member should have his proper place, and complete harmony and social order should ensue. Similarly, he planned an educational scheme for the harmonizing of the individual ; his reproductive power was to be subordinated to nutrition through gymnastics, nutrition to sensation by music, and sensation to reason by means of arithmetic, geometry, and astronomy. Under this system Pythagoras organized a religious brotherhood with certain ascetic and superstitious rules, which for a time proved very successful in Magna Græcia, and eventually became the prototype of many fixed social schemes.

Æschylus, Aristophanes, Xenophon, and others.

As the influence of the sophists began to be felt, other representatives of the reactionary movement also appeared. The aristocratic party naturally held to the old order of things, and advocated a return as the only remedy. Also Æschylus (525–456 B.C.), 'father of tragedy,' attempted to preserve the traditional mythology by interpreting it in an ethical sense, and became the greatest exponent of the old system of institutional

morals in Greece. In comedy, that matchless caricatur-
ist of Athens, Aristophanes (about 445–380 B.C.), used
his plays as a vehicle to parody the new conditions and
contrast them unfavorably with the old. Then, in the
Cyropædia, or *Education of Cyrus*, Xenophon (about
430–370 B.C.) advocated a complete reversion to the ideal
of subserviency to the state. Under the guise of describing the training of a Persian prince, he practically
presented the old Greek plan of education, partly as it
was in vogue at Athens, but mostly as in Sparta. On
the practical side, Pericles endeavored to bring the
Athenians back to an absorption in the welfare of the
state by beautifying Athens in every way, and by interesting them in public exhibitions, and, when these efforts
failed, he appealed to their patriotism by involving them
in the Peloponnesian War.

The Mediators. — But the social process can never
move backward, and a reconstruction on some higher
plane is needed if the effects of destruction are to be
overcome. Some plan to harmonize the interest of the
individual with that of society had to be devised. The
method of obtaining this *desideratum* was the problem
set themselves by Socrates, Plato, and Aristotle. As in
the case of the sophists, they recognized that the traditional beliefs and sanctions, including the gods, the old
social order, and the former ideals and content of education, had been outlived, and that the individual could

not find truth and morality through an institutional system of ethics. At the same time, they felt that the extreme individualism of the sophists was too negative a
basis upon which to build. Without a more socialized
standard of knowledge and morality, they saw that life
could not be satisfactorily interpreted. Thus philosophy began as a means of better social expression.

**How Soc-
rates differed
from the
sophists.**

Socrates. — This mediating effort was begun by Socrates (469–399 B.C.), the homely and abstemious philosopher, who taught contemporaneously with the sophists.
While he started with the formula of Protagoras, he
maintained that the 'man' indicated thereby was not the
individual man. That is, there is a body of truth common to the intelligences of all men, and " man is the
measure of all things " only so far as the knowledge by
which he judges of the truth has this universal validity.
It is not the peculiar view of any individual that represents the truth, but the knowledge that is the same for
every one. The former, which the sophists considered
' knowledge,' Socrates held to be only ' opinion,' and declared that the reason men think so differently is because
they see but one side of the truth, and do not understand
the significance of their own thoughts. He differed
from the sophists, then, in emphasizing in man not his
mere peculiarities, as tested by his sensations, impulses,
and feelings, but rather his rational, and so universal,
self.

Socrates also believed that every one could get at this universal knowledge by stripping off the individual differences and laying bare the essentials upon which all men are agreed. He conceived it to be the mission of the true philosopher to enable the individual to do this, and, accordingly, he endeavored to train the mind of those with whom he came in contact, so that they could form valid conclusions. He felt it necessary to teach them to think rather than load them with ready-made information. Realizing that the 'pouring in' process of the sophists in their lectures could never be effective, he adopted the plan of development through informal conversation.

This method of Socrates has been known as *dialectic* ('conversational'), and was twofold in nature. As the first step, Socrates thought it necessary to dispel the undue assurance of the person he was teaching by a process called *irony* ('dissembling'). He encouraged the individual to make a definite statement of his belief, which he took as a starting-point in the search for truth. Then, through a set of clever questions, he caused the person to develop his thought, until either a self-consistent conclusion was reached, or the individual became so involved in manifest contradictions or an actual *reductio ad absurdum*, that he was forced to admit that his view had been hastily formed, and was mere 'opinion,' after

His 'dia-
lectic'
method:
(1) irony

all.[1] In the latter case, the person was put in the proper

frame of mind to continue the pursuit of truth. In thus developing the logical implications of a person's position, whether they led out to truth or error, he used a procedure that he called *maieutic* ('midwifery'). In this, by means of questions, he caused the individual to see that the opinion he had first expressed was but a single phase of the universal truth, which he had thus helped him to develop or 'give birth to.'

Through this method of developing knowledge, Socrates strove to harmonize the individual welfare with that of the social group. His aim was not so much to fit the individual for immediate practical success as to teach him how to live with his fellows. Accordingly, he applied his doctrine of universal knowledge within each person especially to morals, and made the accomplishment of right living come through the development in consciousness of universal truth. He, therefore, made morality consist in right knowledge, as did Plato after him ; and both left it to Aristotle to make the necessary distinction between the knowledge of an action and the impulse to perform it.

In estimating the value of this method of eliciting knowledge, it is easy to see that it would work well in the formulation of ethical principles,[1] since this is within

---

[1] For a good example, read the account of his interview with the youthful and ambitious Euthydemus in Xenophon's *Memorabilia*, Bk. IV, Chap. II.

the reason of every individual, however unlearned.   But it should also be noted that not everything was, or could be, drawn from the inner consciousness of the individual interrogated, but that Socrates himself contributed much to the progress of the discussion.   Nevertheless, this furnishing of content, which is clearly necessary in all studies that are not purely schematic, does not interfere with the value of the Socratic method for efficient teaching.   If a method arouses and holds the interest of the pupil, he may, without losing an iota of mental activity, be told many facts outright along the lines upon which his curiosity has been excited, especially if he cannot be expected to know them.[1]   The Socratic method contains the germ idea of all modern pedagogy.

But however valid the view of Socrates, it resulted in the death of its promulgator.   He was hated alike by the individualistic sophists, whose shallow and negative opinions he was continually exposing, and by the conservative believers in the old traditions and institutional morality, who felt that Socrates was atheistic and immoral, and the most dangerous among the sophists. Through the traditionalists, Athens was persuaded to give him the hemlock; and thus destroyed the man that

Results of the Socratic teaching.

---

[1] This, however, does not seem to be understood by those educators who state, or imply by their practice, that it is wrong to furnish the pupil with any information whatsoever, under the impression that by the Socratic method he should ' discover ' everything for himself.

might have been her savior.[1]   The spirit of Socrates, however, continued to live, and what he saw but dimly became clearer as time went on.   While it was too late to redeem Athens, his vision remained a great force in the progress of thought.

Plato. — The rather vague formulations of Socrates were accepted by his pupil, Plato.   Like many others, such as the Cynics and Cyrenaics, who made the most diverse interpretations from the somewhat inchoate statements of this master, Plato attempted to develop the thought of Socrates.   He desired to build upon it a complete and fixed system for society, and thus arrest the disintegration that was going on.   He continued the work of Socrates,[2] but modified it in some important respects.   To understand how this occurred will require a brief account of Plato's life and work.

Plato and his philosophy.

Plato (427–347 B.C.) differed greatly in his attitude toward life from the democratic Socrates.   He was by birth and temperament a natural aristocrat; and never mingled indiscriminately with all people, as did his teacher.   He was not, however, out of sympathy with the masses, but his social position may have affected his estimate of their intelligence.   After the death of Soc-

[1] See Plato's *Apology*, which gives Socrates' estimate of the causes of his accusation and condemnation.

[2] In fact, Plato represents Socrates as the chief expounder in practically all his dialogues, except *The Laws*.

rates, he left the state, and, becoming better acquainted through travel with the various philosophic movements of the times, he not only enlarged the character of his master's ethical teachings, but greatly broadened the scope of philosophy itself. Thus he came to plan an ideal state in which there should be more exalted principles, and practice should be in harmony with the highest possible theory.

The Republic. — Plato's description of the ideal state is found especially in that one of his dialogues known as *The Republic*. In this work, he starts with the avowed object of investigating the nature of justice. Finding it difficult to analyze in the case of the individual, he proposes to examine it on a larger scale in the state as a whole.[1] To accomplish this, he undertakes to describe the evolution of a model state and the relations between its inhabitants. He shows how, in society, one industry or occupation after another is differentiated until a special class known as 'guardians' is set aside to protect the state and add to its territory.

Evolution of classes in the model state.

These guardians are to be separated from the industrial classes on the basis of physical prowess and their intellectual and moral endowments, and to be given a suitable education. Apparently he assumes that those who are incapable of becoming guardians should not receive any education beyond apprenticeship. In de-

Elementary education to be similar to that in vogue, but with important reforms.

[1] Bk. II, 368.

scribing the course of study that the guardians are to take first, Plato naturally follows the education in vogue for boys up to eighteen years of age, in the home and at the palæstra, didascaleum, and gymnasium at Athens, but even here, at the start, he would undertake social regulation, and insists upon some rather important reforms. " Our first duty," he says, " will be to exercise a censorship over the authors of fables, selecting their good productions, and rejecting the bad. And the selected fables we shall advise our nurses and mothers to repeat to their children, that they may thus mold their minds with the fables, even more than they shape their bodies with the hand." [1] So he claims that the literary element of the home and school training should be purified of all accounts that lower the character and dignity of the gods or the heroes of the past, or that would tend to create a fear of death. Likewise, music should be confined to the simple patriotic and religious melodies of the Dorians, and to instruments that are not difficult to play. In the matter of gymnastic training, temperate living should be included; and it should be a moral, rather than a physical discipline, since "the two arts of music and gymnastics are not really designed, the one for the training of the soul, the other for the training of the body, but the teachers of both have in view chiefly the improvement of the soul." [2]

[1] Bk. II, 377.   [2] Bk. III, 410.

From this group of guardians are eventually to be selected the ablest and most prudent as magistrates of the state.   The rest are to be regarded as their auxiliaries.   This division is to be determined upon while the guardians are passing through the ephebic or cadet period of education that was customary in Athens [1] between eighteen and twenty.   They are to live in camp in a frugal and hardy way, enforce the laws, and repel the enemies of the state, if necessary.[2]   Those who show themselves capable of further education are to be selected for magistrates, while the others are to be relegated to the auxiliary class. *Secondary education by means of cadet training.*

At this point [3] Plato seems to have completed his search for justice in the state as a whole.   This virtue, he declares, exists for the state, when each class attends to its own business; when the magistrates, in whom is the wisdom of the state, guide both the auxiliaries or soldiery, who possess the courage and so defend the state, and the industrial class, whose only virtue is temperance and whose function is to produce.   This arrangement he now claims to verify by comparing the state to the individual, declaring that justice exists in the individual when his reason, located in the head, which corresponds to the magistrates in the state, controls his spirit, lodged in the breast, and his passions, seated in *Analogy of the state with the individual.*

[1] See pp. 167–168.   [2] Bk. III, 415–417.

[3] Bk. IV.

the abdomen, whose counterparts are the military and industrial classes respectively.

Rule of the philosophers is necessary. Plato's proposition, then, as he soon makes more explicit, is to intrust the entire control of the government to the magistrates, whom he now calls 'philosophers,' for "Until philosophers are kings, or the kings and princes of this world be imbued with a sufficient measure of genuine philosophy,—that is, unless political power and philosophy be united in the same person, . . . there will be no deliverance for cities nor yet for the human race; neither can the commonwealth that we have now sketched in theory ever till then grow into a possibility, and see the light of day." [1] This class alone is capable of abstract thinking, and so possesses real knowledge or universal truth, while the other classes content themselves with mere opinion. This real knowledge Plato describes as coming to the philosophers through a vision of the 'ideas,' [2] which he depicts as existing outside consciousness in a world by themselves and as being the archetypes from which all visible objects are molded. [3]

Higher education for the philosophers, The philosophic class, therefore, requires an education that will enable them to acquire the habit of specu-

[1] Bk. V, 473.

[2] Elsewhere (*Phædrus*, 246 ff., *Meno*, 80 ff., etc.) he more fully develops this doctrine. He holds that in a previous existence the soul lived in the incorporeal world and beheld the 'ideas,' or pure forms of reality, and that a 'recollection' of this vision is produced by a perception of similar corporeal things for those in whom the philosophic impulse exists.   [3] Bk. VI.

lative thinking, or, in Plato's terms, "will turn the eye of the soul from the sensuous to the real." So Plato is now obliged to invent a new course of study for the purpose, as Greek education did not extend beyond the ephebic period or the twentieth year. This additional course, he declares, shall also be graded, in order that a further test of intellectual and moral qualities may be made. Arithmetic, plane and solid geometry, music, and astronomy, are to occupy the first ten years of the course. These subjects, however, are not to be studied for calculation or practical purposes of any sort, but entirely from the standpoint of theory or the universal relations underlying them, since only thus can they furnish a capacity for abstract thought or a vision of the ideas.[1] After this, at thirty, those who show themselves capable of the study of 'real existence,' or dialectic, go on with this subject for five years longer. It then becomes the duty of these highest philosophers to go out into society and guide it until they have reached the age of fifty, when they are to be allowed to retire.[2] Their remaining days are to be spent in study and reflection, which is to be regarded as the highest life of all.[3]

consisting of arithmetic, geometry, music, and astronomy;

and of dialectic for the most capable.

[1] Bk. VII, 522–531. This seems to be the beginning of the theory of 'formal discipline.' Plato's contention is that the precision of mathematics would train one to be exact in judgment about practical affairs in general. See p. 196.

[2] Bk. VII, 532–534.   [3] Bk. VII, 539–540.

Education of women similar to that of men.

In this state, as Plato shows in a digression[1] from the main narrative, women are to receive a similar education to that of the men, even to the extent of wrestling unclad in the palæstra. This is because women are to have the same functions in the state as men. "In the administration of the state neither a woman as a woman, nor a man as a man, has any special function, but the gifts of nature are equally diffused in both sexes; all the pursuits of men are the pursuits of women also, and in all of them a woman is only a weaker man." Women, then, are also to be philosophers, soldiers, or workers according to their ability. In order that they may be freed from the cares of housekeeping and motherhood, all living is to be in common,[1] and the children that are born are to be reared in a state nursery, unless they are undesirable, when they are to be exposed.

How Plato differed from Socrates.

Criticism of The Republic. — In examining this ideal republic, it is first to be noted that Plato hardened the distinction which Socrates made between opinion and real knowledge; and, by a new interpretation, gave the latter an existence of its own outside of consciousness. Also, where Socrates, who constantly mingled with the people, found the basis of this universal truth in every one, Plato, possibly influenced by his aristocratic tendencies, and by his contact with the Pythagorean com-

[1] Bk. V as far as 473, which contains his argument for community in wives, children, and property.

munity, declared that only one class of people, — the most intellectual, could attain to a vision of the ideas, or real knowledge.   And since, like Socrates, he failed to discriminate between the cognitive and volitional, and so identified knowledge with virtue, it seemed to him that the philosophers should guide the conduct of all. Hence his ideal state became a sort of socialistic aristocracy or oligarchy of intelligence, and, in a way, seems to be a return to the old principle of subordinating the individual to the state.

Certainly in his desire to overcome the baneful effects of the extreme individualism of the times, Plato tended to depreciate the products of democracy in Athens. Nor could he realize that, while under a government of this sort there are abuses to be guarded against, and it takes a long time for the average person to reach the level of the most intelligent, yet progress, though slow and uncertain, is sure, and is accompanied by no Waterloo defeats.[1]   In some specific details also Plato seems to have been unable to rise above the most conservative thought of his times.   He permits slavery, and provides no education for the industrial class; family life is abandoned; and he sanctions outright the cruel practice of exposing children.

Aristocratic and conservative tendencies in Plato.

[1] Plato feels, however, that while his republic is difficult of institution, so much so that it may have to be established by force (*Republic*, VII, 540), when once it has been put into effect it will never be overthrown (*Critias*, pp. 120–121).   See also pp. 192–193.

Progressive features of *The Republic*.

Yet The Republic cannot be regarded as a reversion. The scheme advocated at least enables each individual to do that for which he is by nature best fitted; and, while he is to be pushed into his niche in life, rather than allowed to find it, to some extent self-realization is made compatible with social service. Moreover, the reason for allowing a special training and control to one class is not mere enjoyment or gratification of despotism, but because this form of government and this education are considered necessary to enable all classes to fulfill the function for which they are best fitted. And although women are to serve the interests of the state without regard to their own desires, they are not held to be either the slaves or the toys of men, and are allowed the same education as far as they can take it.

Why The Republic had no immediate effect upon education.

But, as a matter of fact, while most inspiring, and of the greatest importance to the development of thought in the long run, The Republic had practically no immediate effect upon education or any other institution of Athens. It was regarded as the visionary conception of a great mind removed from the life of the times. Instead of taking cognizance of the actual conditions of society, it was artificially, though very poetically, based upon a false analogy. Society is not an organism like the human body, and the members of it cannot be knitted together in such a way as to become one.

The Republic quite neglects human will[1] as a factor in society, and assumes that men can be moved about in life like pieces upon the chessboard.   Plato fails to see, too, that each individual really possesses all human characteristics.   The artisans have reason, and the philosophers have appetite.   A human being is not a man unless all these function in him.   But even if all this were the case, the treatise provides no way for an evolution from the current conditions, but plunges society immediately into the new régime.   Plato makes Socrates say that, while this scheme may not be feasible, the object is to have society approach it as nearly as possible, and this can be achieved by the one change of giving all control to the philosophers.   He does not, however, make it clear how this step can be brought about, except to say that every one above the age of ten must somehow be removed from the city.[2]   And if it be further granted that this order of things could be established at once, Plato puts the ban upon all innovation or change, and so closes the door to progress.

The Laws. — In fact, despite the suggestions in this perfected order of affairs, social disorder steadily continued to increase, and Plato himself eventually realized that The Republic was impracticable, and that society

Reversion to tradition in The Laws.

[1] For the place of will in Plato's psychology, see Mary Hay Wood's thesis on *Plato's Psychology in Its Bearing on the Development of Will* (London, 1907).   [2] Bk. VII, 541.   See, however, footnote on p. 191.

O

could be reformed only through the forces that built it. So in his declining years,[1] without denying The Republic as ideal, he wrote the dialogue known as *The Laws*, which was almost as much of a reversion to old traditions and ideals as the doctrine of Pythagoras or the theology of Æschylus. In it he welded together elements from the educational systems of Sparta and older Athens. He replaced the archetypal ideas of The Republic with a pantheon of astronomical gods; the philosophers were supplanted by the priests of these gods, an hereditary ruler, a superintendent of education, and various other officials; their mystic vision of the ideas gave way to intelligence or common sense; and the course of study reached its height with the subject of mathematics, while dialectic was not mentioned.

Influence of Plato. — Thus the efforts of Socrates, as continued by Plato, to obtain the benefit of the growing individualism for society and education without disrupting them, had seemingly come to naught. Nevertheless, Plato has had considerable influence upon the thought and practice of men since the Greek period. The ideal society, where everything is well managed and every one is in the position for which nature intended him, has ever since the day of The Republic been a favorite theme for writers, as witness the *Utopia*

How Plato has influenced thought and practice in general.

---

[1] *The Laws* is generally considered to be the last dialogue written by Plato, but this is questioned by some authorities.

of More, Bacon's *New Atlantis*, and the more modern *Looking Backward* of Bellamy. At times, more or less disastrous attempts to realize these ideals have been made, as in the case of Brook Farm, the Oneida Perfectionists, and a variety of socialistic and communistic colonies. However, even if impracticable for the time, an ideal may yet be of value, as Plato intimated, if it affords us an advanced goal for our efforts. On the other hand, while Plato's comparison of the state to a human organism has in some ways proved most illuminating for writers on social subjects, like Hobbes and Spencer, it has led them into strange fallacies, and is responsible for such phrases to-day as ' social body,' 'body politic,' or ' social organism,' and the various scientific and philosophic errors that have grown out of such implications.

In more specific movements Plato has also left his impress upon the world of thought. The contemplative life of the philosophers, removed from the organization of the state, but inspiring and controlling it, as depicted in The Republic, and afterward made more definite through the ' intellectual virtue ' commended by Aristotle, was the progenitor of a variety of extra-social schools of philosophy. These in their turn prepared the way for an understanding of the mission of Christianity, when it was established, as an institution outside the state, but endeavoring to bring the latter up to its own

More specific influence of Plato:

upon Christianity, monasticism, mysticism, and mediæval realism;

loftier ideals.   So, too, the regimen recommended for
these isolated philosophers, together with a similar practice among the Jews and in the discipline of Pythagoras,
may be held somewhat responsible for 'monasticism'
and 'asceticism' in mediæval times.   It is also apparent
that the doctrine of 'mysticism,' which started in the
early Church, but has somewhat survived in present-day
theology, is a revival of the mystic vision of the ideas,
which was retained in Neoplatonism.   Likewise, the
notion of the ideas as the 'real' things was adopted
by Anselm and other mediæval realists, and died hard
before the onslaught of nominalism and conceptualism.
Again, in the matter of content, Plato's approval of the
music, arithmetic, geometry, and astronomy of Pythagoras, and his adoption of dialectic from Socrates, when
combined with the grammar and rhetoric of the sophists, furnished the monastic schools with their *trivium*
and *quadrivium*.   Possibly, too, it may be held that the
whole notion of 'liberal' studies, and so the doctrine of
'formal discipline,' reaffirmed especially by Locke, goes
back to Plato's idea that the subjects in the special
course for philosophers should never be studied from
a practical point of view; but Aristotle's claim in his
Politics that professional skill should never be attained
in music or other subjects, and particularly his division
of the mind into faculties in his *Psychology*, seem more
clearly the ancestors of this long-lived educational error.

and upon the monastic course of study, and the doctrine of 'formal discipline.'

As a whole, it is evident that Plato has been a factor in educational theory and practice that cannot be overlooked, and The Republic will always remain a masterpiece of general literature and a great educational classic, even though both his theoretical and practical treatises failed to harmonize individualism with the old traditions.

Aristotle. ⎯ A more practical attempt to unify the new with the old in Greek society and education was made by Aristotle (386–322 B.C.), the pupil, and later the rival, of Plato. He came to Athens from Macedon, where his father was the court physician. Partly from his father and the scientific schools of Macedon, but more from his study under Plato in Athens, he obtained an excellent training, which is observable in the way he approaches his problems. Fortunately, the lectures of Aristotle survive in his treatises, as he spent his literary activities in preserving his notes in the form of books, instead of writing dialogues as did Plato. In consequence, while his works lack the imagery and polish of Plato, they treat their subjects much more systematically.

Aristotle waited until his ideas were fully matured before beginning to put them into final form, as he intended to maintain a consistent point of view throughout a complete system of thought. This encyclopædic work could not be finished within the dozen years of life left to him, and many of the treatises he wrote have

Aristotle's life and works.

since been lost, but sufficient material has come down to us to mark him as one of the greatest minds the world has ever known. He gave the first real impulse to biology, physiology, physics, mechanics, and psychology; his *Poetics* was the first attempt at a science of æsthetics; and his treatises on logic, metaphysics, ethics, and politics hold their own among the greatest works ever produced on the subjects.

The Ethics and The Politics. — Aristotle's ideas on education are contained in *The Ethics* and *The Politics*, the one describing how the individual must discipline himself in life, and the other, what social and economic conditions in the state are most favorable for reaching this end. In The Ethics he begins by inquiring what is the greatest good or the 'end' of human action, and declares that, while practically all men hold that this end is 'happiness,'[1] they differ greatly in the content they assign to the term, and that it should, therefore, be more carefully analyzed. He then continues: —

The *summum bonum* is activity of soul in accordance with virtue.

"Probably the best way to arrive at a definition will be to ascertain what is the peculiar function of man, for, as with a flute-player, sculptor, or artisan, and, in fact, any one who has a definite function or course of action, his goodness or excellence seems to lie in this function, so it would seem to be with man, if he has a

[1] I.e. *eudaimonia* ('good fortune'), from which a school of ethical philosophy called 'eudæmonism' is derived.

definite function. . . .   What, then, can this peculiar
function of man be ?   It is not mere life, for apparently
man has life in common with the plants, and we must,
therefore, exclude nutrition and growth.   Next, there is
also sensation ; but this, too, man appears to share with
horses, cattle, and all other lower animals.   There
remains, then, what may be called the practical life of
a being which possesses rationality.   But this rationality
has a twofold meaning; it is rational partly in the sense
of being obedient to reason, and partly in the sense of
exercising reason and intelligence.   This practical life
may, accordingly, be spoken of in two ways, — (from the
standpoint of habit or activity), but the life of activity
seems to be the better way to conceive of it.   The function of man, then, is activity of soul in accordance with
reason, or at least not independent of reason.   Moreover, it has been seen that the functions of a certain
person and of such a person when he is good in his
subject, are the same in kind, so that his excellence
is only a goodness in addition to his function; for
example, it is the function of the harpist to play the
harp, and of a good harpist to play it well.   So if the function of a man is activity of the soul in accordance with
reason, and of a good man it is such activity of a good
and noble kind, it must be true that the greatest good of
man is activity of soul in accordance with virtue." [1]

[1] Bk. I, Chap. VII, §§ 8–12.

The soul is rational and irrational, and the virtues are intellectual and moral.

Having come to this conclusion, Aristotle finds it necessary to analyze 'soul' and 'virtue.' The soul he separates into two parts, — the irrational and rational. The former of these is then divided into nutrition and growth, which are completely without reason, and the impulses and desires, which may or may not be controlled by reason. In so far as they do yield to reason, they are to be classed with the rational part of the soul. Similarly, virtues are to be distinguished as 'intellectual,' such as wisdom, intelligence, and prudence, which belong to the rational soul, and as 'moral,' such as liberality and temperance, where the desires are controlled by reason, and right action has arisen from habit.

Moral virtue is tested by the 'relative mean.'

The moral virtues are discussed before the intellectual, since the formation of moral habits is regarded as the first step toward the unimpeded activity of the reason, and so to the attainment of the higher or intellectual virtues. While man by nature does not possess these moral virtues, he may in early life be impressed by instruction and form moral habits through repeated acts of obedience. The rational principle that is to be applied by the trainer of the child in the formation of moral habits is found in Aristotle's 'relative mean.' According to this doctrine, an impulse becomes a virtue, if held to the mean and so compelled to avoid the extremes of excess and deficiency. For example, —

" He who flees and is afraid of everything, becomes a coward; while he who fears nothing at all, but goes boldly against everything, becomes rash. In like manner, he who indulges in the enjoyment of every pleasure and refrains from none is intemperate, but he who shuns all, as do the dull and boorish, becomes an insensate sort of person." [1]

In this same way he discusses at length all the other virtues. Intellectual virtue, then, which belongs to the rational soul proper, is the outgrowth of moral virtue, and the possession of it has in turn the function of determining the relative mean, the observance of which characterizes moral virtue. The highest of all virtues, therefore, is that of the speculative life, which is found in the philosopher. This virtue is declared in the last book to be that of the gods, for they cannot be supposed to demean themselves with any other activity than speculation. The philosopher, therefore, is nearest to the gods, who are preëminently happy, and is also most beloved by them on that account. [2] But moral virtue, which is secondary, can be attained by all persons, even those who are not capable of becoming philosophers.

Philosophic speculation is the highest of all virtues.

Aristotle thus makes virtue consist primarily in bringing the impulses into harmony with reason, and finds the idea not in a supersensuous world, but within

How Aristotle differed from Plato.

[1] Bk. II, Chap. II, §§ 5–6.   [2] Bk. X, Chap. VIII, §§ 8 and 19–20.

the experience of all.   In this way he welds the dualism that Plato created between sensation and reason.   So, too, The Ethics erases the division line between theory and practice that seems to exist in The Republic, although Plato maintains that the two should never be separated.[1] While with Aristotle, as with Socrates, the greatest good is virtue, with the former this does not consist merely in knowledge, but in a tendency to express one's self in rational action.   Even the highest intellectual virtue or speculation, although it seems to be clearly connected with the vision of the universal truth in Plato, is the result of activity, for philosophy is not held to make one virtuous, except as he puts it into practice.   Aristotle thus unites theory and practice by making clearer the distinction between the cognitive and the conative or volitional aspects of consciousness.

The Politics continues The Ethics.
Aristotle, however, saw that the moral excellence of the individual can be reached only in the life of the community.   "The state," said he in The Politics, "is a creation of nature, and man is by nature a political animal. . . . He who is unable to live in society, or who has no need because he is sufficient for himself, must

[1] See p. 193. Aristotle holds that real existence is not separate from the phenomenal world, but finds its realization in it. His doctrine of 'entelechy' (*entelecheia*) is this self-realization of the essence (*dynamis*) in the actual (*energeia*).

be something more or less than a man,—either a god
or a beast; he is no part of a state. A social instinct
is implanted in all men by nature."[1] So Aristotle's
Ethics should be regarded as introductory to, though
correlative with, his Politics.

In this second work he discusses first the origin
and meaning of a 'state' and a 'citizen.' He shows that
the state grew out of material needs, but is continued
for the sake of the life of reason. Nevertheless, he
defends slavery in the state on the ground that some
races are so inferior by nature as practically to be
born slaves; and holds that the industrial classes should
be excluded from citizenship, since they have no leisure
in which to practice virtue or perform political duties.
Here, also, before describing the perfect state, he
makes a critical analysis of Plato's Republic and Laws,[2]
and analyzes the organization of many other states,
both ideal and actual.[3] He concludes that, while a

Aristotle's model state is theoretically a monarchy; but, because of the possibility of deterioration, a democracy is to be preferred.

---

[1] Bk. I, Chap. II, §§ 9 and 14.

[2] His purpose in this analysis, however, is to show the foundation
for his ideal state in that of Plato.

[3] These analyses and comparisons of governments are found in
Book II. It was in keeping with the inductive method of Aristotle
that, before formulating any theory of the state, he wrote out the consti-
tutions of one hundred and fifty-eight states, that he might see whether
his hypotheses covered the facts. The manuscript of his *Constitution
of Athens* was accidentally discovered in some rolls of papyrus, and
acquired by the British Museum in 1890.

monarchy is theoretically the best type of government, yet, because of the probability of the king's deteriorating into a tyrant, the form most likely to be exercised for the good of the governed and least liable to be perverted is the democracy.[1]   Since, however, it is the expedient rather than the best government, it should be as little democratic as possible, and the power of the people should be minimized wherever it can be done without their perceiving it.[2]   Aristotle then [3] investigates the most fitting life for this model state. {He holds as a general proposition that the ideal state, like the ideal individual, is the one which leads a life of virtue, and thus attains happiness. Passing to details, he considers at length the best natural and social conditions for a state.

Education in the model state must not be purely practical. His final topic among these practical considerations is the proper education for the state, to the end that the citizens may be made virtuous.   But since virtue is of two kinds, moral or practical, and intellectual or speculative, and the former is merely the stepping-stone to the latter, the education needed for the virtue of the state must not, like that of Sparta, be purely a training for war and practical affairs.   It must be primarily intellectual, since war should exist only for the sake of peace, and business for the sake of leisure.

[1] See Bks. III and IV.   [2] Bk. VI.

[3] Bk. VII.

To mark off the periods of education, Aristotle again *Periods of education.* examines the nature of the soul. As in The Ethics, he divides it into the irrational and the rational, but to the former he here assigns only the impulses and desires. Nutrition and growth are now considered functions of the body. From this division it appears that " As the body is prior in order of generation to the soul, so the irrational is prior to the rational. The proof is that anger, will, and desire are implanted in children from their very birth; but reason and understanding are developed as they grow older. Wherefore the care of the body ought to precede that of the soul, and the train- ing of the impulsive side of the soul ought to come next; nevertheless, the care of it must be for the sake of the reason, and the care of the body for the sake of the soul." [1]

The development of the body Aristotle wishes to start *Bodily training.* even before birth, by having the legislator " consider how the frames of the children whom he is rearing may be as good as possible, and make marriage his first care, — at what age his citizens should marry and who are fit to marry." [2] Also he deems it necessary to sanc- tion the usage of his time of exposing all deformed or weakly children; and he goes so far as to recommend abortion for those who would prevent an excess of children. However, his advice [3] concerning the food,

[1] Bk. VII, Chap. XV, §§ 9–10.   [2] Bk. VII, Chap. XVI, § 1.
[3] Bk. VII, Chap. XVII, §§ 1–2.

clothing, and exercise of the children that are to be reared, is much more humane, and in many respects very sensible, even according to modern hygiene. He also holds that the child's games should not be vulgar, tiring, or riotous; and care should be taken that he hear no improper stories or language, and see no indecent pictures. For this reason, boys should come in contact with slaves as little as possible, and should not be allowed to attend satirics or comedy.

The training thus far traced is a preparation for the formal schooling, which is to last from seven to twenty-one, and is divided into two periods by puberty. Education should be public, Aristotle claims, as in Sparta, for it is the business of the state to see that its citizens are all rendered virtuous.[1] However, he has previously maintained that the industrial classes have no need of education, since they are not citizens,[2] and that women, since they are radically different from men, are to be limited in the scope of their training.[3]

Education of the irrational soul: gymnastics, The course of study that he follows is largely the same in content as that in use at Athens, although he recommends some reforms. He discusses gymnastics as a continuation of the bodily training, and the need of music and literary subjects for the irrational soul;

[1] Bk. VIII, Chap. I, §§ 3–4. Compare Bk. V, Chap. IX, §§ 11–12.
[2] Bk. III, Chap. IV, §§ 11–12, and elsewhere.
[3] Bk. I, Chap. XIV, § 15.

but with Aristotle even gymnastics is intended for self-control and beauty of form, and so also has to do with training the irrational soul. The making of neither athletes nor warriors should be the object, since excessive training exhausts the constitution, and martial education is brutalizing, as the history of the Spartans clearly shows. Not until three years after puberty, therefore, should hard exercise and forced dieting begin. During the intervening years the youths are to devote themselves to reading, writing, music, and drawing.

These literary subjects are not to be taught merely for utilitarian reasons. "Children should be instructed in reading and writing not only for their usefulness, but also because many other sorts of knowledge are acquired through them. With a like view they may be taught drawing, not to prevent their making mistakes in their own purchases, or in order that they may not be imposed upon in the buying or selling of articles, but rather because it makes them judges of the beauty of the human form." [1] *literary subjects,*

Music is discussed by Aristotle at considerable length. It may be used for relaxation or for intellectual enjoyment, but higher development is its special purpose. Music inspires us, he claims, with the most vivid imitations of real emotions. "Some melodies make men sad and grave, like the mixed Lydian; *and music.*

[1] Bk. VIII, Chap. III, §§ 11-12.

others enfeeble the mind, like the relaxed harmonies; others produce a moderate and settled temper, which appears to be the peculiar effect of the Dorian; the Phrygian inspires enthusiasm." [1] Since melodies that afford pleasure are connected with noble ideas, and those which give us pain are joined to debased ideas, the study of music "cultivates the habit of forming right judgments, and of taking delight in good dispositions and noble actions." Another moral effect of music, he declares later,[2] is that it produces *katharsis* ('purification'). He explains this term in another treatise,[3] which shows that his meaning here is that music, by arousing in us pity and fear for humanity at large, lifts us out of ourselves and affords a safe vent for our emotions.

He maintains that children should be taught to play and sing themselves, since "it is difficult, if not impossible, for those who do not perform to be good judges of the performances of others," but they should not seek the skill of a professional, for this would be unworthy of a gentleman. He also condemns as immoral the flute and several other instruments, "which are intended only to give pleasure to the hearer, and require extraordinary skill."

Education of the rational soul. Such was the training for the body and the impulsive or irrational side of the soul. How Aristotle would

[1] Bk. VIII, Chap. V, § 22. [2] Bk. VIII, Chap. VII, § 3. [3] *Poetics*, VI.

have advised that the education of the rational soul should be carried on, can only be surmised, for the treatise breaks off suddenly at this point, possibly through his unfulfilled intention to return to it at some later day.   But he elsewhere [1] declares that the citizens should exercise practical functions of two sorts : (1) active service, civil and military, which must be carried on by young and vigorous men; and (2) advisory duties, which would require the matured wisdom of elderly men; and that the very oldest of all, since they have had most experience with divine things, should become the priests of the state.   But he could hardly have been satisfied with merely a practical training.   It is not improbable, from his position in The Ethics and elsewhere, that the citizens, as a means of further efficiency after twenty-one, were to be given a higher training in mathematical sciences and dialectic not unlike that advocated by Plato.   And it is likely that, from his own predilections, he would also have added some physical and biological science to the earlier part of this course.

Criticism of The Ethics and The Politics. — Thus Aristotle, like Plato, endeavored to work out the harmonizing of individual with social interests by the creation of an ideal state.   The greatest good for man, he claimed, depends upon the realization of his peculiar function of rationality, but the state may be so shaped as to

Why The Politics failed to harmonize the individual and the state.

[1] Bk. VII, Chap. IX, §§ 4–9.

P

afford the most complete exercise of this faculty. The state is both means and end; it produces the proper type of individual through its training, and is itself shaped by the acts of these individuals. Hence throughout The Politics, as in The Republic and The Laws, a large importance is attached to the function of education in the state.

Nevertheless, the state of Aristotle, like that of Plato, failed to answer the demand of the times. While it was much less visionary and nearer the actual conditions than The Republic, and was not so hard and fast as to preclude absolutely the introduction of improvement and change, it could not recognize the significance of individualism. The day of the small isolated states of Greece, with their narrow prescriptions for patriotism and social order, had passed forever. While Aristotle seems to feel this vaguely in declaring that the ideal state is a great empire holding broad and diverse interests and having a large-minded monarch at its head, he failed to perceive how rapidly the era of exclusiveness was fading away, and so hoped to achieve some reform by departing but little from existing conditions and reading a sort of philosophy into them.

It is this partial bondage to his times and his lack of imagination that account for his defense of slavery and insistence upon the inferiority of barbarians, the disfranchisement and lack of education for the industrial classes, the subordination of women, and the exposure of children. For this reason, his educational system made practically no advance beyond that of Plato, and there were no forces within the state to put into effect the reforms that he did recommend.

Influence of Aristotle. — Consequently, the work of Aristotle was a failure for the time being. His treatises had little or no effect upon society, and the school of the Peripatetics, which he founded, did little toward developing his philosophy and science. They largely confined their efforts to collecting and interpreting the master's works, and completing them by a combination of the fragments. Early in the third century all his writings were carried to Asia Minor by the head of the school and hidden in a vault to avoid destruction. There they lay for nearly two centuries, when they were taken to the library at Alexandria,[1] and later were brought to Rome.

Little immediate effect of Aristotle.

The ideas of Aristotle, however, were not destined to be without results. While his immediate influence in general was little felt, and the direct effect of his teachings upon education in particular was small, his philosophic and scientific treatises have since been considered of great value, and the method that he formulated has been most important in the development of civilization, especially in the Middle Ages. Instead of trying to

Later influence through his method,

[1] See p. 220.

find truth in a mystic world beyond the senses through an appeal to the individual consciousness, as did Plato, Aristotle investigated the conditions of the objective world and sought to check on the hypotheses he formed by an appeal to the historic consciousness of the race. Thus he regularly sought confirmation of his theories in the statements of the philosophers, the masses, and other exponents of social inheritances. He believed that whatever is attained by the method of introspection, as was seen in the case of the dialectic of Socrates,[1] must be formal and lacking in content. Thus he came to set aside dialectic in favor of the inductive method.

his logic and other sciences,

As a result, through the use of this method, he not only started, or made the first important contributions to, a number of sciences, as was stated at the beginning of this account, but in his *Organon* he also formulated the laws of thought itself. While he accomplished much less in working out induction than deduction, practically nothing has been added to formal logic since his day. Logic was regarded by him not as a separate science, but as introductory to all sciences; and, for this reason, his philosophy and science were universal in nature, and he may be considered the father of the whole progressive search for truth.

and his terminology.

Also, as instruments to assist in fashioning the various sciences, Aristotle forged a complete system of ter-

[1] See p. 183.

minology, which has been of great value in philosophy
and natural science alike ever since his day.   Through
his efforts to systematize thought were created such
pairs as 'matter' and 'form,' and 'mean' and 'extreme,'
and such convenient expressions as 'end' in the sense
of purpose in view, 'final cause,' 'principle,' and
'maxim,' and the common psychological term of 'habit'
and the now outworn 'faculty.'

In definite historical movements also Aristotle's influence has been apparent.   His part in preparing the
way for Christianity through accustoming people to the
idea of an inspirational body outside society, and his
responsibility for the doctrine of 'formal discipline,'
have already been touched upon in summarizing Plato.
But a more important effect of Aristotle's ideas has been
that upon the formulation of doctrine in the Christian
Church.   After Greek learning had been banished from
Europe through the Emperor Justinian in 529 A.D.,
Aristotelianism took refuge in the East.   Eventually,
through the spread of Mohammedanism, which had
largely absorbed the doctrine of Aristotle, it became
generally popular in the twelfth and thirteenth centuries and threatened to overthrow Christianity.   Therefore, Aristotelianism was at first bitterly opposed by the
Church ; but, finding it impossible to suppress it, the
Church finally decided to adopt it and clothe her own
doctrine in it.   The greatest of the schoolmen, such as

*Influence upon histor-
ical move-
ments:
organization
of Christian-
ity; formal
discipline;*

*and Chris-
tian doctrine,
after the
spread of
Mohammed-
anism.*

Alexander of Hales, Albertus Magnus, and Thomas Aquinas, began to study it, and soon made it the effective weapon of the Church by reducing all human knowledge to a finished Aristotelian system with theology at the top. The doctrines of the Roman Catholic Church are consequently decked in an Aristotelian garb to-day. The introduction of Aristotelianism, however, also encouraged the use of reason, and so indirectly led to both the Renaissance and the Reformation.

Triumph of Individualism. — But the irenic attempt of Aristotle was fruitless. While his measures were more practical and scientific than those of Socrates and Plato, and far more progressive than the ideals of Pythagoras, Æschylus, and Xenophon, he likewise failed in the attempt to reconcile with the old and settled order the ever-expanding movement toward individualism. Thus all efforts to control the tendencies of the time were vain. Through the instrumentality of the sophists, the traditional religion and morals had been disrupted, and the masses were unable to grasp the rational moral teachings that were intended to take their place. Corruption in politics and social life, due to the prosperity of Athens, when combined with the denial of every norm of conduct, continued to undermine the foundation until, before long, it tottered and fell. The terrible misfortunes of the Peloponnesian War and the conquest of the Greek states by Philip of Macedon

Failure of Aristotle to reconcile the old with the new order.

were only symptomatic of the complete collapse of corporate life and the inability to reconstruct it successfully.

Later Greek Education. — With the downfall of the polity of Athens, what national pride had remained was lost. All possibility of social unity disappeared, and philosophy no longer considered the individual from the standpoint of membership in society. It was occupied no further with the harmonization of the individual and the state, but concerned itself with the welfare of the individual and the art of living. Individualism was completely triumphant, and education was considered simply as a means to personal development or happiness, without regard to one's fellows. The new theories of life and education were formulated by philosophers or schools of philosophy that kept themselves far removed from society. Where formerly the philosophers had sought a practical ideal for expression in life, the intellectual activity itself now became their ideal. Philosophy had begun as an effort toward securing better social expression, but now the mere pleasure of speculating was sufficient. So any means may tend to harden and become an end in itself.

Later Greek education shows individualism.

Philosophical Schools. — This tendency is noticeable even as early as the foundation of the schools at the Academy and Lyceum, two well-known gymnasia, where Plato and Aristotle respectively had taught.[1] The mem-

Individualistic tendencies in the philosophical schools.

[1] See footnote on page 165.

bers of the latter were commonly known as Peripatetics, from their founder's habit of carrying on his discussions while walking to and fro. But individualistic ideals are much more apparent in several post-Aristotelian schools, such as the Epicureans, Stoics, and Skeptics. The Epicureans considered individual pleasure the goal of life, and while their founder, Epicurus (341–270 B.C.), and his earlier followers, did not mean thereby the pursuit of sensual pleasure, it eventually came to this. With Stoicism, instituted by Zeno (340–265 B.C.), and given a more scientific trend by Chrysippus (280–209 B.C.), the end to be sought was freedom from desire and external wants, and so immunity from the disturbances and trivialities of the world. True satisfaction, the Stoics claimed, lay within the individual mind, and on the basis of this they developed the loftiest ethical code before the time of Christ. When their activities were transferred to Rome, they included most of the great moralists among their adherents. Skepticism, on the other hand, was a complete reaction from the long period of speculation, and represented an absolute distrust of all reason. Pyrrho (365–275 B.C.), the first skeptic, maintained that, since a final decision concerning external things is out of the question, one should take refuge in ignorance and indifference. This was more individualistic and anarchistic than even the doctrine of Protagoras.

None of these 'schools' could be so termed in the sense of offering an education, but rather in the modern usage of a group of adherents to certain teachings. They were merely sects, and did not, through their successive heads, make any serious attempt to construct doctrines beyond those of their founders. They spent their energy, for the most part, in interpreting, elaborating, and lauding the original teachings. The result was a stereotyped dogmatism and a descent from the heights of philosophy. And yet for several centuries these philosophic schools, especially the Stoic and Epicurean, held sway.

Lack of originality.

Rhetorical Schools. — But sects of this character were not the only outcome of the teaching of the sophists. These schools, as has been seen, came about gradually from the speculative tendencies of the sophists as developed through certain famous philosophers, but there also grew up more directly from their efforts to train young men in rhetoric and public speaking a multitude of rhetorical schools, in which a formal study was made of oratory and the knowledge of the day. Their professed object was to make successful men of the world, and they laid little claim to teaching anything solid or profound, much less to forming any philosophic habits. They succeeded in spreading a popular education among a people that had lost all hope of political life and had found their highest means of expression in polite society.

Origin of rhetorical schools.

Isocrates and
his school.

One of the earliest of these schools, and the most reputable and influential of all, was that of the florid Isocrates (436–338 B.C.). He had been a pupil of Socrates, but became distrustful of the value of abstract speculation as a means of making the thoughtful man and efficient citizen. Accordingly, he started to prepare young men for public life through a study of rhetoric and the prudential philosophy of the world. As he was a man of large political interests and general culture, the training he afforded was broad and rational, except for its attitude toward philosophy and science. He believed that eloquence is the product of the virtuous soul, and that a beautiful style is the handmaid of virtue in the individual and of justice in the state. Hence he held that the entire higher education should be linguistic and literary. In this way he helped the philosophers make Athens a great literary center.

Later schools
of rhetoric.

But the rhetorical schools soon degenerated into narrow and formal methods. The later rhetoricians attempted to hasten oratorical training and preparation for life by teaching their pupils ready-made speeches and dialogues together with isolated pieces of information. The students thus acquired a certain glibness and a superficial knowledge of questions of the day in addition to the mere technique of oratory. Nevertheless, these schools flourished for several centuries and closely rivalled those of the philosophers.

Universities. — From these two classes of schools, the philosophical and the rhetorical, the fame of Athens spread rapidly, and from the fourth century before Christ onward the numbers of young men from all over the civilized world who came there to study steadily increased.   In Athens itself the old ephebic training was gradually modified so as to allow the youths to attend courses of one or more philosophers or rhetoricians in the intervals between their active duties, and about the time of the Macedonian conquest the whole physical training was first narrowed to a single year and then made optional.   About the same time the intellectual education was made compulsory.   Thus from the union of physical and intellectual training sprang a regular institution or university, which the Athenian youths were compelled to attend, and to which students from outside might come.   As many of the latter had received but little preparation for the work, there arose a number of private teachers as dependent or subordinate officers of the university.

Before long, the Hellenic world boasted other universities, such as those at Rhodes, Pergamon, Alexandria, and Rome.   Nevertheless, Athens, until almost 300 A.D., remained the chief intellectual center of civilization.   It afforded the best opportunities for philosophical, scientific, literary, grammatical, and rhetorical work, and continued to attract students from all parts of the Roman

Empire.   But the tendency of higher education there was toward the study of rhetoric alone; and, while great teachers like Isocrates had been able to maintain the union between education and real life, even after style rather than knowledge had become the object, artificiality grew apace, and decay finally resulted.

Alexandria and her university.

In consequence, some time during the third century after Christ, Alexandria displaced Athens as the center of culture, and her university became the leading one of the world.   This university had grown out of the museum and library founded about 300 B.C. by the Ptolemies.   These institutions were maintained in pursuance of the policy of Alexander to make of his namesake a city of predominant influence in the Greek world. Here were collected the most remarkable sets of Greek, Egyptian, Babylonio-Assyrian, and Jewish manuscripts that had ever been known; and here the most distinguished scholars of the day lectured on philosophy, letters, and science.   About the library and museum gathered the various philosophic sects to study and discuss, and the doctrines promulgated were not limited to Greek thought, but included beliefs from Egypt and the Orient.

Its intellectual productions:

Hence it was naturally here that the higher abstract Greek philosophy united with the more concrete beliefs of the Orient, including especially Zoroastrianism, Judaism, and Christianity.   Thus there flourished at this center the various systems of religious philosophy known collectively as 'Hellenistic,' such as Neopytha- goreanism, Neomazdeism, Philonism, Gnosticism, and Neoplatonism.   Consequently, it was at Alexandria that the more liberal of the Christian fathers, Pantænus, Clement, and Origen, started their school.   But science was equally well represented with philosophy and theology.   Considerably before Alexandria had be- come preëminent in philosophy, there had been developed at the same center the Ptolemaic theory of the universe, which held until the days of Copernicus. Other noted investigations, like those of Euclid in geometry, some of those of Archimedes in physics, of Eratosthenes in astronomy and physical geography, and, much later, of Diophantus in algebra, also bear witness to the intellectual activity of this university. However, much formalism and fruitless commentaries also emanated from here, as they did from all the other academic centers in Hellenistic times.

Hellenistic philosophy,

and scientific investigation.

Extension of Hellenic Culture. — It can be seen, how- ever, from the very extensiveness of mental activity after the Macedonian conquest, that the downfall of Greek society and national life had only prepared the way for a larger intellectual influence.   As Alexander had extended his yoke over one Eastern country after another, he had carried with him all the culture of Greece, and within a century of his death the whole

Hellenizing of the Orient

Orient seems to have been saturated with Greek ideas. These are noticeable first in externals, such as the Greek palæstræ, gymnasia, theaters, stadia, and baths that appeared in every portion of the East. But soon the deeper culture, — the literature, philosophy, art, and learning, became common throughout the Orient; and Greek customs, institutions, and education were ingrained everywhere.

Continuation of Greek culture by the Romans. Similarly Rome, which had come somewhat into contact with Greece before conquering her, had been tinctured with Greek life and learning; and, after her absorption of Macedon and Hellas, she fell under the spiritual thrall of the subjugated people. After 146 B.C. the history of Greek civilization and education was speedily so amalgamated with the Roman that it can scarcely be distinguished from it, and Greek thought was by this means further spread throughout the world. The Greek philosophical and rhetorical schools were continued in Rome, Roman youths made up a great body of the attendance at the universities of Athens and Alexandria, and the Roman emperors did much for the support and extension of the work in these institutions of learning.

Its expanding ideals. **Survey of Greek Education.** — But before following the continuation of Greek education and culture among the Romans, it may be well to take a bird's-eye view of the development of this training in the land that gave it birth. The history of Greek education is a record of ever-expanding ideals. It portrays a gradual elevation of the individual from bondage to nature or convention to freedom of expression and complete realization of the self, although this resulted in an extreme reaction toward the satisfaction of the individual without regard to society, and the downfall of Greek independence.

Each stage in this educational development was accompanied by corresponding social and political conditions, and was characterized by definite ideals. In the prehistoric times the people were still somewhat bound by the blood-tie and the worship of gods representing natural forces. Their morality was that of the community; and the aim of education, while more elastic and advanced than that of primitive man, and, in some respects, of the barbarian peoples, was to fit the youth for the practical life of war and the council.

Even during the older historic period, when the city-state had been generally organized, and the ownership of land had become the social bond, education had service to the state as its only purpose. While in Sparta this ideal was based more upon principles than upon precepts like those of the Orient, and at Athens it was felt that the best personal development would be of most assistance to the social whole, in the one state, education included practically no literary, scientific, or artistic development, and in the other the intellectual portion of the curriculum was still rather formal and prescribed. These older historic times also resembled the Orient somewhat in having a pantheon of gods, and rising gradually to henotheistic conceptions.

During the 'new' period the development of Athens was made manifest by a greater recognition of personality, which enlarged the culture and prosperity of the state. The old traditional theogony was replaced first by ethical interpretations of the gods, then by investigations into the physical nature of the universe, and finally by attempts at metaphysical interpretations of matter and mind. The old sanctions were disrupted, and confusion resulted. Extreme individualism became the order of the day, and the aim of education was to secure happiness for the individual, with little regard to the welfare of the state. This destructive influence of individualism, the best minds of the times, both conservative and progressive, endeavored to stay, but without success. Even philosophic speculation soon became an end in itself rather than a means to social improvement. All efforts toward a return to the old, or a harmonization with the new, failed; and the gradual disintegration of the state that had been going on was soon made manifest at the onset of Philip. The citizen and the man had been hopelessly sundered, and the aim of the philosophical and rhetorical schools that existed after Aristotle was purely to secure the happiness of the individual apart from society. Yet it was the political downfall of Greece that enabled her to spread her ideal of individualism throughout civilization, and give a broader impulse to progress.

Corresponding to the enlarged ideals, the content of Greek education was constantly expanding, and far outstripped that of the Orient or Judæa. At first the curriculum consisted simply of the attainment of skill in practical pursuits; but gradually it came to include a wide range of gymnastic, literary, musical, scientific, and philosophical subjects without regard to their immediate utility, and, with Plato and Aristotle, on the strength of their very remoteness from concrete living. Thus philosophical speculation was to be engaged in for its own sake, and not as a means of improving society.

Advance in (1) content, (2) method, and (3) organization of education.

The method of teaching, too, which in the early days was merely imitation of a living example or of an heroic embodiment of the proper ideals, became more elaborate as time went on, and made clear the reason underlying each concrete act and habit. Although during the prehistoric period there was no formal means of training the youth, education soon organized into regular schools for the different stages, and culminated in the foundation of universities.

In this way it came about that the Greeks more than any other ancient people showed the world the advantages of individualism. From their history we may

Greek contributions to progress.

Q

learn that only by permitting variations in the social, as in the biological, world, can there be evolved and fixed new types that will answer to changed conditions, and so allow growth and progress without the intervention of conflict or cataclysm. Through the Greeks it has thus become evident that the individual should not only not be suppressed, consciously or unconsciously, but should be encouraged, if the social welfare is to be consulted and social progress to go on. From these people has developed the principle that the expression of the individual is essential to real stability and progress alike.

As specific illustrations of this principle, Greece has furnished us with examples of individualism that have been the source of much development since. On the intellectual side, she first recognized that the truth should be sought for its own sake, and that knowledge should no longer be connected merely with theology and largely limited to the priesthood. Hence arose the idea of a society not controlled by a sacerdotal class, and to this is due the real debt that civilization owes to Greek science and philosophy. On the emotional side, through the medium of the fine arts, — sculpture, music, painting, and poetry, the concrete expression by the individual of some general truth, ideal, or experience, also culminated with this people. From the Periclean age on there was permitted in these arts the highest degree of individualism known to the ancient world. Similarly, from this country also came the first encouragement of volitional expression, as can be seen in her ideas of moral freedom and responsibility, and the search for principles of conduct not based on any stereotyped system, but upon reason.   Naturally enough, all these forms of expression grew up in connection, on the institutional side, with the first instances of political individuality, as found in the self-governing states of Greece.

But this was the first extensive essay at individualism, and it can hardly be supposed that it was completely successful.   Inasmuch as the industrial class was allowed neither the franchise nor education, foreigners were despised as inferiors, and slavery was sanctioned, some nine-tenths of the male population of Athens must have been absolutely excluded from the rights of individualism.   While women were kindly treated, they were always regarded as subordinate to men, and only those of questionable reputation were ever outside the household.   Children had absolutely no rights of their own, but were held subservient to the interests of the state or their parents, and might be exposed when they were deformed or supernumerary.

Limitations of the times.

Moreover, the Greeks never obtained a complete conception of personality, as, with the exception of the later Stoics, they never approached the moral consciousness of the Jews.   Their ethics consisted mostly in a counterbalancing of the rights of individuals, and not the comparison of self with a superior self through a divine ideal. Consequently, the future life with them was, except for the great philosophers, a conception but little more developed than with the Orientals.

However, it is well that all worth living for was not worked out at once, and that social evolution did not close with the Greeks. It is sufficient that one people and age should have given to civilization so many lofty ideas concerning what a free man should be and what education best befits him. Whatever their achievements may have been, the Greeks should be credited with the greatest impulse to progress, for they started the belief in the necessity of individualism, and so furnished the first real dynamic conception of life.

SUPPLEMENTARY READING

I. SOURCES

ARISTOPHANES. *The Clouds* and *The Frogs*.

ARISTOTLE. *Ethics*, *Politics*, and *Poetics*.

HERODOTUS. Books VI and VII.

HOMER. *Iliad* and *Odyssey*.

ISOCRATES. *Against the Sophists* and *On the Exchange of Estates*.

PLATO. *Apology, Critias, Crito, Gorgias, Meno, Phædo, Phædrus, Protagoras*, and *Republic* and *Laws*.

PLUTARCH. *Lycurgus* and *Moralia* (especially *The Nurture of Children*).

THUCYDIDES. Books II, VI, and VII.

XENOPHON. *Hellenica, Cyropædia, Œconomicus*, and *Memorabilia*.

Also Monroe's *Source Book of the History of Education* (*Greek and Roman Period*).

II. Authorities

ADAMSON, J. E.   *The Theory of Education in Plato's Republic.*

BECKER, W. A.   *Charicles.*   Scene First and Excursus on Education.

BLÜMNER, H.   *Home Life of the Ancient Greeks.*   Chap. III.

BOSANQUET, B.   *The Education of the Young in Plato's Republic.*

BRYAN, W. L.   *Plato the Teacher.*   Pp. 181–409.

BURNET, J.   *Aristotle on Education.*

BUTCHER, S. H.   *Some Aspects of Greek Genius.*   Pp. 1–84.

CAPES, W. W.   *University Life in Ancient Athens.*

DAVIDSON, T.   *Education of the Greek People.*

FREEMAN, K. J.   *Schools of Hellas from 600 to 300 B.C.*

GROTE, G.   *History of Greece.*

KELLER, A. G.   *Homeric Society.*

LANE, F. H.   *Elementary Greek Education.*

LAURIE, S. S.   *Pre-Christian Education.*   The Hellenic Race.

MAHAFFY, J. P.   *Greek Life and Thought.*   Chap. XIII.

MAHAFFY, J. P.   *Old Greek Education.*

MAHAFFY, J. P.   *Social Life in Greece.*   Chaps. IX–XI.

MONROE, P.   *Text-book in the History of Education.*   Chap. III.

NETTLESHIP, R. L.   *Theory of Greek Education in Plato's Republic.*

SEYMOUR, T. D.   *Life in the Homeric Age.*

TUCKER, T. G.   *Life in Ancient Athens.*   Chap. IX.

WILKINS, A. S.   *National Education in Greece.*

ZELLER, E.   *Plato and the Old Academy.*

ZELLER, E.   *Socrates and the Socratic Schools.*

CHAPTER XIII

ROME AND THE ROMAN WORLD

THE name of Rome is still suggestive of power and organization. These characteristics seem to have been innate; but the significance of Roman development to the history of progress and education was largely due to the fact that, in her spread over the civilized world, the Eternal City amalgamated the Greek civilization with her own. Until then her ideals of life, while effective in conquest, had been narrow and little adapted to the development of individuality or a cosmopolitan civilization. Unconsciously realizing the need of broader ideals, she absorbed those of Greece. But Rome could not be Hellenized without making some contributions to the result from her own genius, and for that reason it is important to learn something of Roman civilization and education, crude as they were, before they came into contact with Greek culture.

The
Kingdom.

Survey of Roman History. — At the time of its alleged foundation, 753 B.C., Rome probably consisted of a federation of Latin clans on the Palatine and adjacent hills. It was governed by a war-chief or king, who was also judge and high priest in times of peace; a senate, composed of the heads of the three hundred clans; and a popular assembly, made up of all freemen capable of bearing arms. These came to be known as *patres* ('fathers') or patricians, in distinction to the *plebs* ('people') or plebeians, who had afterward settled in Rome, and were not represented in the assembly.

After about two hundred and fifty years the kings were expelled (509 B.C.) and most of their power transferred to two consuls elected for one year and to the aristocratic senate. As the plebs had no part in the government, almost immediately a struggle to secure recognition began, and continued with little intermission for two and a quarter centuries. Some reforms were gradually secured by the plebeians, the most important of which was the revision and codification of the laws in 451 and 450 B.C. by decemvirs elected for the purpose. The resulting code included the laws concerning property, political rights, and religion, that had been previously approved by the senate and assemblies. Until then the laws had been known and administered exclusively by the patricians, but they were at this time cut upon bronze tablets, set up in the market-place, and ever afterward known as the *Twelve Tables*.

Notwithstanding this extension of popular rights, the senate remained the real force, as the assembly was unwieldy, and the magistracies divided their powers and

The Republic and the struggle of the plebs.

The Twelve Tables.

were brief of tenure. This caused the senate to feel a responsibility for the preservation of the state, and produced a stability and continuity of policy that made possible large conquests, and eventually the Empire. Even during her internal struggles Rome gained the hegemony of the Latin tribes, and soon extended her sway over the rest of Italy. Then, in the second quarter of the third century B.C., she began to advance beyond the peninsula. In the three Punic wars (264–241, 218–202, and 149–146 B.C.), the Romans not only conquered, but exterminated their rival, Carthage; they humbled Macedon and divided her Hellenic kingdom (197 and 168 B.C.); conquered Asia Minor (190 B.C.) and Illyricum (167 B.C.); and reduced Greece to a province (146 B.C.).

Extension of Roman dominion.

Thus supremacy over the entire Mediterranean country was obtained, and great social changes began to appear in Rome. The religious faith and the old stern ideals of duty and training gradually broke up, and in their place ideas of religion and philosophy, harmony and culture, were introduced from Greece. A new set of patricians, who obtained their position by wealth rather than descent, sprang up. The power of the senate, and with it the old purity and patriotism, vanished; and the last century of the Republic was filled with struggles centering about great individuals, — the Gracchi, Marius and Sulla, Pompey and Cæsar, Antony and Octavius. The old representative constitution

Changes in society, and establishment of the Empire.

could not stand the strain, and gave way.   In 48 B.C.
Julius Cæsar was made perpetual dictator, and would
have become monarch, had not his ambition been evident and led to his assassination.   The opportunity was
thus left to his successor, Octavius ; but not until 27 B.C.
did the latter lay aside the exceptional powers that he
had assumed four years previously as *imperator* ('dictator'), and become emperor in real earnest with the title
of 'Augustus.'   Even then he preserved all the old
republican forms, but while magistrates continued to
be elected, their powers and those of the senate were
gradually assumed by the emperor.

While Rome was undergoing such a political and
moral transition, the Greek influence had started that
brilliant period of letters known as the *Age of Augustus*.   This development reached its height in the last
years of the Republic, while the old Roman ideals were
still somewhat in force.   Much literature, especially
history and oratory, was produced.   These were the
days of Cæsar, Sallust, Nepos, and Cicero.   Also poetry
was not lacking, as the philosophic verse of Lucretius,
the lyrics and elegies of Catullus, the epic and bucolics
of Vergil, and the odes, satires, and epistles of Horace,
bear witness.   Philosophy was likewise produced by
Cicero, a striking work on education by Quintilian,
and a whole encyclopædia of knowledge by Varro.
In fact, while the Romans could not equal their

Age of Augustus.

Greek models in quality, they far surpassed them in quantity.

Despite this intellectual flowering, Rome was declining, although for almost two centuries the decay is not at all apparent. On the contrary, during the reign of the Twelve Cæsars, her empire was greatly extended; while much peace and prosperity resulted from the rule of the Five Good Emperors, who succeeded them. Toward the end of the second century A.D., however, political conditions became most unstable, and the emperors put aside all pretense of observing the constitution. Although reforms were later introduced by Diocletian (284–305 A.D.) and Constantine (312–337 A.D.) which delayed the final downfall, from this time on corruption was widespread. The emperor had become a complete despot, except as far as a large and extravagant army dominated even the throne; a bureaucracy controlled the government; the court was sunk in all the luxury and vice of the Orient; and tax officials and governors cheated and ground down the provinces. Through bribery and favoritism, men were raised to senatorial rank. This class had now, of course, no political functions, although it was exempt from taxation and had many other privileges. It was self-indulgent, and blind to the sufferings of the less fortunate, and deaf to their needs. Roman citizenship, formerly sought so eagerly and so proudly claimed, now came to be regarded as a misfortune, and something to be avoided, if possible. Those who remained among the *curiales*, or ordinary class of citizens, had to support the government, municipal and imperial, and the army. To escape from these burdens, Romans that could not attain senatorial rank entered the army, the monasteries, or clerical positions in the Church, or enrolled themselves as serfs of some great estate.

Dissolution was not long delayed. In 395 A.D. the sons of Theodosius divided the Empire into two districts, nominally for the convenience of administration, but really because of radical differences in type of civilization. The Roman or Western division came gradually under the control of German tribes that invaded it, and finally, in 476 A.D., the German leader, *Odovaker*, or Odoacer, deposed the youthful Romulus Augustulus, and had the imperial purple sent to the emperor at Constantinople as a sign of the reunion of the empire. Odoacer himself, however, became king of Italy, and the real power of the Western empire was thereafter in the hands of the Germans. Italy was never fully recovered; and while the Eastern or Greek division of the empire continued until Constantinople was taken by the Turks in 1453 A.D., the days of ancient Rome and the Roman world had passed forever.

Odoacer becomes king of Italy.

Practical Aim of Education in Early Rome. — Obviously, a people with such an environment, traditions, and history as the Romans would have a very different set of ideals in life and education from the Greeks. In the early days they were animated almost entirely by an intense patriotism, reverence for law, and love for military life, and felt that each citizen was bound to merge his identity in that of the state. In the surrender of individuality they were, to be sure, not unlike the Spartans, although they believed that this subordination should be brought about voluntarily rather than by compulsion of law and state organization. But with such a love as theirs for mere material achievement, the Athenian ideal of a full and harmonious development of one's whole nature could scarcely be expected to make any appeal. They looked not for harmony, proportion, or grace, but for stern utility. All the æsthetic pleasures and the finer sides of life were held in contempt by them, and they regarded the Greek thinkers as mere visionaries. They showed none of the youth and impulsiveness that was characteristic of the Athenians, but were sedate, grave, stern, and serious. Their education was, accordingly, practical, prosaic, and utilitarian.

Voluntary subordination of the individual to the state.

Utility, rather than harmony or grace, appealed to the Roman.

Informal Acquisition of Abilities and Virtues. — Until the Greek institutions began to be adopted, there were practically no schools in Rome, and it was much later before anything approaching a public school system came into existence. At first, education consisted simply of a practical training in certain abilities and virtues that were bound up in the Roman ideals and every-day life. The chief means for obtaining this education was the home, which was the most important of old Roman institutions.

The home as the chief means of education.

In striking contrast to the Spartans and theorists like Plato, the family was regarded by the Romans as almost sacred, and the power of the father (*patria potestas*) often extended beyond the maturity of the son or the marriage of the daughter. While the wife was subordinate to her husband (*in manu eius*), her authority within the family was scarcely less than his, and she exerted a great influence upon her boys as well as upon her girls. The traditional picture of Cornelia, the mother of Tiberius and Gaius Gracchus, is a graphic illustration of this. In early life the boys and girls alike were given a physical and moral training by the mother, but, as the boy grew older, he went more in the company of his father, and learned efficiency in life informally through his example and that of other older men. In a similar way the girl was trained at home by her mother.

If the boy belonged to a patrician family, he might acquire much knowledge concerning Roman custom and law by seeing his father receive the *clientes* ('dependents ') each morning and give them advice **and aid.** He could likewise learn a great deal from the older men at the banquets to which he went with his father.[1] He might also receive an apprenticeship training from his parent or some other older man in the profession of soldier, advocate, or statesman. In case he was born in a less exalted station, he would accompany his father during his daily duties at the farm or the shop, and so learn the occupation of his parent.[2] The Roman girl, whatever her social status, stayed at home with her mother, and was trained in morals and the domestic arts, especially spinning and weaving wool for the family clothing.

Reading,
writing, and
literature
were also
learned
through the
family.

Through their parents the children probably learned also whatever reading and writing would be necessary for them in every-day life. They also committed to memory stories of prominent men of the past, ballads, and martial and religious songs.[1] After the codification of the *Twelve Tables*, the national laws had especially to be memorized by the young Romans. Physical training was secured mostly by games, which were largely in imitation of future occupations. Gymnastics were employed only as a training for war; the

[1] According to Cicero (*Tusculanae Disputationes*, I, 2, 3) and Varro (quoted by Nonius, p. 77), at the banquets, where the boys often accompanied their fathers, each guest was required to sing a song in praise of the old heroes.

[2] Industrial life was not, as in Greece, considered a disgrace, and did not deprive one of his citizenship.

Athenian ideal of athletics for the sake of grace and ease would have appeared absurd to the old Romans. The literature, music, and dancing of the Greek curriculum seemed similarly unpractical; and all humanities, learning, and art were scorned as subject-matter for education. Culture for its own sake was an ideal quite foreign to the Roman.

The usages of religion at home and in public did much toward furnishing a training for the youth. The faith of the Romans was of a very practical order, and consisted largely of requirements and observances. Almost every activity or portion of an activity in life, as plowing, sowing, reaping, gathering the harvest, vintage, or fruits, was presided over by some deity whom it was necessary to propitiate when engaging in it. So birth, marriage, and death had special divinities, who must be worshiped at the proper times. Even Jupiter, their chief deity, was regarded only as a generalization of Roman manhood, as was Juno of the womanhood of Rome, while Mars, their next greatest god, was a personification of war. This can hardly be considered a lofty religion; in fact, it was little beyond the ceremonies of primitive people, but it was associated with their morals and kept their consciences active. The ethical system, to be sure, was of an institutional sort, but it sanctified family ties, patriotism, and duty, and recognized the sacredness of oaths.

Training was likewise obtained through religious observances.

The first contact the Roman boy had with religion
was at home in the offerings to the *Lares* and *Penates*,
who typified the unity of the family. The Lares, or
spirits of departed ancestors, were considered the pro-
tectors of the family estate; while the Penates, or
deities of the household, guarded the provisions and
stores of the family. The shrine was at the hearth,
where was placed the image of the chief *Lar* ('lord')
between two Penates. Sacrifices were made to these
divinities each morning by the head of the family as
priest, and special exercises were held upon the occasion of birthdays, marriages, the assumption of the
toga virilis ('garb of manhood'), which marked arrival
at maturity, and upon the return of a member of the
family that had been long absent. Moreover, the *gens*
('clan') was regarded merely as a larger family, and
had a common altar and sacrifices; and the state was
similarly considered a union of clans with sacrifices
and ceremonies in common. The priestesses known
as the *Vestal Virgins* acted for the whole state.
They guarded the public hearth, which, with its fire
that was never allowed to die, was located in a temple
representing an *atrium*, or the main room of a Roman
house.

Religion in early Rome was, therefore, not an individual matter, but a means of holding together family and
state. Originally the king was the chief priest; and,

after the Republic was established, a *pontifex maximus* was appointed to represent the state. All priests were, in general, regarded as civil functionaries rather than as members of a sacerdotal class, and religious observances became a species of training in citizenship.

Thus education in early Rome was practical, and, to a great extent, occupational. It was calculated to produce efficiency as fathers, citizens, and soldiers. It consisted in training the youths to be healthy and strong in mind and body, and sedate and simple in their habits; to reverence the gods, their parents, the laws, and the institutions; and to be courageous in war, and familiar with the traditional agriculture, or the conduct of some business. Hence the virtues for which they struggled and which constituted the abstract material of their training, were *pietas*, which included the observance of filial duty and patriotism as well as worship of the gods ; *constantia*, or stability of character ; *gravitas*, signifying seriousness and dignity; the valorous quality of *fortitudo* or *virtus*, and the practical business virtue of *prudentia*.[1]

Abstract virtues at which Roman education aimed.

Imitative Method of Training. — The method of their education clearly was not through instruction, but informal training. Definite abilities and virtues were

Living example was followed.

---

[1] Clarke adds to this list of desirable virtues, *pudor* ('modesty'); while Monroe includes *honestas* ('fair dealing in all economic relations'). All these ideals are largely inferred from the laws on the *Twelve Tables*.

R

inculcated by means of imitation. "Long is the road through precepts; short and effective, through examples," is Seneca's epigrammatic way of approving the Roman method. While, however, it consisted in following a living example that was perfectly possible of attainment, and in this way gave more play to personality than the literal obedience to the sacred books of the Oriental training, it does not compare with the method of assimilation in the Athenian education, which came through the media of literature, music, and art, and permitted of so much latitude. Neither did the Roman method include any subsequent explanation of the acquisitions, as the Greek training did, and so lacked largely in rationality.

Their training was effective for a small state, but required the Hellenic ideals when the Romans had spread over Italy.

Effect of the Education of Early Rome. — This education of the early Romans produced a nation of warriors and loyal citizens, but it inevitably tended to make them calculating, selfish, overbearing, cruel, and rapacious. They never possessed either lofty ideals or enthusiasm. Their training was best adapted to a small state, and became unsatisfactory when they had spread over the entire peninsula. With their conquest of Italy, the golden age of valor and stern virtue largely departed, and they began unconsciously to seek a more universal culture. While such a people regarded the Greeks as visionary, just as the Greeks looked upon them as barbarians, they felt instinctively that only by absorption of the Hellenic ideals could their cosmopolitan ambitions be carried out. On the other hand, it was through the organization which the Romans were able to furnish, that the great ideals formulated by the Greeks were destined to be rendered effective and become a matter of value and concern to civilization ever since.

Absorption of Greek Culture. — The gradual infiltration of Greek culture into Rome must have begun very early. Even before the foundation of the city there were Hellenic colonies in Sicily and Magna Græcia, and in the middle of the fifth century the decemvirs are said to have gone to Greece for advice concerning their code of laws.[1] Not, however, until the spread of Hellenism through the conquests of Alexander in the latter half of the fourth century could the Romans have come into extensive contact with the Greeks. Even then, although commercial and diplomatic intercourse must have increased immensely, and the expanding power of Rome was necessitating a larger type of civilization, the Greek influence does not seem to have been very great. But after the humiliation of Carthage in the third century, and, still further, the downfall of Macedon in 168 B.C., Greek ideals must have made considerable headway. This is evidenced by the encouragement given to Crates of Mallos, a Stoic philosopher, who

The Romans began early to absorb the Greek culture,

[1] See p. 231.

came to Rome in 167 B.C. as an ambassador, and, being detained by an accident,[1] was persuaded to lecture to the Roman youth; and by the crowds that flocked to hear Carneades, the Academic, and Dionysius, the Stoic, a dozen years later. Suetonius tells us further of a number of other Greek teachers in Rome about this time. It is supposed, too, that Cato's treatise, *De Liberis Educandis* ('How Children should be Educated'), shows that the stern old censor felt that the Greek innovations were getting too influential, and thought it necessary to protest against them by emphasizing the old practical training for a farmer, warrior, orator, or advocate.

but not until the middle of the second century was the opposition to Hellenism really removed.

Finally, with the death of Cato in 148 B.C., and the conquest of Greece two years later, the last barrier to Hellenism may be considered to have been removed. Greeks came over to Rome in large numbers, and introduced more and more their philosophy, religion, art, science, and education. It became obvious that the Romans could not successfully rival or oppose the Greek culture; and, as no other seemed cosmopolitan enough to suit their purpose, they began rapidly to accept it. There followed a rapid adaptation of Greek ideals, both in intellectual and political life. By the beginning of the first century, if we may judge from Cicero's statement that the old training had completely disappeared during

[1] See Suetonius, *De Grammaticis*, II.

his early life, this transformation must have become complete. How thoroughly it was accomplished is well illustrated by comparing the old simple training advocated in the educational work of Cato with the treatise of Varro *On the School Sciences*, which seems to have included all the Greek studies, — grammar, rhetoric, dialectic, arithmetic, music, geometry, and astronomy, as well as medicine and architecture.

This new type of education may be said to have remained almost unmodified until toward the end of the second century A.D., when, as previously recounted,[1] the Roman Empire began most rapidly to deteriorate. Hence, during the last century before Christ and the first two centuries of the present era, a new type of Hellenized education had come to prevail in Rome, in marked contrast to that which was indigenous.

Schools of the Hellenized Roman Education. — The absorption of the Greek learning and culture was largely aided by the fact that Rome had no distinct educational institutions of her own, except possibly the rude elementary school called the *ludus*, and she was, therefore, the more readily influenced by those of the Greeks. A fairly complete and scientific account of all these schools of the time can be found in Quintilian's *De Institutione Oratoria* ('On the Principles of Oratory'). In spite of the title, this work is not limited to a description of pro-

Rome had practically no schools of her own, and readily adopted those of the Greeks.

[1] See pp. 234–235.

fessional training, but treats all stages of education. This treatise, with *De Grammaticis* ('On the Grammarians') and *De Rhetoricis* ('On the Rhetoricians') by Suetonius, Cicero's *De Oratore* ('Concerning the Orator'), and the vituperative *Dialogus de Oratoribus* ('Dialogue on the Orators') by Tacitus, furnishes most of our information concerning the Hellenized Roman education, as well as a description of the educational institutions of the period.

Elementary Schools. — Elementary schools may well have existed before the process of Hellenization even began, but this is doubtful. The assumption is largely based upon Livy's[1] account of the seizure of Virginia while on her way to school. Dionysius[2] similarly describes the occurrence, and the tradition may have had some foundation. If the *ludus* ('play' or 'exercise'[3]), as the elementary school was called, did exist as far back as this first century of the Republic, it must have been intended simply to supplement the more informal training of the home. From the name given it, the early Romans would seem to have considered it something of a diversion and not a necessary part of the regular education.

Whenever they did originate, these schools probably taught at first only reading, writing, and rudimentary

If Rome had elementary schools in early times, they were supplementary in purpose.

Old practical content gradually

[1] Bk. III, 44. [2] Bk. XI, 24.
[3] Compare '*ludus gladiatorius*,' '*ludus militaris*,' '*ludus fidicinus*,' etc.

calculation, as in the home, through the medium of historical anecdotes, ballads, religious songs, and the Twelve Tables. Hence they were sometimes known as the school of the *litterator* ('teacher of letters'). But, as the Greek influence crept in more and more, the literary content was somewhat extended. About the middle of the third century B.C., Livius Andronicus translated the *Odyssey* into Latin; and a number of epics, dramas, and epigrams were composed after Greek models about the same time, or a little later, by Nævius, Ennius, Pacuvius, Plautus, and Terence. The effect of this stimulation of Latin literature is seen in the gradual introduction of parts of these works into the curricula of the ludi, and the eventual displacement of the Twelve Tables about the beginning of the first century B.C. by the Latinized Odyssey of Andronicus.

became more literary.

In this elementary education the Roman boys were taught first the names and alphabetic order of their letters, without learning anything with regard to their significance or even shape. This method is sensibly criticised by Quintilian on the ground that it "hinders their recognition of the letters, as, while they follow their memory, they do not fix their attention on the forms of the letters. . . . It will be best for children, therefore, to be taught the appearances and names of the letters at once, as they are taught those of men." [1]

Methods of teaching reading, writing, and calculation.

[1] Bk. I, I, 25.

After learning their letters, the pupils seem to have committed all the possible combinations in the way of syllables, and were then taught reading and writing by means of exercises dictated by the master. This was because books were scarce and expensive [1] until toward the close of the second century B.C. After that time a large number of slaves were employed as copyists, and each boy was enabled to have his own book. When they had learned to read, special attention was given to clear and correct pronunciation, even to the extent of practicing the boys on difficult combinations of words,[2] and to intelligent expression.[3] Writing was usually taught by copying and tracing on wax-tablets with a stylus, while the hand was at first guided by the teacher.[4] Sometimes bits of parchment were also used for practice. The calculation taught was but rudimentary, as the Roman numerals were very cumbrous; and it was learned by counting on the fingers, or by means of pebbles, and, after the pupils had some facility, with an *abacus* on which pebbles or sand had been placed.[5] Eventually their sums were also worked upon wax-tablets. There seem to have been special teachers of arithmetic, who sometimes taught in schools of their own, although generally also in the regular ludi.

---

[1] Books would have been much more rare, had it not been for the speed with which skillful slaves were able to copy them.

[2] Quintilian, Bk. I, I, 37.

[3] Quintilian, Bk. I, VIII, I.

[4] Quintilian, Bk. I, I, 27.

[5] Persius, I, 131.

Thus the elementary education remained somewhat *memoriter* and imitative. The pupils generally repeated their letters and syllables aloud until they had committed them. As a reënforcement of interest under these circumstances, it is not surprising that discipline was severe. The rod (*ferula* or *virga*), the lash (*scutica* or *lorum*), and the more brutal whip (*flagellum*) are mentioned as if in frequent use in the Roman schoolroom; and throughout Latin literature schoolmasters have such suggestive adjectives connected with their names as *sævus* ('ferocious'), *iracundus* ('irascible'), *acerbus* ('harsh'), *clamosus* ('bawling'), and *plagosus* ('fond of blows'). So Juvenal declares that he, like others, has 'flinched from the rod'[1] at school; and a more telling method of punishment is shown in a fresco of Herculaneum, in which one boy appears on the back of another with his legs held by a third, while the master beats him on the bare back. While corporal punishment probably remained throughout Roman history the orthodox method of securing attention, in the time of Augustus a milder type of extraneous interest was introduced, when rewards in the shape of books, or even pastry, began to be offered. Theory, too, was in advance of practice, for Quintilian, the great educationalist of the times, says: "I by no means approve of corporal punishment, though it be

Memoriter character of the methods and severity of the discipline.

[1] "et nos ergo manum ferulæ subduximus," *Satires*, I, 15.

a received custom, and Chrysippus[1] makes no objection to it: first, because it is a disgrace, a punishment for slaves,[2] and an affront; secondly, because, if a boy's disposition be so abject as not to be amended by reproof, he will be hardened even to stripes; and lastly, because, if one who regularly exacts his tasks be with him, there will not be the least need of any such chastisement."[3]

Qualifications, remuneration, and social status of the teacher.

Under these conditions, elementary teaching could hardly be recognized as a profession, and the social standing of the teacher was low. No license or qualifications were required to teach in the elementary schools, and the remuneration was very small. The work was undertaken largely by slaves or freedmen.

The *pædagogus*.

The Greek custom of having the boy accompanied to and from school by a slave soon came to be imitated by the Romans. This functionary was sometimes called *pædagogus*, but often the Latin name of *pedisequus* ('attendant') or *custos* ('guardian') was used. The purpose, as in Athens, was to look after the manners and morals of the boys; but, while the slave was more carefully selected than in Greece, he was too often one that was incapacitated by age or physical disability. Usually Greek or Syro-Greek slaves filled

---

[1] The greatest formulator of Stoic doctrine.

[2] Compare Plutarch, *De Liberis Educandis*, XII.

[3] Quintilian, Bk. I, III, 14.

the rôle, and besides attending to the character of their charges, they often taught them a little conversational Greek. When their duties had been satisfactorily completed, these slaves were not infrequently manumitted.

These elementary schools had but poor material equipment. They were not held in regular schoolhouses or in buildings intended for educational purposes, but in a single room of a building put to other uses, or in a sort of booth or veranda (*pergula*), which was roofed in, but open at the sides. Good illustrations of the structures were found in the frescoes at Pompeii. The pupils sat on the floor, or, if the school were on the street, upon stones, and rested their tablets upon their knees. The schools were quite bare of adornment.

Material equipment of the schools was meager.

School began very early in the day. "What right have you to disturb me, abominable schoolmaster," cries Martial, "object abhorred by girls and boys alike? Before the crested cocks have broken silence, you begin to roar out your savage scoldings and blows." [1] The hours often lasted, too, until nightfall, with only a short intermission in the middle of the morning for a luncheon. There were, however, no home lessons, and the holidays for religious and public festivals, as well as every *nundinæ* ('ninth day'), or market day, were numerous. Probably also there was a consider-

School hours were long, but holidays were numerous.

[1] Martial, *Epig.*, Bk. IX, LXVIII.

able break in the hottest season,[1] and no attendance during the harvest and vintage.

Grammar Schools. — A higher training was given in the secondary or 'grammar'[2] schools. These were undoubtedly of Greek origin, and were taught by a *grammaticus* ('grammarian') or *litteratus* ('liberally educated'). "The appellation of *grammaticus*," Suetonius states, "was borrowed from the Greeks; but at first the Latins called such persons *litterati*." And then he continues: "Some distinguish between a *litteratus* and a *litterator*, as the Greeks do between a *grammaticus* and a *grammatistes*, applying the former term to men of real education, the latter to those whose pretensions to learning are moderate."[3] Evidently the grammar schools gave more of a literary training than the ludi, but it is difficult to say exactly where the work of the litterator ended and that of the litteratus began. For example, the *grammatodidascaleum*, which was opened by Spurius Carvilius[4] as early as 230 B.C., was probably not a real grammar school, although it may have gone somewhat beyond the ordinary elementary work.

Secondary education was more literary than that of the ludi.

---

[1] Martial, *Epig.*, Bk. X, LXII.

[2] The term is used here, as in England, or during the early days of the American colonies, of a secondary school; and must not be confused with the 'grammar' schools of the United States to-day, which constitute the higher elementary schools.   [3] *De Grammaticis*, IV.

[4] See Plutarch, *Quæstiones Romanæ*, 59.

Probably the grammar schools were differentiated gradually from the elementary. Grammatici, who taught their pupils to speak and write Greek, began to appear. At first the language was used merely for practical purposes, and no idea of the literature was given, but it was soon extended so as to include a study of the greatest works, especially Homer, as in Greece itself. During the second century Crates[1] of Mallos gave instruction, and some twenty other grammatici started schools at Rome. They embodied great improvements in method, and insisted upon wide learning as necessary for the understanding of the poets. Up to this time secondary education had not existed for the masses, and even the aristocratic had to secure it at home through Greek tutors.

Grammar schools taught Greek literature.

By the beginning of the first century Latin grammar schools began to arise, as the Latin language had become well fixed, and Rome possessed considerable literature of her own. The first was that of Lucius Ælius Præconinus, sometimes called *Stilo* ('the penman'), who is said to have had Cicero among his pupils. The young Roman attended both the Greek and the Latin grammar school. As regards the order of attendance, Quintilian says: "I prefer that a boy should begin with the Greek language, because he will acquire Latin, which is in general use, even though we tried to pre-

Latin grammar schools.

[1] See p. 244.

vent him; and because at the same time he ought first to be instructed in Greek learning, from which ours is derived. Yet I should not wish this rule to be so superstitiously observed that he should for a long time speak, or learn, only Greek, as is the custom with most people; for hence arise many faults of pronunciation, which is viciously adapted to foreign sounds, and also of language, in which, when Greek idioms have become inherent by constant usage, they keep their place most pertinaciously, even when we speak a different tongue. The study of Latin ought, therefore, to follow at no long interval, and soon after to keep pace with the Greek." [1]

The grammatical and literary courses in these schools.

While the head of each grammar school determined his own curriculum, and the state did not interfere in any way, the schools were quite uniform, since the teachers, when not Greeks themselves, had been trained by them, or had their course approved by them. The effort of these schools was to secure a mastery of the language and correctness of expression through familiarity with the best Greek and Latin authors. The curriculum consisted, according to Quintilian, of 'the art of speaking correctly,' and 'the interpretation of the poets'; [2] or, in other words, of a training in grammar and literature. Grammar, which, with the practical Romans, composed the larger part of the course, must

[1] Bk. I, I, 12–14. Compare Bk. I, IV, 1. [2] Bk. I, IV, 2.

have included all the philology that was known at the time, phonetic changes, and derivations, as well as drill on the parts of speech, inflections, syntax, and prosody, and practice in composition and paragraphing.

Literary training was obtained by writing para- phrases of the authors, both through abbreviation and expansion of the original; by textual and literary criticism; by commenting on the authors; and by exercises in diction and verse-writing. The commen- taries included not only interpretation of meaning, but explanations of the allusions to ancient mythology, re- ligion, history, and geography. Hence great learning was expected of the grammaticus, and Quintilian says: "It is not enough to have read the poets only. Every kind of writer must be studied, not only on account of the history contained in them, but also for the lan- guage; for words often derive their rights from the authorities that sanction them. Further, grammar can- not be complete without a knowledge of music, as we have to treat of meters and rhythms; nor if a man is ignorant of the stars can he understand the poets, who, to pass over other points, so often use the risings and settings of constellations as indications of time. Nor can the teacher of literature be ignorant of philosophy, not only because of many passages in almost all poems derived from a close and exact knowledge of the prob- lems of nature, but also because of the poems of Em-

Exercises in the literary training.

pedocles in Greek, and Varro and Lucretius in Latin, who have taught the doctrines of philosophy through verse." [1]

Authors read.

The authors that furnished the material for literary criticism were mostly poets. Cicero tells us: "We (Romans), who have all our learning from Greece, read and learn these works of theirs (*i.e.* the poets) from our childhood; and look on this as a liberal and learned education." [2] Homer was generally read for the inspiration of his theme and the loftiness of his style. Hesiod, with his prudential ethics and practical sense, naturally appealed to the Romans, while various dramatists, and epic and lyric writers, are advised by Quintilian. [3] Among the Latin poets Vergil stood first. Shortly after his death, his works were introduced into the curriculum, and soon took the place of the Homeric poems. During the Empire there was a reaction against the old poets, and Horace, Lucan, and Statius were given prominent places in the curriculum of the grammar schools.

Text-books on grammar.

Although there early appeared Latin treatises on grammar for schools, such as those of Præconinus and Lucilius, no text-books suited to pupils existed throughout the Republic. Consequently, some Greek text, especially that of Dionysius of Thrace, was adopted by

---

[1] Bk. I, IV, 4.   [2] *Tusc. Disp.*, Bk. II, XI, 27.

[3] Bk. I, VIII, 5-11.

the grammaticus. The first Latin grammar for schools must have appeared early in the first century of the Christian era. It was written by Palæmon, the teacher of Quintilian, who probably embodied the substance of it in his own treatise. After this many other texts were produced.

Toward the close of the Republic there was a tendency to keep the boys longer in the grammar schools and encroach upon the field of the higher training of the rhetorical schools by exercising them in declamation on ethical and descriptive topics. Quintilian[1] complains of this as bad pedagogy, since the pupils undertook oratory before they were ready, and neglected the more solid preparation of linguistic and literary drill for the sake of a precocious display. Their productions, however, were often fairly good, as a definite method of writing the declamations was laid down for them. It consisted of some seven steps, beginning with a praise of the writer or man of prominence who had furnished the theme, and closing with a hortatory peroration.

Encroachment of the grammar schools upon the rhetorical curriculum.

The grammar schools included other studies from the Greek learning, but gave them a practical bearing. As arithmetic had previously been studied to enable them to make business calculations, now geometry was learned for the sake of mensuration, and astronomy to enable them to form a calendar. A crude geography was also

Other studies in the secondary curriculum.

[1] Bk. I, I, 24–25.

S

sometimes studied for practical purposes. Likewise, music was taken up from the standpoint of rhythm and meter, to secure the proper intonation in oratory. It was not studied as an art or for playing an instrument, but for chanting the simple melodies of the Roman religion. For a long time there was no training in gymnastics, as this was believed to contribute to idleness and immorality,[1] and encroach upon one's time and strength;[2] and, until the time of Nero, no athletic festivals were held. Some exercises for the sake of health and strength were at length added to the curriculum, but they were adapted mostly to military training. Dancing was more violently opposed, and even Cicero implies that he who dances must be either crazy or drunk.[3] In spite of this criticism, it is probable that dancing appealed to the youth and was found useful as a means of exercise and improvement of the carriage. Thus, with the exception of the literary training, most of the subjects in secondary education were studied superficially and entirely from a utilitarian standpoint.

Method of study and discipline.

The attitude of the pupils in learning the literary subjects was quite passive. The passages were read first by the teacher and then by the pupils. The teacher probably marked the ictus in every foot of the verse by

---

[1] Cicero, *De Republica*, IV, 4. [2] Seneca, *Epistulae*, XV.

[3] "Nemo enim fere saltat sobrius, nisi forte insanit." See Cicero, *Pro Murena*, VI, 13.

snapping his fingers or stamping his foot.   After the
reading an interpretation was given, which the pupil was
obliged to take down *verbatim* in his note-book.   Explanations, often trivial and pedantic, of all incidents and
allusions were made by the teacher, and the text and
style were critically examined.   A commentary of Pris-
cian on the first dozen lines of Vergil's *Æneid*, which is
still extant, shows rather accurately in what this literary
training must have consisted.   With such a burden of
memorizing, it is not surprising that the brutal discipline
of the elementary schools was largely continued in the
secondary.

The accommodations for the grammar schools, however, were much superior to those of the elementary.
The schoolhouses were generally additions to larger
buildings, and opened on the street.   They were furnished with benches for the pupils and a higher seat for
the teacher, and were often adorned with paintings and
sculpture, especially portraits or busts of authors and
scenes from history or mythology.

Material equipment.

Rhetorical Schools. — About the time of the conquest
of Greece by Rome, a higher education through the
foundation of schools of rhetoric or oratory began to
grow up.   This completed the Hellenization of the
Roman training.   Suetonius says: "Rhetoric also, as
well as grammar, was not introduced amongst us till
a late period, and with still more difficulty, inasmuch

*Develop-
ment of
Greek and
Latin rhetor-
ical schools,
in spite of
opposition.*

as we find that, at times, the practice of it was even prohibited. In order to leave no doubt of this, I will subjoin an ancient decree of the senate as well as an edict of the censors." [1] Then he gives the senatorial decree of 161 B.C., which banished all Greek philosophers and rhetoricians, and the edict of Gnæus Domitius Ænobarbus and Lucius Licinius Crassus, issued in 92 B.C., disapproving of the schools of the Latin rhetoricians. Rhetoric would thus seem to have been imported during the second century to Roman soil from the Greek rhetorical schools, which had resulted [2] from the sophistic training. It "gradually manifested itself to be a useful and honorable study, and many persons devoted themselves to it both as a means of defense and of acquiring a reputation." [1] The first Roman to attain distinction from public speaking through the study of rhetoric was Porcina, who flourished during the latter half of the second century and was looked to as a model by the Gracchi. As also indicated in the passage from Suetonius, Latin rhetorical schools, such as those of Plotius and Blandus, appeared during the first century B.C. as a sort of continuation of the declamation in the grammar schools, but were shallow as compared with those of the Greeks. In spite of this and the disapproval of the censors, the movement survived, although rhetorical schools of either sort were not

[1] *De Rhetoricis*, I. [2] See 217–218.

at all common until the time of the Empire. Only the first families availed themselves of this education, and the schools were patronized mostly by those who intended to become orators and statesmen.

But while these schools afforded a legal and forensic training, and were decidedly professional as compared with the cultural work of the grammar schools, they were by no means narrow, if one may judge from the descriptions of Cicero and Quintilian.[1] These authors hold that the orator is not to be merely a pleader at the bar, but should take an interest in all public matters. Fluency, eloquence, and an acquaintance with law and history will not suffice for him; he must have these qualifications, but he must also possess wide learning, grace, and culture, a knowledge of human emotions, good judgment, a good memory, and, above all, virtue. He is simply a philosopher, who, through preference and special fitness, is engaged in practical affairs. So these schools of rhetoric, besides a knowledge of the technique of oratory, furnished a linguistic, literary, and scientific education of broad scope, and even a training in philosophy, especially Stoicism. They thus covered all the subjects later included under the Seven Liberal Arts, — grammar, rhetoric, and dialectic, and music, arithmetic, geometry, and astronomy, although, as would be

Cultural as well as professional content.

[1] See Cicero, *De Oratore*, Bk. I, V–VI, and XIV; Quintilian, Bk. II, XXI, and Bk. XII, I.

expected, these studies were all given something of a practical turn. Music, Quintilian shows, will help the orator with his gestures, collocation of words, and inflections of the voice ; geometry aids him to determine boundaries in lawsuits; and dialectic assists him in argument and the detection of fallacies; while astronomy enables him to understand the movement of the heavenly bodies, and not be misled by superstition.[1]

Method of training in oratory. From Cicero [2] we may gather something of the method employed in the technical training in rhetoric. It seems to have consisted first of exercises in declamation on ethical and political subjects. These themes were intended to bring out the fine distinctions of which Roman law and ethics were capable, and much ingenuity was shown in inventing instances where legal or moral principles would come in conflict. After this, more advanced work, accompanied by lectures, was engaged in. The students were given practice in three types of speeches : deliberative, which considered what ought to be done under given circumstances; judicial, in which the pupil assumed the rôle of an advocate for the plaintiff or defendant; and panegyric, in praise or censure of some one. Attention was given to all the various factors in making a successful oration : the matter;

[1] See Quintilian, Bk. I, X, 22, 37, and 46.
[2] *De Oratore*, Bk. I, XXXI–XXXIV.

arrangement into exordium, statement, argument, amplification, and rebuttal; the style; accuracy in memorizing; and dignified and graceful delivery.

The Roman youth that received a rhetorical education usually began when he laid aside his boyhood dress, the *toga prætexta*, to assume the garb of manhood, or *toga virilis*, that is, at about the age of sixteen. The length of time that he studied depended largely upon his ability and the school to which he went, but it seems to have been usually a matter of two or three years. Age for rhetorical training.

Education beyond the Rhetorical Schools. — Besides the training of the rhetorical school, many of the wealthy homes of Rome had a philosopher attached, with whom the youth of the family came in contact and learned much informally while still in school. Moreover, when the young man had completed his course at a rhetorical school, he might, if he were very ambitious, go to the university at Athens, Alexandria, or Rhodes. Soon other universities sprang up at Rome and elsewhere throughout the Empire. Alexandria had a second museum added to it by Claudius in 54 A.D. In 408 A.D. Theodosius II increased the number of professors and strengthened the university at Constantinople, which was known as the *Capitolium*. In Asia Minor a number of universities arose. The Greek influence caused most of these institutions to be located in the East, but Some of the wealthy families kept a philosopher to train their youth. University training.

the flourishing university at Massilia [1] was an exception to the rule.

Origin and work of the universities. Many of these Roman universities found their nucleus, somewhat as Alexandria did, in one of the many libraries that were started with books brought from the sacking of Greece and Asia Minor, and were added to after the Roman literature itself began to come to its zenith. The university of Rome was one of these. It sprang from a library founded by Vespasian in the Temple of Peace about 75 A.D., and half a century later, through the addition of professors and a splendid building, Hadrian organized it into the *Athenæum*. Here at first courses in liberal arts, especially grammar and rhetoric, were given; and, somewhat later, professional work in law, medicine, architecture, and mechanics was added. There was, however, no effort at philosophic speculation or scientific investigation.

Women were often given considerable training, although they had not equal privileges. **Education of Women.** — After the early days women were given a great deal of liberty and often had considerable culture. The girls probably attended the same elementary schools as the boys. Women were not, however, able to obtain equal opportunities with men, and generally had to secure any higher training through tutors at home, or possibly, after marriage, from their husbands. Nevertheless, the attitude of the times was very liberal. Musonius, who wrote in Greek upon edu-

---

[1] Now Marseilles.

cation, and fragments of whose work appear in the
Anthology of Stobæus, took special interest in the education of women, as the following quotation shows :—

Recommen-
dations of
Musonius.

" The philosopher (after referring to the analogy furnished by the identical training received by both the
males and females of two of the species of animals employed by men to render them active service, — horses
and dogs) asks whether men ought to receive any
special education and training superior to those allowed
to women, as if both alike should not acquire the same
virtues, or if it is possible for the two sexes to attain the
same virtues other than by the same education. . . . If
any one asks me what science is to preside over this instruction, I shall reply that, as without philosophy no man
can be rightly instructed, so neither can any woman."

Education Subsidized and Systematized.—Thus through
the gradual adoption of the institutions of the Greeks,
Roman education became thoroughly Hellenized. Although all the types of schools spread everywhere
throughout the empire, there was no real public school
system, except as the government gradually came to
subsidize the schools and so acquire control. This was
accomplished in various ways, — by contributing to
school support, paying the salaries of certain teachers
or granting them special privileges and distinctions, or
offering scholarships to a given number of pupils. Thus
Julius Cæsar, who intended to inaugurate a universal

Imperial
aid to the
schools
through
salaries,
scholarships
and privi-
leges.

empire, granted the franchise to all foreign teachers already in Rome, and offered it to any others who should
come; and Augustus, in banishing foreigners from
Rome, made an exception in favor of teachers. Vespasian (70–79 A.D.), however, established the first real
endowment of education by paying salaries of one hundred sestertia ($4000) from the imperial treasury to
each Greek rhetorician in Rome, Quintilian probably
being the first to receive the benefit.

Throughout the second century, this policy was continued, especially by Hadrian; extended by Antoninus
Pius to the provinces; and enlarged by Marcus Aurelius,
who, in addition, granted a public salary to two rhetoricians and two teachers of philosophy in each of the four
schools at Athens. Trajan also gave scholarships to five
thousand children. Besides paying salaries, Antoninus
Pius exempted from taxation, both imperial and municipal, and from army service and support of the soldiery
a given number of philosophers, rhetoricians, and grammarians in all cities, somewhat in accordance with their
size.

Even the later emperors paid great attention to the
extension of educational privileges. During the reign
of Alexander Severus (222–235 A.D.) many schools and
scholarships were founded. Constantine in three different decrees (321–333 A.D.) extended considerably the
privileges of teachers, and thereby laid the foundation

for the special rights afterward granted the clergy. Gratian (378–383 A.D.) went still further in subsidizing education, and offered to give a like amount with each municipality toward the salaries of the grammarians and rhetoricians in each of the seventeen capitals. His coadjutor and successor, Theodosius, gave the profession its final advancement by raising the most distinguished of the rhetoricians to the rank of count.

In this way the control of the schools came more and more into the hands of the imperial government. Julian the Apostate, shortly after becoming emperor (361 A.D.), demanded the right to pass upon all teachers; and it was at length promulgated by Theodosius and Valentinian in 425 A.D. that the emperor was the sole authority entitled to establish schools, and that a penalty would be exacted from any one else assuming this prerogative.

Control of the schools by the emperor.

Decay of Education. — Before this control had been established, however, Roman education had greatly deteriorated. With the political and moral decay of the empire previously [1] described, education declined correspondingly. It became a mere form and mark of the aristocracy. It was a necessary qualification for entering the senatorial class, which was now composed mostly of the favorites of the emperor or of merely wealthy men. Thus education had lost its real purpose. There was no longer any occasion for a training in oratory, as the emperor controlled all the func-

Anachronistic condition of education.

[1] See pp. 234–235.

tions of government and law; and, while the schools still existed and taught oratory, it was simply as a survival, and they were not intended to furnish a training of any value in life.

The careful grammatical and literary preparation recommended by Quintilian was more and more shirked. Philosophy and law were no longer taught, and most of the time was spent upon rhetoric, with a modicum of grammar. Vergil was almost the only author read, and his work was analyzed and dissected rather than appreciated. Rhetoric no longer dealt with real life, but aimed at an exhibition in the theater or before a private audience, and consisted of an abundant vocabulary, superficiality, and glibness. While the grammarians and rhetoricians were still held in high esteem, they contented themselves with mere display. Wandering lecturers, similar to the sophists, went from town to town, but more for the purpose of entertaining than teaching, and people rushed to hear them declaim, much as moderns flock to hear a popular preacher. Glittering phrases, epigrams, and other artificialities took the place of instruction and argument.

Predominance of the Christian schools. Gradually the Christian schools combined with the old Græco-Roman training, and eventually replaced it. After the fourth century, ecclesiastical education through the episcopal and monastic schools became predominant; and by the middle of the sixth century the monasteries were in full control of the situation, and the period we know as the Middle Ages was well under way.

Effect of Roman Education upon Civilization. — But the Roman education and civilization had left their impress upon the world. This was accomplished by the practical nature of the Roman, and the amalgamation of this characteristic with the ideals and culture of the Greeks. The Romans were originally trained in certain definite duties and virtues through an informal and imitative education in the home and the activities of life; but when they had become Hellenized and had absorbed the Greek educational institutions, they in turn modified the great ideals presented to the world by the Greeks, and through their practicality supplied the means of carrying out those ends.

Combination of Roman practicality with Greek ideals,

The Hellenic concepts of intellectual power and æsthetic enjoyment and the Jewish ideal of moral force were made concrete and furnished with institutions that enabled them to be useful to civilization and progress. Through them the Greek notion of a federated government was expanded into that of a universal empire, and the organization that made this possible was elaborated. This practical concept has been influential throughout the world's history, as can easily be seen from the idea of a reunited empire held by Charlemagne, Otto, and Napoleon, and reflected in the titles of the German and Russian monarchs to-day. Similarly,

and the effect upon progress.

the concept of law originating with the Greek philosophers became in the hands of the Romans a great system of principles that underlies and guides all our present civilization. Roman jurisprudence is the foundation of modern law everywhere. Finally, it was by means of the Roman genius for organization that a despised religious sect was institutionalized and expanded into the position of the greatest world religion. Through the administrative power of Rome, Christianity became the means of saving Europe from sinking into barbarism, and ever since it has been the schoolmaster of civilization.

So if it be true that Judaism furnished the world with its most exalted religious ideals, and from Hellenism came our most striking intellectual and æsthetic concepts, it is as worthy of note that the institutions for realizing these ideals originated with Rome. Despite the economic and moral decay and the political dissolution that followed closely upon the absorption of Hellenism and the growth of universal empire, Rome's ideals and social products still stand as monuments in the world's civilization.

SUPPLEMENTARY READING

I. Sources

Scattered references to education during the different periods appear throughout the Roman writers, but more extended descriptions are found in the following works : —

AURELIUS, MARCUS. *Meditationes.*

CICERO. *De Officiis, De Oratore, De Republica, Pro Archia,* and *Disputationes Tusculanæ.*

MARTIAL. *Epigrammaton,* IV, IX, X, and XII.

MUSONIUS. See *Anthologion* of Stobæus.

PLINY. *Epistulae.*

QUINTILIAN. *De Institutione Oratoria.*

SENECA. *Epistulae Morales.*

SUETONIUS. *Divus Augustus, De Grammaticis,* and *De Rhetoricis.*

TACITUS. *Agricola, Annales,* and especially *Dialogus de Oratoribus.*

The *Twelve Tables* afford an idea of the content of early education.

MONROE'S *Source Book of the History of Education (Greek and Roman Period)* should be consulted.

II. AUTHORITIES

BECKER, W. A. *Gallus.* Scene First and Excursus on Education.

CLARKE, G. *Education of Children at Rome.*

DAVIDSON, T. *Aristotle.* Bk. IV, Chap. II.

DAVIDSON, T. *Education of the Greek People.* Chap. IX.

DILL, S. *Roman Society from Nero to Marcus Aurelius.*

DILL, S. *Roman Society in the Last Century of the Western Empire.*

JULLIEN, E. *Les Professeurs de Littérature dans l'ancienne Rome.*

LAURIE, S. S. *Pre-Christian Education.* The Aryan Races (D).

MAHAFFY, J. P. *The Greek World under Roman Survey.*

MARQUARDT, J. *Das Privatleben der Römer.*

MOMMSEN, T. *The History of Rome.*

MONROE, P. *Text-book in the History of Education.* Chap. IV.

SANDYS, J. E. *A History of Classical Scholarship,* Vol. I (second edition).

THOMAS, E. *Roman Life under the Cæsars.* Chaps. IX–XI.

WILKINS, A. S. *Roman Education.*

With these
peoples
began a con-
sideration
for ideals
and the
future, and
so for indi-
vidualism,

Beginnings of Individualism among the Jews, Greeks, and Romans. — The three great peoples of antiquity, the Jews, Greeks, and Romans, through their civilization and educational practice, jointly made a large contribution to progress. With each are evident the beginnings of a consideration of the future rather than of the past, and an attempt to develop humanity in accordance with ideals rather than traditions. Among the Jews the world's loftiest conceptions of religion, and of moral personality and responsibility, had their beginning; out of Hellenism have developed the most advanced intellectual and æsthetic ideas that civilization has known; while the means of rendering all these ideals practical and of carrying them into effect sprang largely from the organizing power of the Romans. Through these peoples the value of the individual to progress became evident for the first time in history, and no longer was he held absolutely subservient to the social whole. From this time on society can no longer be described as entirely in bondage to nature or convention, or as practically tied to the present or the past.

The emphasis upon individuality and the future has begun.

Naturally these first essays were not completely successful. With the Athenians and the Romans, never more than one tenth of the entire population at best could obtain the advantages that paved the way to individuality in thought and conduct; and, while Judæa was quite democratic in theory, the proportion of those eligible among her people was not much larger, and the magnitude of her development was obscured by ceremonial and formalism. Each of these peoples, too, possessed its own narrow group of traditions, customs, and laws, its own language, and its own gods. While some prophets and philosophers[1] may have caught a vision of the brotherhood of man and the immanence of the divine, such an idea was regarded largely as a dream. With each of the three, all other peoples were considered inferior and beyond the pale. Slavery was widely sanctioned, and, although some possibility of manumission was believed in, it was held that always some people are by nature slaves. Not only were the masses and foreigners disregarded or enslaved; but women, while sometimes kindly treated, were generally regarded as man's subordinates, and among the Greeks

but it failed to become universal.

---

[1] Especially Socrates, in whose teachings, whether he was conscious of it or not, was implicit the conception of the brotherhood of man. See Davidson, *The Education of the Greek People*, p. 118.

T

and Romans it was held that children might be slain or exposed to die at the convenience of their parents or the state.

Larger Ideals of Christianity. — The world had need of a wider view and a larger bond of unity. Judæa, Greece, and Rome had to pause after establishing the beginnings of individualism and progress. But new ideals were destined to be found in the principles of Christ, which were first promulgated about this time in an obscure corner of the Roman Empire. These teachings had their roots in Jewish soil; they recognized the one living God spoken of by the prophets, the faith in humanity, and the joy of heart common to the Israelites; but they tended to strip away the ceremonialism and peculiar observances as unessential, and inculcated a broader interpretation of humanity. Without pretense at philosophic statement, Jesus suggested the fatherhood of God as the basis of human unity. As a corollary to this lofty conception, with its incumbent ideals of gratitude and love, he taught the brotherhood of all mankind. "These things I command you," said he, "that ye love one another." "Therefore, all things whatsoever ye would that men should do to you, do ye even so to them." This law was destined to obliterate the distinction between bond and free, rich and poor, and under it not only could no social classes consistently exist within a people, but national lines themselves

Christianity recognized the brotherhood of man, and gave to women and children their rights, and thus made individualism universal.

would eventually be considered artificial. Similarly, woman would have to be regarded as one half of mankind, and become the companion and equal of man. The sympathetic attitude of the Master toward women, and the respect that he felt should be shown them, appear at all times in his ministry. Again, to those moved by the spirit of Christ, it seemed no longer possible that children should be exposed, slain, or brutally treated, but that they should be considered as the especial gift of God. He expressly declared: "It were better for him that a millstone were hanged about his neck, and he cast into the sea, than that he should offend one of these little ones." Such is essential Christianity. While it was not altogether understood by the primitive Christians, and since their day has often been overlaid with trappings and subject to misconception, through it the road to universal individualism was opened, and full recognition given to personality and the right and need of every one to work out his own salvation.

Vicious Conditions That Christianity Needed to Reform. — The actual social conditions amid which the religion of Christ was born, and which it was destined to reform, were most degraded. As a result of the transition through which it was passing, the Roman world appears [1] to have been sunk in vice and corruption, espe-

The Roman virtues were civic, and failed with the rise of the Empire, when Rome became corrupt and immoral.

[1] See pp. 234–235.

cially at its capital. The virtues of the Romans had been civic for the most part, and consisted in patriotism, bravery, and service to the state, and even these ideals largely disappeared with the development of the Empire. There was not much incentive to patriotic service, where the whole power of government was vested in the emperor, and the state existed only as a means of collecting taxes; while the employment of mercenaries prevented the rise of valor and the willingness to sacrifice one's self for the country. The superabundance of slaves shut the citizens out from industrial pursuits, and enabled them to be supplied in their idleness with food and amusement. The people naturally fell more and more into vicious tastes and habits, especially as the example set them by the upper classes was most depraved. Divorce became frequent and common to all strata of society; children were destroyed by exposure and infanticide; public ceremonials of the most immoral sort, together with the most disgusting wantonness in private, were practiced under the guise of religion; while at regular intervals occurred the bloodiest of gladiatorial shows.

Other philosophies and religions were ineffective in checking this corruption,

To check this widespread depravity, the old state religion of the Romans, with its system of legal, institutional, and parental duties, could no longer prove effective. Nor could the Greek thought itself, even the highest, such as Aristotle's 'well-being' and 'well-doing,' accomplish much, since it was too intellectual and philo-

sophic to make the necessary emotional appeal. On
the other hand, the Eastern religions, which Rome had
admitted in her easy-going skepticism, were productive
of anything but good results. Most of them appealed
only to the worst instincts and passions; and while the
Persian and Egyptian doctrines, which had become more
rational through combination with Greek philosophy,
met with many converts, they were too gloomy and
bizarre for general acceptance. Judaism, however, especially in the Hellenized form given it by Philo,[1] cap-
tured a large number of proselytes; and, although it was
somewhat impaired as a religion by its philosophic
development, must have accomplished considerable good.
And the Romans themselves must instinctively have felt
the need of some regenerating force, as is shown by the
developments of Stoicism worked out by Seneca, Epictetus, and Marcus Aurelius, in which conscience and
duty were almost deified. While these concepts also
seemed too cold and dead, and could reach only a limited class of people, about the time of Christ they had
produced a marked effect; and, together with Judaism,
they enabled Christianity to enter the Roman world
upon a rising tide in morals, and to find a receptive
environment.

Nevertheless, none of these forces could have accom- but Chris-
plished a successful reform in Roman society, without tianity made
a more

[1] See footnote on p. 135.

the stimulus and wider appeal of the Christian teachings. Christianity was the ethical and universal religion needed as a leaven. Its truths were based on faith rather than understanding, and its appeal was to the instinctive promptings and emotions rather than to the intellect. It appealed to sympathy for one's fellow-man and the love of an ideal character, as well as to the desire to enter the kingdom, and the emotion of fear lest one miss this everlasting happiness. This made it democratic, and enabled it to reach the masses as the more philosophic system of ethics and the various national religions could not, for everybody can feel and have faith, even where he cannot understand. It could be grasped and applied to the conduct of all, and it found a large work ready for it.

The earliest
education for
Christians
consisted in
their ' other-
worldly '
manner of
living.

The Earliest Christian Education. — Thus it came about that, while the earliest Christians were without schools of their own and were largely illiterate, their religion itself served as an education. They were practically deprived of intellectual development, but they received moral training of a very high order. The very dishonor and unpopularity of the Christian religion, and the segregation of their church membership, gave *the Christian life* itself all the effect of a species of school.

The early Christians showed an extreme reaction to the vicious morals of the time, and endeavored to cultivate in their life the higher ideals that they believed to be inculcated by the teachings of Christ. They had gathered from the statements of the Master that he would soon return and the world would come to an end, and they concerned themselves almost entirely with a preparation for 'Jerusalem the golden' and the 'life everlasting.' They had little or no regard for the things of this world. Mundane pleasures and satisfactions were to be sacrificed for the good of their souls. Hence the ideal of this most primitive education through the Christian life may be described as 'otherworldly.'

The Catechumenal Schools. — When, however, the Church began to extend itself rapidly, it seemed necessary to insist upon some sort of instruction as preliminary to Church membership. It was also deemed wise to fix a period of probation after the profession of one's faith in Christ, in order that informers might not be admitted to the services, or the Church disgraced by apostasy or the lapses of those who had not well considered the step. These demands were met by the gradual institution of popular instruction in Christian principles for the Jewish and pagan proselytes, who were known as *catechumenoi* ('those caused to hear'). While some effort was made to lift the pupils of these *catechumenal schools* from the bondage of ignorance, the catechumen was primarily

The same ideal was maintained in the schools for catechumens, which were soon instituted,

trained in those things which were needed for his soul's salvation. Thus the ideal of Christian education remained prevailingly 'otherworldly.'

The course in the catechumenal schools was for only two years at first, according to Origen; but, as the children of believers also came to be trained in this way, it was extended to four. The catechumens themselves were grouped into four grades: (1) those who had just expressed their desire to enter the Church; (2) *audientes* ('hearers'), who were admitted to part of the worship, but had to withdraw after the reading of stated passages and the sermon or exhortation; (3) *genuflectentes* ('those bending the knee'), who joined in the prayers of the faithful; and (4) *electi*, who were ready for baptism and full communion upon the next occasion of admission. As time went on, there was a general tendency to remain in the body of catechumens indefinitely, in order that one might not be guilty of sinning after entrance upon Christian life, and to be baptized, and so purified from transgression, only shortly before death. Some of the most famous men of the Church were themselves guilty of this abuse, but it was finally stopped.

and which became the prototype of parochial schools.

The instruction of the catechumens was carried on in the portico or some special portion of each church; and consisted in moral and religious teachings, the reading, writing, and memorizing of the Scriptures, together with some training in early psalmody.   The meetings in the church were held several times a week, or even every day, and were supplemented by the strict religious and moral training of the home.   The teachers were known as *catechists*, and were generally the most able men in the Church.   This catechumenal instruction became the forerunner of the *parochial* ('parish') schools of to-day.

Amalgamation of Christianity with Græco-Roman Culture. — But while the Christian ideals and training were developing and crystallizing, the Greek philosophy in its Roman form was being continued and expanded.   This movement has been seen to be very different from early Christianity in its general purpose.   It concerned itself chiefly with life in this world.   The problem that it attempted to solve was how one should live so as to get the most satisfaction out of life.   It had culminated in philosophy and given birth to truths based upon reason. Because only a few could understand it, or possessed the leisure to seek 'well-being' consciously, the Græco-Roman movement, as previously noted, was as essentially aristocratic as the Christian was democratic ; and, since they were organized so as to prepare for the enjoyment of this life, the Hellenized Roman schools may be accounted as 'worldly' as the Christian were 'otherworldly' in their aim.

A general feeling of the marked difference in purpose and organization between Christianity and the contempo-

The Græco-Roman schools were, on the other hand, aristocratic and 'worldly.'

The Greek Fathers at first favored Greek philosophy,

raneous Græco-Roman culture was destined to cause an opposition to the pagan learning to spring up among the Christians, and to produce a conflict between ideals in the Christian schools themselves. For some time, however, this is scarcely noticeable, especially in the Eastern empire, where it was felt that philosophy was, like Christianity, a search after truth; and, as far as it went, confirmed the Bible. Justin Martyr, as late as the middle of the second century, declared that "the teachings of Plato are not alien to those of Christ, though not in all respects similar, for all writers (of antiquity) were able to have a dim vision of realities by means of the in-dwelling seed of the implanted word."

and there was a tendency for Christianity to unite with it.

There was even a tendency to unite the two movements. In the earliest days the Christians were closely bound together by a common enthusiasm, and had not found it necessary to organize the Church, or formulate an explicit system of doctrine. But as the new religion spread throughout the Roman world, and was compelled to defend itself against the charges of immorality, atheism, and treason, the educated converts attempted to set forth the Christian teachings in terms of Greek thought, and to solve speculative problems that had never been considered by Jesus and his disciples.

The Apologists.

Hence, the first Hellenizing Christians like Justin were naturally *Apologists*, since their efforts were directed toward reconciling Christianity with the Græco-Roman philosophy. In general, these philosophers mingled Stoicism with the teachings of Jesus. They utilized especially the Stoic doctrine of the *Logos* ('word'), taking it more directly from the combination with Judaism found in Philo. With Philo this Logos is represented as the reason within every man, which is also the reason of God, but the Christian philosophers emphasized more clearly than Philo the personal aspect of the Logos and the position of John that "the Word was made flesh and dwelt among us." Others besides the Apologists, who had previously been Hellenistic philosophers, and naturally continued after becoming Christians to think in those terms, carried the union to such an extent that it seemed for a time as if Christianity might become a mere intellectual system instead of a religion. The teachings of Pythagoras, Plato, Aristotle, and the Stoics were all more or less amalgamated with those of Christ. Perhaps the most extreme of these philosophic positions within Christianity was that Gnosticism. tendency known as *Gnosticism*. This movement was a combination of the Hellenized forms of Oriental religion with Christianity. It was intended to be a sort of esoteric 'knowledge,' [1] which should show the relation of Christianity to other religions and to the universe. In most cases it began with the Platonic doctrine of ideas,

[1] I.e. *gnōsis*.

and so made a metaphysical distinction between the material world, which was imperfect and evil, and the spirit or God, who was perfect.   As this spiritual God could not have created the world of matter from which he was by nature so removed, the Gnostics had to reject the idea that the transcendent Jehovah was the Creator, and, accordingly, to modify the Old Testament Scriptures.[1] Likewise, they selected the Gospel of Luke and the writings of Paul from among the contemporary Christian documents.

The Alexandrian Christians.   In this way, during the second and third centuries, all the Christians at Alexandria, which had become the great center of the various syncretic movements known collectively as Hellenistic philosophy, were influenced by their environment and tinctured with Greek thought. Clement (150–215) held that the Gospels were simply 'perfected Platonism,' and that philosophy was a 'pedagogue to lead the world to Christ;' while his pupil, Origen (185–253), carried his admiration for philosophy to such an extent as to maintain that the real spiritual Christianity could be apprehended only through the forms of Greek thought.   Ammonius Saccus (165–241) and his pupil, Plotinus (205–270), went even farther and reverted to Hellenism.   They are generally considered

[1] Hence, too, their formulation of a whole hierarchy of intervening powers, which had emanated from God in a series until one was sufficiently akin to matter to create the world.

the founders of the school of philosophy known as Neoplatonism.

The Catechetical, Episcopal, and Cathedral Schools. — As the Christians came to absorb the Greek philosophy and culture, higher training became a necessity. For more than a century and a half they were unable to obtain any real literary education, except by attending pagan schools, but, with a view to affording higher instruction for Christian teachers and leaders, a sort of theological, or 'catechetical' school, was gradually organized at Alexandria during the latter half of the second century. It had no building of its own, and the students met at the teacher's house, but they were able to take advantage of the facilities of the University of Alexandria. In addition to their theological training, the pupils were allowed to study all types of Greek philosophy, except the degrading Epicureanism, and also the classical Greek literature, grammar, rhetoric, dialectic, arithmetic, music, geometry, astronomy, and other higher subjects common to the pagan schools, but from a different point of view. Thus the Græco-Roman and the Christian movements had formed an alliance in education, and in this catechetical school we find a complete union and harmonization of the 'otherworldly' ideal with the 'worldly.'

The founder of this institution was probably Athenagoras, one of the Apologists; but it first became of

Catechetical schools were organized at Alexandria and elsewhere, where Christianity began to amalgamate with Greek philosophy,

importance under Pantænus, 179, who had been converted from Stoicism, and was a man of wide learning. He was succeeded by his pupil, Clement, and he in turn by Origen. These last two were among the most noted of the Eastern Fathers in the philosophic interpretation of Christianity, and their school at Alexandria contributed no little to heretical doctrine as well as to Christian theology. Origen was finally expelled for heresy, and opened a new school of the same sort at Cæsarea, where he was kindly received. Other *catechetical schools* then sprang up rapidly at Antioch, Edessa, Nisibis, and elsewhere throughout the East, where the Christians were more sympathetically disposed toward the Greek philosophy.

d later jecame known as episcopal or cathedral schools.

Before long the catechetical schools came to be used regularly by the bishops in training their clergy, and promotion in the Church began to depend upon having had this education. So these schools came to be an institution in every bishopric at the see city; and thus became known eventually as *episcopal* (' bishop's ') *schools*, or, in the West especially, from their location at the bishop's church, as *cathedral schools*. These names, however, are not generally attached to the catechetical schools until the general foundation of monastic schools in the sixth century.

Christianity gradually grew sus-

Opposition of Christianity to the Græco-Roman Culture. — However, by the century after the foundation of the catechetical school at Alexandria, the Christians picious of Greek culture, had begun to grow suspicious of Græco-Roman culture and the 'worldly' ideal in education. Even the Eastern Fathers appear to have cooled considerably in their attitude toward philosophy. Basil of Cæsarea wrote: "Are we then to give up literature? I do not say that, but I do say that we must not kill souls. . . . If you can unite both advantages, do so all means; but if not, choose the more precious." d Chrysostom of Antioch, in the fourth century, say f the Greek learning: "I have long ago laid aside follies, for one cannot spend all one's life in child's y."

The Western or Latin Fathers 1 to have been especially among the Western Fathers; bitterly opposed to pagan culture eve rlier. Roman Christians could not forget the immor an of those who had been connected with this culture, nor the abuse and insults that these pagans had heaped upon the Christians. They felt, too, that the one great mission of the Church was ethical, and that philosophy was somewhat impertinent. Moreover, the belief that the second coming of Christ was close at hand, and the consequent reaction against all the pleasures of the world, greatly strengthened their disposition to regard learning as of trivial importance.

"The simpler-minded," said Tertullian, somewhere toward the end of the second century, "not to say ignorant and unlearned men, who always form the majority of believers, are frightened at the Economy (*i.e.* the philosophic explanation of the Trinity)." And he elsewhere shows himself so much in sympathy with this view as to ask: "What resemblance is there between a philosopher and a Christian, — between a disciple of Greece and a disciple of heaven?" A century later, Jerome, the most scholarly of the Christian Fathers and the author of works on a variety of topics, narrates a dream in which his claim to being a Christian was rebuked by the Almighty on the ground that no one could be of the faithful and at the same time 'a Ciceronian.' Similarly, Augustine (354–430), who until nearly the middle of his life was a teacher and had written a great treatise on dialectic, later, as an ecclesiastical administrator, condemned the very works that had broadened his mind, and spent much of his energy fighting philosophic heresies. The principle of 'authority' contained in his *City of God* and his *Confessions*, together with his personal influence, was largely instrumental in bringing about the Council of Carthage (401), at which the clergy were forbidden to read all pagan literature; and so helped to make possible the edict of Justinian (529), by which all pagan schools were closed and the Middle Ages ushered in.

and all pagan literature was forbidden, and the pagan schools closed.

Influence of Greece and Rome upon Christianity. — Nevertheless, in spite of the growth of opposition *t*o

But, as a result of Greek in-

pagan culture and its eventual suppression, primitive
Christianity could not endure in its simplicity after it
had been in contact with the advanced intellectual concepts of the Greeks as modified by the organizing
genius of the Romans. Both Greece and Rome had
left a permanent impress upon Christianity; and,
though dead, they yet live in the Christian Church.
While the Græco-Roman culture had been rejected, its
influence is seen in the formulation of a system of Christian doctrine and the institutionalizing of the Church.
Christianity no longer rested solely upon upright conduct and religious fervor. An authoritative creed and
a canon of approved writings had begun to appear.

fluence, Christianity adopted formal creeds, and selected a canon of sacred writings.

During the second century, the nucleus of the *Apostles' Creed* developed. It was not at first supposed
that the apostles had a common confession, but in time
the belief naturally arose that this creed had come down
from them through unbroken tradition. By the earliest
part of the third century the Church had also selected
a canon of sacred writings, which overlapped that of
the Gnostics somewhat, but omitted some works and
added others. This *New Testament* was now recognized as on a par with the Jewish Scriptures, which
the orthodox Christians had never rejected, and, taken
together, they were considered to make up the *Bible*,
or 'book' of authority. While creed and canon were
not completely shaped for several centuries, both were

early regarded as final on the ground of being the product of revelation.   Henceforth, the assent to a body
of doctrine, rather than one's conduct, became the
test of Christian membership.   In this way, a century
before Augustine, the idea of 'authority' appeared;
and the Gnostics and other Hellenists were viewed
as heretical.   But the formulation of Christian doctrine
could not stop with the Apostles' Creed and the Bible.
There was much speculation with regard to the person
of Jesus.   The party of Arius held that Jesus was not
'consubstantial' with the Father, as was maintained in
the doctrine of Athanasius and his followers.   To settle
this controversy, a Church council was called together
at Nicæa in 325; and, as the result of the defeat
of the Arians, a new creed was formed, known as the
Nicene Creed, which was perfected during the following centuries.   In the Western Church the Apostles'
Creed was preferred, while in the East that of Nicæa
prevailed.

In other
ways, too, the
theology and
customs of
Christianity
were in-
fluenced
by Greek
thought and
practice.

The Greek influence upon Christianity, however, has
not been limited to the production of the Gnostic and
other heresies, or to the Gospel of John, the Nicene
Creed, and similar orthodox works.   It appears throughout the theology and customs of the Church.   Many
other doctrines, especially of the Platonists and Stoics;
the Greek tendency to attribute universal validity to
their inspired writings, and to interpret them allegori-

cally; and the pomp, ceremonies, and mysteries of the old Hellenic worship, are all more or less apparent in various ecclesiastical tenets and usages. Likewise, the early Christian practice of spontaneous utterance, with the belief that the mouth would be filled by the Holy Ghost, gave way during the fourth century to the Greek custom of careful preparation. The artificial structure, elaborate phraseology, and bid for applause in the preaching of Basil and Chrysostom remind us somewhat of the later rhetoricians of Hellenized Rome.[1]

But Christianity was not modified by Hellenic influence alone. The Roman concepts of law and administration specifically played an important part in reshaping Christianity. The institution of definite tests, like the creeds and the canon of Scriptures, had been possible only through the Church's becoming more and more organized on the plan of the Roman civil polity. At first there seem to have been no appointed officials in the Church; the apostles wandered from place to place, the prophets announced, and the teachers taught by no authority save the moving of the divine spirit. Gradually the various congregations came to see the need of having officers to administer the funds of the churches, and apparently followed the pattern of the *episcopi* ('overseers') of the pagan benevolent societies on the one hand, and of the *presbyteri* ('elders')

Christianity was influenced also by Roman organization.

[1] See pp. 218 and 268.

of the Jewish synagogue upon the other. As the enthusiasm and prophesying of the early days died out, and it became necessary to have regular teachers, it was only natural that the churches should turn to the overseers and elders to perform this function in addition to their stewardship. The names 'overseer' and 'elder' seem to have been used at first interchangeably, but before long the president of the board of elders alone was known as overseer or bishop, and became a sort of superior teacher. Before the end of the second century, bishops were believed to have succeeded the apostles in a direct line, and to have a supernatural apprehension of the truth. Then the bishops were thought of together as the heads of the Church, and met as a body from the neighboring cities of a given province to approve and defend doctrines. By the third century had begun that powerful organization of bishops, clergy, and laity known as the *Catholic* ('universal') Church; and any one selecting a belief outside of that authorized by the Church, such as Arianism, was considered a heretic and debarred from salvation.

This federation of the Church seems to have closely paralleled the Roman civil organization, the presbyters and bishops ordinarily corresponding to district and city magistrates respectively. Only a visible head of the entire Church, with a position similar to that of the emperor, was needed to make the comparison complete, and this was eventually accomplished in 445 through the recognition by Valentinian III of the supremacy of the Bishop of Rome, who by the sixth century came to be generally known as the *Pope* ('father'). From this time on the terms 'Catholic' and 'Roman' became practically synonymous.

Effect of Organized Christianity upon Society. — Thus to-day the genius of both Greece and Rome is given a new lease of life through its incorporation in the doctrine and government of the Christian Church. If one would find the continuation of Greek philosophy, he must look not to the schools of Alexandria, where it ran into a blind alley, but to the theology of Christianity; and if he would trace the organizing power of the Romans, he will find the best present illustration not in a mighty empire, which died before the sixth century, and which neither Charlemagne nor Napoleon could revive, but in the living Church of Catholic Christianity.

Greek and Roman thought have, therefore, found their continuance in Christianity.

Conversely, it must be admitted that for centuries Christianity has not been the pure unadulterated religion of Christ, and that many of the doctrines and forms of Church government are outgrowths of more ancient thought. Nevertheless, while this substitution of dogma for a free spirit of devotion, love, and service constituted a lowering of standards and a loss to true religion, it seems to have been absolutely necessary, if Christianity were to accomplish its mission. After the traditions of the personality of Jesus had somewhat faded, and the enthusiasm had been diluted by the accession of great hordes of converts, especially among the German barbarians, some system of organization and doctrine was necessary to bind the heterogeneous mass together. Christianity was preserved at a lower level, but it was preserved.

The Monastic Schools. — Thus it has been seen how the two great movements of Græco-Roman culture and Christianity arose independently, in time united, and later separated, although after separation each is discovered to have been influenced by the other. That is to say, as we view the education of premediæval Christianity, we find first that the catechumenal schools illustrate the nature of primitive Christianity, with its 'otherworldly' ideal. Then the union of Hellenism and Christianity, — the 'worldly' with the 'otherworldly,' appears in the catechetical schools. Finally, through the alienation of the Christians from the Greek learning, which culminated in 529 with the decree of Justinian and the downfall of the pagan schools, the Christian education seems to have been left alone in the field, but to have been somewhat affected by its long association with Græco-Roman culture.

It then found its chief means of expression in the *monastic schools;* and there was naturally in these institutions a tendency to revert to an ascetic or 'other-

The alienation of Christianity from the Græco-Roman culture resulted in the prominence of monastic schools and a reversion to the 'otherworldly' ideal.

worldly' ideal, and leave intellectual attainments largely out of consideration. The curriculum became fixed and somewhat barren. It consisted mostly in learning to read and write the Scriptures, sing psalms, work out enough mathematics and astronomy to calculate holy days, together with a mere taste of the old Græco-Roman culture through the medium of the Seven Liberal Arts.

These monastic institutions remained the most important influence in education until the Revival of Learning and a wider educational content appeared. But the discussion of monasticism and the monastic schools belongs rather to the Middle Ages than the period of Early Christianity.

Summary of Premediæval Progress. — It may be well at this point to summarize in briefest terms what progress was effected in education before the dawn of modern times. In general, it may be stated that during the day of primitive man no distinction at all was made between society and the individual, and practically all advancement was impossible, for no one looked beyond the present. With the appearance of the transitional period in the Oriental countries, the individual had begun to emerge, but was kept in constant subjection to the social whole, for man was quite enslaved to the past. As the Jewish, Athenian, and Roman civilizations developed, the beginnings of individualism were for the first time revealed, and some regard was had for the future.

Finally, in the teaching of Christ, there came a larger recognition of the principle of individualism and the brotherhood of man. Owing to the necessity for spreading these enlarged ideals among a barbarous horde of peoples, individualism for a time was forced back, and throughout the Middle Ages the leaven lay hidden in the lump. But in a variety of ways its influence increased during this seemingly dormant period, until, in the fourteenth, fifteenth, and sixteenth centuries, we catch the unmistakable signs of an awakening. Such a *Renaissance* ('new birth') was inevitable, for development cannot be permanently arrested, and only through a universal possibility of expression can progress be insured. In the spiritual, as in the biological world, variation is essential.

SUPPLEMENTARY READING

I. SOURCES

Christian Fathers: Athanasius, Athenagoras, Basil, Chrysostom, Clement of Alexandria, Clement of Rome, Cyprian, Eusebius, Gregory of Nazianzus, Gregory Thaumaturgus, Hegesippus, Hippolytus, Ignatius, Irenæus, Jerome, Justin Martyr, Lactantius, Marcion, Minucius Felix, Origen, Polycarp, Tatian, Tertullian, and Theophilus.

Hellenized Jew: Philo.

Neoplatonist: Plotinus.

Stoics : Marcus Aurelius, Epictetus, and Seneca.

The Apostles' Creed; *The New Testament*; *The Nicene Creed*; *The Teaching of the Apostles*; *Epistle of Barnabas*.

II. AUTHORITIES

ADDIS, W. E.   *Christianity and the Roman Empire.*

ALLEN, A. V. G.   *The Continuity of Christian Thought.*

CAIRD, E.   *Theology in the Greek Philosophers.*

DILL, S.   *Roman Society in the Last Century of the Western Empire.*   Bk. V especially.

DÖLLINGER, J. J. I.   *Jew and Gentile.*

FARRAR, F. W.   *Early Days of Christianity.*

HARRISON, JANE E.   *Prolegomena to the Study of Greek Religion.*

HATCH, E.   *The Influence of Greek Ideas and Usages upon the Christian Church.*

HAUSRATH, A.   *History of New Testament Times in the Apostolic Period.*

HODGSON, GERALDINE.   *Primitive Christian Education.*

KUENAN, A.   *Judaism and Christianity.*

MILMAN, C.   *History of Latin Christianity.*   Bk. III.

NEANDER, A.   *General History of the Christian Religion and Church.*

ORR, JAMES.   *Neglected Factors in the Study of the Early Progress of Christianity.*

SCHÜRER, E.   *History of the Jewish People in the Time of Jesus Christ.*

TAYLOR, H. O.   *Ancient Ideals.*

TAYLOR, H. O.   *Classical Heritage of the Middle Ages.*

TOY, C. H.   *Judaism and Christianity.*

WENLEY, R. M.   *The Preparation for Christianity.*

INDEX

Academy, the, 165 (footnote), 215.

Achaia, 146.

Acropolis, 144.

Æschylus, 144, 172, 178.

Ahriman, 94.

Aim of education. *See* Purpose.

Alcibiades, 144.

Alexander, 145.

Alexandria, university of, 219 f.; museum and library, 220, 263; Christians at, 284 f.; catechetical school at, 285 f.

Ammonius Saccus, 284 f.

Amon, 25, 36.

Ancestor worship, 11.

Andronicus, Livius, 247.

Angas, 85.

Animism, 9, 117.

Anthropomorphism, in Judæa, 119.

Apologists, 282 f., 285.

Apostles' Creed, 289.

Architecture, of Egypt, 29 f.; Babylonio-Assyria, 47 f.; Greeks, 143 f., 222.

Aristides, 144.

Aristophanes, 144, 172, 179.

Aristotle, educational theory, 198 ff., 276 f.; influence of, 211 ff.

Arius, 290.

Art, of Egypt, 31 f.; Babylonio-Assyria, 47 f.; China, 62; Greeks, 143 f.

Aryans, 77 f.

Assyria, 43 ff.; social conditions, etc. *See* Babylonia.

Aten, 25.

Athanasius, 290.

Athenagoras, 285.

Athens, history of, 142 ff.; education of, 157 ff.

Augustine, 288.

Augustus, Age of, 233 f.

Ba'al, 118, 120.

Babylonia, 43 f.; social conditions, 44 f.; religion and ethics, 45 f.; science, 46 f.; architecture and art, 47 f.; literature, 48 f.; education, 49 f.

Barbarism, 20 f.

Basil, 287, 291.

Beth ham-Midrash, 126.

Bhandarkar, Professor, quoted, 85.

Bible, 289 f.

Bishop of Rome, 293.

Bishops, 291 f.

Blandus, 260.

Blood tie, 9.

Book of the Dead, 26.

Brahmanism, 78 ff.

Brotherhood of man, 273, 274.

Buddhism, 60, 79 f.

Carvilius, Spurius, 252.

Castes, in India, 80 f.

Catechetical schools, 285 f.

Catechists, 281.

Catechumenal schools, 279 ff.

Cathedral schools, 286.

Catholic Church, 292, 293.

Cato, 244, 245.

Children, in China, 65; India, 80; Persia, 96; Judæa, 135; Sparta, 149 ff.; Athens, 157 ff.; *The Republic*, 186; *The Politics*, 205 ff.; Christianity, 275.

China, 55 f.; religion and ethics, 58 ff.; culture, 61 f.; education, 62 ff.; effect upon civilization, 73 ff.

Christianity, larger ideals of, 274 f.; its universal appeal, 278; amalgamation with Græco-Roman culture, 281 ff.; opposition to pagan learning, 286 ff.; influence of Greece upon, 288 ff.; influence of

299

Rome upon, 291 ff.; effect upon society, 293 f.

Christian schools, 278, 279 f., 285 f., 294 f.

Chrysippus, 216, 250 (footnote).

Chrysostom, 287, 291.

Cicero, 233, 246, 253, 256, 258, 261, 262.

Cimon, 144.

Citharistes, 161, 163, 165 (footnote).

Classes of society, in Egypt, 27 f.; Babylonio-Assyria, 44 f.; India, 80 f.; Persia, 96.

Clement, 284, 286.

Cleon, 144.

Confessions before Osiris, 26.

Confucius, 56 ff.

Conscious evolution, education as, 1 f.

Constitution of Athens, 203 (footnote).

Content of education, 6; in primitive society, 14 f.; Egypt, 35 ff.; Babylonio-Assyria, 49 f.; Phœnicia, 54; China, 69 ff.; India, 83 ff.; Persia, 98 ff.; transitional people, 106; Judæa, 123 ff.; prehistoric Greece, 146 f.; Sparta, 150 ff.; Athens, 157, 159 ff.; *The Republic*, 186 ff.; *The Politics*, 205 ff.; Rome in early days, 237 ff.; ludi, 246 f.; grammar schools, 252 ff.; rhetorical schools, 259 ff.; university, 264; Christian schools, 278 f., 279 ff., 285 f., 295.

Corporal punishment, in Egypt, 38 f.; China, 73; India, 88; among Jews, 132 f.; Spartans, 151, 153; Athenians, 165, 166; Romans, 249 f., 259.

Corruption, at Rome, 234 f., 245.

Council, at Carthage, 288; Nicæa, 290.

Crates of Mallos, 243, 253.

Curiales, 235.

Cyropædia, 99 (footnote), 179.

Dancing, 152, 155, 163, 258.

Decemvirs, 231, 243.

Degrees, in China, 66 ff.

Delos, Confederacy of, 143.

Dialectic, 181, 189.

Didascaleum, 161, 186.

Dionysius, of Thrace, 256 f.

Discipline, of schools. *See* Corporal punishment.

Double, conception of the, 9 f.

Education, purpose of, 5; matter, 6; method, 6; organization, 6; results, 7.

Egypt, 22; engineering, 23 f.; religion and ethics, 25 ff.; classes of society, 27 f.; position of women, 28; architecture, 29 f.; art, 31 f.; sciences, 33; literature, 34; education, 34 ff.

Eiren, 154.

Elementary schools, in China, 64 f.; India, 84; Judæa, 126 f.; Sparta, 150 f.; Athens, 158 ff.; *The Republic*, 185 f.; *The Politics*, 205 ff.; Rome, 246 ff.

Engineering, in Egypt, 23 f., 33.

Entelechy, 202 (footnote).

Ephebus, 167 f., 175.

Epicureans, the, 216.

Episcopal schools, 286.

Episcopi, 291 f.

Erechtheum, 144.

Ethics, in Egypt, 26 f., Babylonio-Assyria, 45 f.; Phœnicia, 53 f.; China, 58 f.; India, 78 f.; Persia, 93 f.

Ethics, The, 198 ff.

Euripides, 144, 172.

Examinations, in China, 65 ff.

Exposure of children, 149 f., 158, 191, 205, 211, 275.

Family, as means of education, among savages, 14 f.; Jews, 123; Greeks, 147, 150, 158, 186, 205 f.; early Romans, 237 ff.; Christians, 278.

Five Classics, 57.

Formal discipline, 189, 196, 213.

Four Books, 57 f.

Future, consideration for, 109, 272 f.

Future life, belief in, among Egyptians, 26; Babylonio-Assyrians, 46; Persians, 96.

Gemara, 116.
Gilgamesh, Epic of, 46, 48.
Gnosticism, 283 f., 289, 290.
Græco-Roman culture, absorption of, 281 ff.
Grammar schools, in Rome, 252 ff.
Grammaticus, 252.
Greece, history of, 139 ff.; education in, 146 ff.; influence of, upon Christianity, 288 ff. *See also* Athens and Sparta.
Greek culture, absorption of, 221 f., 281 ff., 288 ff.
Greek Fathers, 281 ff.
Gymnasia, 165, 175.
Gymnastæ, 165.

Hammurabi, 43, 49.
Han-lin, 66.
Hapi, 25.
Hebrews. *See* Jews.
Hellenistic philosophy, 221, 284 f.
Helotes, 141, 150.
Henotheism, in Egypt, 26; Babylonio-Assyria, 45 f.; Israel, 118, 122; Greece, 224.
Herodotus, 144.
Hesiod, 164, 256.
Hieroglyphs, Egyptian, 37 f.
Higher education, in China, 65 ff.; India, 84 ff.; Judæa, 125 f.; Sparta, 153 f.; Athens, 165 ff., 175 f.; *The Republic*, 189; *The Politics*, 208 f.; Rome, 259 ff.; early Christianity, 285 f.
Hinduism, 80.
History of education, value of, 2; how to study it, 2 ff.
Home, as means of education. *See* Family.
Homer, 140, 147, 152, 164, 253, 256.
Horace, 233, 256.
Horus, 25.

Ideal of education. *See* Purpose.
Ideals, how developed, 3 ff.; how realized, 5 f.; beginnings of consideration for, 272 f.
Ideographs, 37 f., 50, 61.

Imitation, as method of education, primitive peoples, 16; Egypt, 38; Babylonio-Assyria, 50; China, 72; India, 87; Persia, 100; transitional peoples, 107; Jews, 131; prehistoric Greece, 148; Athens, 164; Rome, 241 f., 248 f.
India, 77 f.; religion, 78 ff.; castes, 80 ff.; education, 83 ff.; effect upon character, 88 f.
Individualism, in primitive society, 15, 18; Egypt, 40; Babylonio-Assyria, 51; Phœnicia, 54; China, 75; India, 88 f.; Persia, 101; the transitional peoples, 105; prehistoric Greece, 148; Sparta, 155; Athens, 157, 159; of the sophists, 176 f.; Plato, 191 ff.; Aristotle, 209 f., 214 f.; the Greeks, 226 ff.; the beginnings of, 272 f.; in Christianity, 274 f.
Industrial class, in Egypt, 28; in Babylonio-Assyria, 44 f.
Initiatory ceremonies, 15.
Irony, of Socrates, 181 f.
Isis, 25.
Isocrates, 218.
Israel. *See* Jews.

Jahweh. *See* Jehovah.
Jehovah, 111, 113, 133.
Jerome, 288.
Jews, history of, 110 ff.; religion, 117 ff.; education, 122 ff.; effect on civilization, 133 ff.
Johnson, Samuel, quoted, 8.
Josue ben Gamala, 104.
Judæa. *See* Jews.
Justin, 282.
Justinian, edict of, 288, 294.

Ka, the, 26.
Karnak, 29.
Katharsis, 208.

Lares, 240.
Latin Fathers, 287 f.
Laws, The, 194.
Liberal studies, 196.
Literature, of Egypt, 34; Babylonio-

Assyria, 48 f.; China, 61; India, 85; Persia, 97 f.; Jews, 115 f.; Greeks, 143 f.; Romans, 233 f.
Litterator, 247, 252.
Litteratus, 252.
Locke, 196.
Logos, 283.
Lucilius, 256.
Lucretius, 233, 256.
Ludus, 245, 246 f.
Luxor, 29.
Lyceum, 165 (footnote), 215.
Lycurgus, 142, 152.

Maccabees, the, 116.
Macedonian conquest, 145.
Maieutic, 182.
Manu, Code of, 85.
Martin, Dr., quoted, 65.
Matter of education. *See* Content.
Mazdeism, 93 f.
Means of education. *See* Organization.
Melleiren, 153.
Memoriter method, 38, 50, 71, 87, 129 f., 164, 249.
Metempsychosis, 78.
Method, of Socrates, 181 f.
Method of education, 6; in primitive society, 16; Egypt, 37 f.; Babylonio-Assyria, 50; China, 71; India, 86; Persia, 100; Judæa, 129 ff.; prehistoric Greece, 148; Sparta, 150 ff.; Athens, 164; Rome, of early days, 241 f.; ludi, 247; grammar schools, 258 f.; rhetorical schools, 262 f.
Micah, quoted, 119.
Military class, in Egypt, 27 f.; Babylonio-Assyria, 44; India, 80; Persia, 91, 98.
Mishna, 116.
Mnemonics, among Jews, 130.
Monastic schools, 294 f.
Monitorial system, 87 f.
Monotheism, among Jews, 120.
Musonius, 264 f.
Mycenæ, 140.
Myron, 144.

Natural forces, savages' inability to control, 12.
Nature peoples, 12, 18.
Nazarites, the, 120 (footnote).
Neomazdeism, 221.
Neoplatonism, 196, 221, 285.
Neopythagoreanism, 221.
New Period, education at Athens, 170 ff.
New Testament, 289 f.
Nicene Creed, 290.
Nicias, 144.
Nile, effect on Egypt, 23 f.; as deity, 25.

Occupational content, 106.
Old Period, education at Athens, 157, 169 f.
Organization of education, 6; in primitive society, 14; Egypt, 35 f.; Babylonio-Assyria, 49 f.; Phœnicia, 54; China, 63 ff.; India, 83 f.; Persia, 98; among transitional peoples, 107; Jews, 125 ff.; prehistoric Greeks, 147; in Sparta, 150 ff.; Athens, 157 ff.; Rome of early days, 236 ff.; ludi, 246 f., 251; grammar schools, 252 f.; catechumenal schools, 280; catechetical schools, 285.
Organon, The, 212.
Origen, 284, 286.
Ormazd, 94.
Osiris, 25.
Ostracism, 143.

Pædagogus, 158, 250.
Pædonomus, 150.
Pædotribes, 160.
Palæmon, 257.
Palæstra, 159.
Panchatantra, 84.
Pancratium, 151, 166.
Pantænus, 286.
Parishads, 84.
Parochial schools, 281.
Parthenon, 144.
Patria potestas, 237.
Patricians, 231.

Pedisequus, 250.
Peloponnesian war, 144 f.
Penates, 240.
Pentathlum, 160.
Pericles, 143 f., 179.
Periœci, 141, 150.
Peripatetics, the, 211, 216.
Persia, 91 f.; government, 92 f.; religion and ethics, 93 ff.; education, 98 ff.
Persian wars, 143.
Phidias, 144.
Philip of Macedon, 145.
Philonism, 135 (footnote), 221, 276, 283.
Philosophical schools, 215 ff.
Philosophic class, in *The Republic*, 188 f.
Philosophy, inadequate to check vice, 276 f.
Phœnicia, achievements, 52 f.; character of people, 53 f.; education, 54; influence upon civilization, 54.
Phonetic alphabet, 53.
Physicians, in Egypt, 33, 37; Babylonio-Assyria, 47.
Plato, 184 ff., 215.
Plebeians, 231.
Plotinus, 284.
Plotius, 260.
Poetics, The, 198, 208 (footnote).
Politics, The, 198, 203 ff.
Polydemonism, 117.
Polygnotus, 144.
Practical education, of savages, 13.
Præconinus, 253, 256.
Presbyteri, 291 f.
Present, savages tied to the, 17.
Priestly class. *See* Sacerdotal.
Primitive education, purpose of, 12 ff.; organization and content, 14 ff.; method, 16; results, 17 f.
Primitive society, 9 ff.
Progress, premedieval, 295 f.
Prophets, schools of, 113, 119 ff., 124 f.
Protagoras, 174, 177.
Ptah-hotep, Aphorisms of, 27.
Puberty rites, 15 f.
Purpose of education, 5; in primitive society, 12 ff.; Egypt, 34 f.; Babylonio-Assyria, 49; Phœnicia, 54; China, 62 f.; India, 83; Persia, 98; among transitional peoples, 105 f.; Jews, 122 f.; prehistoric Greeks, 147; in Sparta, 149; Athens, 157; Socrates, 181; Plato, 190 f.; Aristotle, 198; Rome in early days, 236; ludi, 246; grammar schools, 254; rhetorical schools, 259 ff.; catechumenal schools, 279; catechetical schools, 285; monastic schools, 294 f.
Pyramids, in Egypt, 30 f.
Pyrrho, 216.
Pythagoras, 178 f., 194.

Quintilian, 233, 245 f., 247, 249, 253, 254, 255, 257, 261, 262, 266, 268.

Rê, 25.
Rechabites, the, 120 (footnote).
Relative mean, of Aristotle, 200 f.
Religion, in primitive society, 9 ff.; Egypt, 25 f.; Babylonio-Assyria, 45 f.; Phœnicia, 53 f.; China, 58 ff.; India, 78 ff.; Persia, 93 ff.; of Jews, 117 ff.; Greeks, 152, 162, 171; Romans, 240 f.; Christians, 274 f., 277 f.
Renaissance, 296.
Republic, The, 185 ff.
Restricted ideals, 105 f.
Results of education, 7; in primitive society, 16 ff.; Egypt, 39 ff.; Babylonio-Assyria, 50 f.; Phœnicia, 54; China, 73 ff.; India, 88 f.; Persia, 101 f.; among transitional peoples, 107 ff.; Jews, 133 ff.; in Sparta, 155 ff.; Athens, 169 ff.; Socrates, 183 f.; Plato, 194 ff.; Aristotle, 211 ff.; early days of Rome, 242 f.; later Rome, 269 f.
Rhetorical schools, 217 f., 259 ff.
Rhodes, university at, 219, 263.
Rome, history of, 230 ff.; education in early days, 236 ff.; religion, 239 ff.; influence of Greece upon, 243 ff.; ludi, 246 ff.; grammar

schools, 252 ff.; rhetorical schools, 259 ff.; university, 263 f.; effect of education upon civilization, 269 f.; influence of, upon Christianity, 291 ff.

Sacerdotal class, in Egypt, 27; Babylonio-Assyria, 44; India, 80; Persia, 94.
Sacerdotal organization, 107.
Satraps, 93.
Savages, chief characteristics. *See* Primitive society and Primitive education.
Schoolrooms, in Egypt, 36; Babylonio-Assyria, 50; China, 64; India, 84; Judæa, 125 ff.; Athens, 159 ff., 165; Rome, 251, 259.
Science, in Egypt, 33; Babylonio-Assyria, 46 f.; Phœnicia, 53; China, 62; India, 86; among the Jews, 126, 135; prehistoric Greeks, 147; in Athens, 174; Plato, 189; Aristotle, 198; Alexandria, 221; Rome, 245; rhetorical schools, 261 f.; university, 264.
Scribes, in Egypt, 36 f.; Babylonio-Assyria, 44; among Jews, 115 f., 121.
Seven Liberal Arts, 261, 295.
Simon ben Shetach, 127.
Skeptics, the, 216.
Smith, Dr. A. H., quoted, 71, 73.
Socrates, 180 ff.; method of, 181 f.
Sopherim, 116.
Sophistæ, 173 ff.; influence of, 175 f.
Sophocles, 144, 172.
Sophronistes, 166.
Sparta, 141 f., 144 f.; education, 149 ff.; effect upon civilization, 155 ff.
Static results, 107 f.
Stilo, 253.
Stoics, the, 216.
Subsidizing of education, at Rome, 265 ff.
Suetonius, 246, 259.
Synagogues, 125 f.

Tacitus, 246.
Talmud, 116.
Taoism, 60.
Teacher, in primitive society, 17; Egypt, 38, 41; Babylonio-Assyria, 50; China, 65, 71 ff.; India, 87 f.; among transitional peoples, 107; Jews, 123 f., 125 f., 127, 131 f.; in Persia, 150; Sparta, 160, 161, 165, 173 f.; Rome, 247, 252 f., 260, 263, 265 ff.
Tertullian, 287 f.
Theban supremacy, 145.
Themistocles, 144.
Theoretical education, of savages, 15 f.
Theseum, 144.
Thorah, 112, 115, 116, 129.
Thucydides, 144.
Totemism, 10, 117.
Traditions, evolution of, 3 f.
Trial and error, 16.
Twelve Tables, The, 231, 238, 247.

Universities, among the Greeks, 219 f.; the Romans, 263 f.

Varro, 233, 245, 256.
Veda, 85.
Vergil, 233, 256, 259, 268.
Vestal virgins, 240.
Vice, at Rome, 234, 275 ff.

Women, in primitive society, 15; Egypt, 28; Babylonio-Assyria, 45; China, 59; India, 82; Persia, 98; among transitional peoples, 106; the Jews, 129; in Sparta, 154 f.; Athens, 168 f.; *The Republic*, 190; *The Politics*, 206; Rome, 264 f.; Christianity, 275.

Xenophon, 99 (footnote), 144, 179.

Zarathushtra, 94.
Zend-Avesta, 97.
Zeno, 216.
Ziggurat, 47.
Zoroaster. *See* Zarathushtra.

A LIST OF BOOKS FOR TEACHERS

Published by The Macmillan Company

ADAMS, John. Exposition and Illustration in Teaching.
Cloth. viii + 428 pages. $1.25 net.

ARMSTRONG, Henry E. The Teaching of Scientific Method and Other Papers on Education.
Cloth. xxvii + 504 pages. $1.75 net.

ARNOLD, Felix. A Text-book of School and Class Management. I. Theory and Practice.
Cloth. 12mo. xxii + 409 pages. Index. $1.25 net.

II. Administration and Hygiene.
Cloth. xii + 292 pages. $1 00 net

—— **Attention and Interest.**
Cloth. viii + 272 pages. $1.00 net.

BAGLEY, William Chandler. Classroom Management : Its Principles and Technique. By William Chandler Bagley, Director, School of Education, University of Illinois.
Cloth. 12mo. xvii + 352 pages. $1.25 net.

—— **The Educative Process.**
Cloth. 12mo. xix + 358 pages. $1.25 net.

BROWN, John Franklin. The American High School. By John Franklin Brown, Ph.D., formerly Professor in Education and Inspector of High Schools for the State University of Iowa.
Cloth. xii + 498 pages. 12mo. $1.25 net.

BUTLER, Nicholas Murray. The Meaning of Education, and Other Essays and Addresses. By Nicholas Murray Butler, President of Columbia University.
Cloth. 12mo. xii + 230 pages. $1.00 net.

CHUBB, Percival. The Teaching of English. By Percival Chubb, Principal of High School Department, Ethical Culture School, New York.
Cloth. 12mo. xvii + 411 pages. $1.00 net.

COLLAR, George, AND CROOK, Charles W. School Management and Methods of Instruction. By George Collar and Charles W. Crook, London.
Cloth. 12mo. viii + 336 pages. $1.00 net.

CRONSON, Bernard. Methods in Elementary School Studies. By Bernard Cronson, A.B., Ph.D., Principal of Public School No. 3, Borough of Manhattan, City of New York.
Cloth. 12mo. 167 pages. $1.25 net.

—— **Pupil Self-Government.**
Cloth. 12mo. ix + 107 pages. $.90 net.

CUBBERLEY. Syllabus of Lectures on the History of Education. With Selected Bibliographies and Suggested Readings. By Ellwood P. Cubberley. Second Edition, revised and enlarged. In two parts.
Part I, v + 129 pages, $1.50 net; Part II, xv + 361 pages, $1.50 net.
Complete in one volume, $2.60 net.

DE GARMO, Charles. Interest and Education. By Charles De Garmo, Professor of the Science and Art of Education in Cornell University.
Cloth. 12mo. xvii + 230 pages. $1.00 net.

—— **The Principles of Secondary Education.**
Vol. I, Studies. Cloth. 12mo. xii + 299 pages. $1.25 net.
Vol. II, Processes of Instruction. xii + 200 pages. $1.00 net.
Vol. III, Ethical Training. x + 220 pages. $1.00 net.

DEXTER, Edwin Grant. A History of Education in the United States. By Edwin Grant Dexter, Professor of Education in the University of Illinois.
Cloth. xxi + 665 pages. 8vo. $2.00 net.

DUTTON, SAMUEL T. **Social Phases of Education in the School and the Home.** By Samuel T. Dutton, Superintendent of the Horace Mann Schools, New York.
Cloth. 12mo. ix + 259 pages. $1.25 net.

DUTTON & SNEDDEN. **The Administration of Public Education in the United States.** By Samuel Train Dutton, A.M., and David Snedden, Ph.D. With an Introduction by Nicholas Murray Butler, Ph.D., LL.D.
Cloth. viii + 595 pages. Bibliography. Index. 12mo. $1.75 net.

FITCH, SIR JOSHUA. **Educational Aims and Methods.** Lectures and Addresses by Sir Joshua Fitch, late Her Majesty's Inspector of Training Colleges.
Cloth. xii + 448 pages. 12mo. $1.25 net.

—— **Lectures on Teaching.** *Cloth. xiii + 393 pages. 16mo. $1.00 net.*

FOGHT, HAROLD W. **The American Rural School.** By H. W. Foght, Professor of Education, Midland College. *Cloth. xxii + 366 pages. $1.25 net.*

GANONG, WILLIAM F. **The Teaching Botanist.** By William F. Ganong, Ph.D., Smith College. *Cloth. 12mo. Rewritten ed. xii + 444 pages. $1.25 net.*

GILMAN, MARY L. **Seat Work and Industrial Occupations.** A Practical Course for Primary Grades. By Mary L. Gilman, Principal of the Clay School, Minneapolis, Minn., and Elizabeth L. Williams, Principal of the Holmes School, Minneapolis, Minn. *Fully illustrated. Cloth. 141 pages. Square 12mo. $.50 net.*

GRAVES, FRANK P. **A History of Education before the Middle Ages.** By Frank Pierrepont Graves, Ohio State University.
Cloth. 320 pages. Bibliography. $1.10 net.

—— **A History of Education during the Middle Ages.** *Cloth, 376 pages, $1.10 net.*

HALLECK, REUBEN POST. **The Education of the Central Nervous System.** A Study of Foundations, especially of Sensory and Motor Training.
Cloth. 12mo. xii + 258 pages. $1.00 net.

HANUS, PAUL H. **A Modern School.** By Paul H. Hanus, Professor of the History and Art of Teaching in Harvard University.
Cloth. 12mo. x + 306 pages. $1.25 net.

—— **Educational Aims and Educational Values.** By Paul H. Hanus.
Cloth. 12mo. vii + 221 pages. $1.00 net.

HENDERSON, ERNEST N. **The Principles of Education.** By Ernest Norton Henderson, Professor of Education and Philosophy in Adelphi College, Brooklyn.
Cloth. 8vo. xiv + 570 pages. $1.75 net.

HERBART, JOHN FREDERICK. **Outlines of Educational Doctrine.** By John Frederick Herbart. Translated by Alex. F. Lange, Associate Professor of English and Scandinavian Philology and Dean of the Faculty of the College of Letters, University of California. Annoted by Charles De Garmo, Professor of the Science and Art of Education, Cornell University. *Cloth. Large 12mo. xi + 334 pages. $1.25 net.*

HERRICK, CHEESMAN A. **The Meaning and Practice of Commercial Education.** By Cheesman A. Herrick, Ph.D., Director of School of Commerce, Philadelphia Central High School. *Cloth. xv + 378 pages. 12mo. $1.25 net.*

HORNE, HERMAN HARRELL. **The Philosophy of Education.** By Herman Harrell Horne, Assistant Professor of Philosophy and Pedagogy in Dartmouth College.
Cloth. 8vo. xvii + 395 pages. $1.50 net.

—— **The Psychological Principles of Education.** *12mo. xiii + 435 pages. $1.75 net.*

—— **Idealism in Education.** *Cloth. 12mo. xxi + 183 pages. $1.25 net.*

HUEY, EDMUND B. **The Psychology and Pedagogy of Reading.** By Professor Edmund B. Huey, of the Western University of Pennsylvania.
Cloth. 12mo. xvi + 469 pages. $1.40 net.

JONES, OLIVE M., LEARY, ELEANOR G., and QUISH, AGNES E. **Teaching Children to Study.** The Group System applied.
Illustrated. Cloth. viii + 193 pages. 12mo. $.80 net.

KILPATRICK, VAN EVRIE. **Departmental Teaching in Elementary Schools.**
Cloth. 12mo. xiii + 130 pages. 16mo. $.60 net.

KIRKPATRICK, EDWIN A. **Fundamentals of Child Study.** By Professor Edwin A. Kirkpatrick, Principal of State Normal School, Fitchburg, Mass.
Cloth. 12mo. xxi + 384 pages. $1.25 net.

—— **Genetic Psychology.** *Cloth. xv + 373 pages. $1.25 net.*

LAURIE, S. S. **Institutes of Education.**
3d ed. Cloth. xii + 391 pages. $1.90 net.

MAJOR, DAVID R. **First Steps in Mental Growth.** A Series of Studies in the Psychology of Infancy. By David R. Major, Professor of Education in the Ohio State University. *Cloth. xiv + 360 pages. 12mo. $1.25 net.*

THE McMURRY SERIES *Each, cloth, 12mo.*

General Method

—— **The Elements of General Method.** By Charles A. McMurry.
323 pages. $.90 net.

—— **The Method of the Recitation.** By Charles A. McMurry and Frank M. McMurry, Professor of the Theory and Practice of Teaching, Teachers College, Columbia University. *xi + 329 pages. $.90 net.*

Special Method. By Charles A. McMurry.

—— **Special Method in Primary Reading and Oral Work with Stories.**
vii + 103 pages. $.60 net.

—— **Special Method in the Reading of English Classics.** *vi + 254 pages. $.75 net.*

—— **Special Method in Language in the Eight Grades.** *viii + 192 pages. $.70 net.*

—— **Special Method in History.** *vii + 291 pages. $.75 net.*

—— **Special Method in Arithmetic.** *vii + 225 pages. $.70 net.*

—— **Special Method in Geography.** *xi + 217 pages. $.70 net.*

—— **Special Method in Elementary Science.** *ix + 275 pages. $.75 net.*

—— **Nature Study Lessons for Primary Grades.** By Mrs. Lida B. McMurry, with an Introduction by Charles A. McMurry. *xi + 191 pages. $.60 net.*

Course of Study in the Eight Grades.

Vol. I. Grades I to IV. vii + 236 pages. $.75 net.
Vol. II. Grades V to VIII. v + 226 pages. $.75 net.

MONROE, PAUL. **A Brief Course in the History of Education.** By Paul Monroe, Ph.D., Professor in the History of Education, Teachers College, Columbia University. *Cloth. 8vo. xviii + 409 pages. $1.25 net.*

MONROE, PAUL. **A Text-book in the History of Education.**
Cloth. xxiii + 277 pages. 12mo. $1.90 net.

—— **A Source Book of the History of Education.** For the Greek and Roman Period.
Cloth. xiii + 515 pages. 8vo. $2.25 net.

O'SHEA, M. V. **Dynamic Factors in Education.** By M. V. O'Shea, Professor of the Science and Art of Education, University of Wisconsin.
Cloth. 12mo. xiii + 320 pages. $1.25 net

—— **Linguistic Development and Education.**
Cloth. 12mo. xvii + 347 pages. $1.25 net.

PARK, JOSEPH C. **Educational Woodworking for Home and School.** By Joseph C. Park, State Normal and Training School, Oswego, N.Y.
Cloth. 12mo. xiii + 210 pages, illus. $1.00 net.

PERRY, ARTHUR C. **The Management of a City School.** By Arthur C. Perry, Jr., Ph.D., Principal of Public School, No. 85, Brooklyn, N.Y.
Cloth. 12mo. viii + 350 pages. $1.25 net.

ROWE, STUART H. **The Physical Nature of the Child.** By Dr. Stuart H. Rowe, Professor of Psychology and the History of Education, Training School for Teachers, Brooklyn, N.Y.
Cloth. 12mo. vi + 211 pages. $.90 net.

ROYCE, JOSIAH. **Outlines of Psychology.** An Elementary Treatise with Some Practical Applications. By Josiah Royce, Professor of the History of Philosophy in Harvard University.
Cloth. 12mo. xxvii + 392 pages. $1.00 net.

SHAW, EDWARD R. **School Hygiene.** By the late Edward R. Shaw.
Cloth. vii + 255 pages. 12mo. $1.00 net.

SHURTER, EDWIN DuBois. **The Rhetoric of Oratory.** By the Associate Professor of Public Speaking in the University of Texas.
Cloth. 323 pages. 12mo. $1.10 net.

SINCLAIR, S. B. and TRACY F. **Introductory Educational Psychology.** A Book for Teachers in Training.
Cloth. 180 pages. $.90 net.

SMITH, DAVID E. **The Teaching of Elementary Mathematics.** By David E. Smith, Professor of Mathematics, Teachers College, Columbia University.
Cloth. xv + 312 pages. 12mo. $1.00 net.

SNEDDEN AND ALLEN. **School Reports and School Efficiency.** By David S. Snedden, Ph.D., and William H. Allen, Ph.D. For the New York Committee on Physical Welfare of School Children. *Cloth. 12mo. xi + 183 pages. $1.50 net.*

VANDEWALKER, NINA C. **The Kindergarten in American Education.** By Nina C. Vandewalker, Director of Kindergarten Training Department, Milwaukee State Normal School. *Cloth. xiii + 274 pages. Portr., index, 12mo. $1.25 net.*

WARNER, FRANCIS. **The Study of Children and Their School Training.** By Francis Warner.
Cloth. xix + 264 pages. 12mo. $1.00 net.

WINTERBURN AND BARR. **Methods in Teaching.** Being the Stockton Methods in Elementary Schools. By Mrs. Rosa V. Winterburn, of Los Angeles, and James A. Barr, Superintendent of Schools at Stockton, Cal.
Cloth. xii + 355 pages. 12mo. $1.25 net.

THE MACMILLAN COMPANY

Publishers   **64–66 Fifth Avenue**   **New York**